RN

WASHOE COUNTY LIBRARY

3 1235 0

D0021090

DUE

RENO
DOWNTOWN
BRANCH

SOLD SHORT

UNCOVERING DECEPTION IN THE MARKETS

MANUEL P. ASENSIO

WITH JACK BARTH

John Wiley & Sons, Inc.
New York • Chichester • Weinheim • Brisbane • Singapore • Toronto

This book is printed on acid-free paper. ∞

Copyright © 2001 by Manuel P. Asensio. All rights reserved.

Published by John Wiley & Sons, Inc.
Published simultaneously in Canada.

No part of this publication may be reproduced, stored in a retrieval system or transmitted in any form or by any means, electronic, mechanical, photocopying, recording, scanning or otherwise, except as permitted under Sections 107 or 108 of the 1976 United States Copyright Act, without either the prior written permission of the Publisher, or authorization through payment of the appropriate per-copy fee to the Copyright Clearance Center, 222 Rosewood Drive, Danvers, MA 01923, (978) 750-8400, fax (978) 750-4744. Requests to the Publisher for permission should be addressed to the Permissions Department, John Wiley & Sons, Inc., 605 Third Avenue, New York, NY 10158-0012, (212) 850-6011, fax (212) 850-6008, E-Mail: PERMREQ@WILEY.COM.

This publication is intended to provide accurate and authoritative information in regard to the subject matter covered. It is sold with the understanding that the publisher is not engaged in rendering professional services. If professional advice or other expert assistance is required, the services of a competent professional person should be sought.

Library of Congress Cataloging-in-Publication Data:
Asensio, Manuel P., 1954–
    Sold short : uncovering deception in the markets / by Manuel P. Asensio.
      p. cm.
    ISBN 0-471-38338-4 (cloth : alk. paper)
    1. Short selling. 2. Speculation. 3. Stocks. I. Title.

HG6041.A82 2001
332. 63'228–dc21   00-068043

Printed in the United States of America.

10   9   8   7   6   5   4   3   2   1

Para ti.
Que con una sonrisa
Me enseñastes a
cambiar mis ideas.

RENO
DOWNTOWN
BRANCH

Preface

I run a securities brokerage whose primary business is proprietary trading. A part of my business has involved researching, short selling (an investment technique in which one profits from a stock's decline), and publishing on the Internet information about high-flying stocks. Some people might call me a professional investor. Others, including the normally docile financial press, have referred to me using less than kind words. That's because those high-flying stocks that I researched and panned had lots of supporters, and when things didn't go as those supporters had hoped, those stocks crashed. Few heard us tell of the impending crash, because the events we foretold were like skywriting: easy to see, but you needed to look up.

I'm a fundamental, "bottom-up" securities analyst, cautious and deliberate. I don't invest based on market trends, which change uncontrollably and unpredictably. And I don't purchase stocks based on relative valuations. I purchase only stocks that are reasonably priced, based on reasonable multiples of conservatively projected growth and earnings.

In the late 1990s, there were few such animals available. And even if you managed to find that elusive bargain in a mature, long-term bull market, it was more likely to continue underperforming than to show itself to have been unjustly undervalued. These market conditions, and my desire to limit risk, are what led me to short selling.

While a long-term bull market leaves few companies absolutely undervalued, it does breed companies—some might say whole industries—that are *over*valued. Sometimes overvaluations occur naturally, despite complete and accurate disclosures about a company's risks and prospects. But sometimes overvaluations occur because investors are buying based on false statements and/or the omission of material negative facts. I call these misrepresented companies "grossly overvalued." In these cases, astute analysts can determine with a great deal of certainty why and maybe even when these stocks will decline.

When I find a grossly overvalued company, I thoroughly research every aspect of its history, management, products, market, and earnings potential. In some cases my research leads me to conclude that omissions and false statements are the primary reason for a company's gross overvaluation—in some cases these misleading statements are responsible for the company's *entire* valuation.

These companies are known as stock promotions. A stock promotion is not the same as a stock that is being promoted. All companies have employees or entire departments dedicated to informing the public about the company and promoting its stock. A stock promotion, however, is a stock whose price is based not on fundamentals—on the company's actual sales and profits and an assessment of the future potential of its business—but solely on the ability of its promoters to conjure up schemes to sell its shares.

These shaky shares aren't always dumped onto the little guy. My firm has had its largest, longest battles with the perma-bulls at some of Wall Street's most distinguished institutions. These billion-dollar gorillas have been known to risk other people's money with about as much compunction as a spoiled teen raiding the mall with Daddy's credit card.

When I find a grossly overvalued company, perhaps one that is an outright stock promotion, I do enough deep research to develop the high degree of conviction I need to sell short, even in a raging bull market. Among the companies we choose to sell short are some whose promoters perpetrate such egregious omissions and patently false claims that we elect to publish our research. We post our research on the Internet, where it is freely accessible to anybody who wants it. In doing so we fully disclose the fact that we and our clients are short selling the stock and have a negative opinion about the company.

Once we make this disclosure, it's a sure bet that any time the media or the target companies refer to our opinions and research, it will be qualified with the statement that we're short sellers. The implication is that, as short sellers, we have a conflict of interest, or, worse, we have an incentive to lie, and therefore our research must somehow be biased or false.

Naturally, any grossly overvalued company is going to have its "true" believers—shareholders who will retreat into denial when confronted with the cold, hard evidence that their company is not what they thought it to be. And their first reaction is usually to shoot the messenger. Their second reaction is "How can it be legal for Asensio to *say* these things?!"

It strikes me as odd that my right to publish an opinion on a company that has solicited and obtained money from the *public* by telling the *public* about its business could ever be questioned by that same *public*. I would think that all shareholders would welcome being told that they should take a closer look at their prized possession. A bum stock is like a straying partner: You may not want to hear about it, but you need to know.

Many principles and laws protect my right to publish and to use my research to trade. Over the years many lines have been written about public debate over the value of public corporations—a vital facet of free capital markets. In the U.S. Supreme Court case of *Virginia Pharmacy Board v. Virginia Citizens Consumer Council Inc.*, the judges wrote: "So long as we preserve a predominantly free-enterprise economy, the allocation of our resources in large measure will be made through numerous private economic decisions. It is a matter of public interest that those decisions, in the aggregate, be intelligent and well informed. To this end, the free flow of commercial information is indispensable."

PREFACE

In some cases, our factual reports and fact-based opinions—part of the "free flow of information" endorsed by the Supreme Court—have been tied to a stock's sudden, rapid, and steep decline. This has led to an immense amount of controversy and media coverage. I have been portrayed in the media as a "stockbuster," "demolition man," "Attila the Hun," and "a company's worst nightmare." Large public companies have issued press releases and held conference calls to discuss (read: confuse) the issues raised in our reports and in many cases to cast aspersions on our firm's short interest in their companies.

In extreme cases, these companies will drag me and other members of my firm through the courts in an effort to deplete our time and resources. Despite the assurances of the Supreme Court just cited, despite the guarantees of the First Amendment, despite the despicable nature of some of the scams you will be reading about, by the time these cases reach a point where hopefully a judge can toss them out, I've had to spend time and money that I can never recoup.

Some people will try to undermine these commercial speech protections with glib, knee-jerk statements like "The First Amendment doesn't guarantee you the right to shout 'Fire!' in a crowded theater." Well, guess what: It's the scamsters who are doing all the yelling. Ours is but a tiny voice of opposition. Actually, upon reflection, I've never had any company offer this particular argument; it's too sophisticated for them. Their attitude is more along the lines of "Shut this guy up. Spend as much as it takes. What the heck, it's other people's money anyway."

Asensio & Company has been providing in-depth research and practicing this brand of short selling for over five years. Time and again the events we foretold, though diametrically opposed to the projections of the companies and their promoters, came to pass. Furthermore, once the events occurred as we foretold, those events materially impacted in a negative way the value of those stocks. Nonetheless, each time we issue an initial report on a new company, we are met with the same denial, hostility, threats of litigation, and dismissal by the media as nothing more than compromised short sellers. I do not expect more. I understand there is no way for others to know immediately who's right and who's wrong.

When we issue a report, we have a definite opinion as to the value of a company's stock and firmly believe that the stock's price will change to properly reflect its fair value. We never know the impact our reports will have on a stock's price, however, or how long the stock will continue to trade above the price we calculate as its fair value. Yet I always think about the potential impact of a report before it's issued. And whether I'm right or wrong, I'm never surprised. In retrospect, we can always identify good reasons that help us reconcile the market price with our view of the shares' fair value. Here are some of the things we examine:

- How wide is the variance between the events we are predicting and the events predicted by management?
- How much negative sentiment already exists about the company?
- How has the stock's price reacted to previous news?
- How legitimate is the market for the stock's shares? Is there legitimate (as opposed to manipulated) trading volume? Is it difficult to short-sell the stock?
- Does the company have sales and tangible assets, or is it all promises?
- What is the quality of analyst coverage for the stock?
- What is the reputation and history of the company's management?
- What is the company promoting?
- Who's doing the promoting?
- Who holds the stock, and how much do they really know about the company?

- Is the company known in its industry?
- How wide is the variance between our calculated fair value and the stock's current price?
- How strong is our evidence? Have we presented it well? Is it easy to understand?

In this book I'll guide you through our procedures. You may not be able to practice our brand of hostile, adversarial short selling, but you will learn how to identify companies that may be grossly overvalued, and you'll see how a stock promotion plays out. You will be better able to avoid scam stocks and learn that all scams look sweet going in but ultimately turn sour. This is a book about people who engage in deception, who try to shelter themselves from the efficient market's invisible hand. The good news is, in the end they can't.

Although I may be perceived as antiestablishment or contrarian, I'm actually a great supporter of the courts and of the securities industry's self-regulation system. I'm not fighting these institutions; I'm fighting those who abuse them.

Free markets are at the heart of a successful capitalist society. These markets must be transparent and open. The Efficient Market Theory (EMT) states that in a pure, open market, every security reaches its proper price—its point of perfect balance between buyers and sellers. The flourishing American securities markets reflect the beauty of the EMT. Only through extreme lies and manipulation can someone subvert the EMT and temporarily deceive the market. But in the end, material facts will outweigh relentless fabrication. And unfettered short selling—the ability of investors to react at will on a stock they consider overpriced—is an important element in maintaining a efficient market.

There's a prevailing, pernicious attitude in some quarters of Wall Street that short selling is somehow a dirty business—that it is about tearing down companies that are trying their best to produce value for investors and contribute something to the world. This rankles me to no end.

First of all, at Asensio & Company we issue fact-based analysis—information for investors. How can that possibly be interpreted as a negative on any level? Furthermore, we do not rely on company information on the companies we sell short. All we use are facts, not stories. This is the opposite of a long-side investment firm that releases analyst reports that are often nothing more than secondhand puff pieces reiterating company statements. When we issue a report, we are obligated to disclose the fact that we have sold the stock short or have advised our clients to do so. The subject companies and the media then label us "acknowledged short sellers." Have you *ever* read a qualifier on a bullish analyst's quote that labels him or her "an acknowledged stock promoter"? How about a clear and precise statement that the investment house also handles the subject company's investment banking business, which is worth $X to them?

We don't offer concurrent opinions on a spectrum of companies. We don't make statements about any stock unless we have spent months researching it. And we must have concrete evidence. As a result, we've issued opinions on an average of only six new stocks per year. We don't even offer opinions on stocks we covered in the past unless we have kept up with them.

But even if we're not talking about the sort of short selling we do at Asensio & Company, all short selling should be viewed as a legitimate and vital component of a free and open market. If a short seller has done no research and just has a hunch that a stock is heading down, why should he or she be any less free to speculate than someone on the long side taking an uninformed flutter?

During my 24 years in finance I've been an investment banker, an analyst, and a trader. I know of no Wall Street group that works harder, adds more value, and performs less selfishly than short sellers. Short sellers are constantly at odds with the collective, uncontrollable forces that call the shots. I know of short sellers—private investors who don't make public statements—who profitably managed large pools of capital dedicated to short selling during the entire late 1990s.

This is the story of one company that issues bold, no-nonsense opinions on stocks—controversial opinions that have been proven correct. It's a story of good research consistently producing abnormally positive short-selling returns during the most furious bull market in history. Some will say: How could this be true? How could so many respectable institutions, pillars of Wall Street, have been so wrong? Others will point to the Efficient Market Theory and claim it's impossible. If there ever was an Alice in Wonderland story of finance, this is it.

MANUEL P. ASENSIO

New York, New York
March 2001

Acknowledgments

Many people worked closely with Asensio & Company on the jobs chronicled in this book. They're all interesting characters. But because short sellers approach the markets as skeptics rather than as cheerleaders, they are misunderstood at best, feared and reviled at worst. For this reason, many of them choose to remain anonymous. Nonetheless, their thinking and judgment impacted the results of every story in this book. A little of each of them is part of us.

One very special person in particular must be mentioned. Dr. Judy Stone was a mother of six and a doctor who got her medical degree in 1973. She gave birth to her first two children while still in medical school. In 1993, after 20 years of practice, specializing in oncology, she began a new career on Wall Street as a professional investor.

Judy soon established a reputation as an extraordinarily detailed analyst and an astute judge of character. Her brilliant, scientifically trained mind cut through Wall Street crap like a laser scalpel. Her delightful good humor found something amusing in each day. But she had zero tolerance for those who compromised on good principles.

On April 18, 2000, Dr. Stone passed away, and New York City lost one of its dearest citizens. Judy was literate, musical, beautiful, and high-spirited.

Two talented young people have been with Asensio & Company since we began short selling. Chehrazad Mamri, our calm and collected controller, awes me with her ability to shut out the madness and get on with her work. Charles Stewart, besides handling our trading desk, has helped on so many bogus stocks that it's probably

ACKNOWLEDGMENTS

no surprise that he refuses to do any trading for his own account. Charles also provided the research backbone for this book.

Our editor, Pamela van Giessen, approached me with the idea of doing this book after reading some of our press. It was a long and bumpy road from that first conversation, but Pamela never wavered in her enthusiasm for the project.

Until the laws change, an unfortunate by-product of what we do is that some companies will use their ill-gotten shareholder money to sue us in an attempt to prevent us from disseminating information about their omissions and misstatements. We have never given in. Our voice has always gotten stronger in these cases. This has made the difficult work of our attorneys even harder. Steve Agus has been my attorney for over 10 years, and I shudder to think where I'd be without his realism, good-hearted nature, and intelligence. Larry McMichael and Thomas Biemer of Dilworth Paxson have been on the front lines of the ugliest, most malicious and protracted legal battle of my life. It can't be a fun job by any means, but it's one that absolutely has to be done.

Victor A. Kovner, of Davis Wright Tremaine LLP, provided legal guidance and review.

I must also thank Mike Wilkins and Dave Scially for their wisdom, instincts, and savvy. And Jack Barth, who assembled thousands of documents and random shards of memory into a cohesive and, surprisingly often, pretty damn funny manuscript.

M. P. A.

Contents

CONTENTS

SOLD SHORT

CHAPTER ONE

DIANA DAY AFTERNOON

Octtober 15, 1996, was a make-or-break day for Asensio & Company. We were a tiny brokerage firm, less than three years old. Even though we had thus far achieved solid results for our investors, we were just another struggling, small business. Few, if any, had ever heard of us. Earlier in the year we had struck off into uncharted territory—short selling high flyers in the hottest sectors of a bubbling market. Our new direction was to discover hyperpromoted, grossly overvalued companies, research them seven ways to Sunday, and take a trading position.

But that's not all. Although promotions that rise on hot air will eventually fall to earth, many short sellers have gone broke waiting for the laws of gravity to take effect. In fact, the object of our disaffection had already cost the shorts a bundle. Many had begun to short this puppy at $10 only to see it rise to $120, despite a flurry of major negative news stories. Instead of just sitting back and waiting, our plan was to escalate the fight, to get all the facts, and then to publish the straight, fully documented story and our opinions directly on the Internet, with no wishy-washy middleman.

Ready or not, here come the New Wave shorts.

We first issued a *sell* advisory on the Diana Corporation on May

29, 1996, when its stock was trading over $100, giving the company a market capitalization of more than $500 million. The overall stock market had since inflated so much that this may seem like peanuts, but back in 1996 this was the big enchilada of stock promotions. This meat distributor turned sizzling tech avatar had risen in only nine months from $5 a share to an intraday high of $120 on May 24. It was one of the sexiest playthings on Wall Street: volatile, high volume, high short interest, and price action like a late '90s dot-com initial public offering (IPO). The company was promoting an Internet access switch that would allegedly provide huge savings and productivity gains for Internet Service Providers (ISPs). But of all the investors and prominent analysts pumping up the stock, apparently not one had done the research to learn that it was all just an elaborate scam.

In the months following my first report, the stock sank like a bag of Sakrete, dropping to as low as $20 per share. Investors who followed Asensio & Company's advice to short Diana collectively made millions. But the institutional wise guys promoting the stock, whether aware of its true nature or not, just didn't quit. Five months after our initial report, the promote became reinvigorated, and the stock charged back up as high as $50 again.

The stakes in Diana had grown massive and the climate nasty. On October 15, 1996, it all came to a head: apparent stock manipulation by front-running, fat-cat investment bankers; high-level corporate skullduggery; choruses of traders from both the short and the long side beseeching me for information; and the complete inability of the world's most respected stock market, the New York Stock Exchange, to maintain a fair and orderly market.

Diana's resurgence had kicked off what some call a short squeeze on Wall Street. This happens when a large number of investors have sold the stock short—that is, borrowed the stock from their brokers to sell with the intention of buying the shares back on the market at a future date. The short sellers are betting the stock price will fall and that they will be able to buy it back at a lower price than what they sold it for, pocketing the difference.

When the Diana battle was raging, the regulatory climate allowed for liberal interpretation of the short selling rules. As a result, the company's efforts to keep the shorts out of its stock had failed and Diana became one of the most heavily shorted companies on Wall Street.

Investors, whether they are professional money managers or individuals overseeing their personal investments, tend to think of the stock market in terms of *buying* stock—and generally holding it. Short selling, on the other hand, is about selling—without first buying—to make a profit. When a lot of traders have gone short and the stock price begins to rise, a certain number will panic, leaping to buy the stock and cut their losses. This can send the stock price even higher.

There were more than 3 million shares short in Diana and only 5 million total shares outstanding—a huge short interest. This means that an inordinate number of traders had chosen to short Diana, expecting its price to fall. A large short interest in a stock usually indicates negative investor sentiment and should be a blinking caution light to anybody thinking of buying the stock. Sure, all those short sellers might be wrong, but as a group short sellers have always been accorded a grudging respect on Wall Street for the quality of their research. In this case, the large short interest also meant that there might be more "weak hands" out there holding short positions who could be induced to panic and buy if the stock price were to rise suddenly and steeply.

Amid this "squeeze," we hired a software expert and a hardware expert—unfortunately, both must remain anonymous—with intimate knowledge of Diana's switch and other switches that actually worked. With their input I began preparing an extensive plain-language 16-page engineering report detailing the flaws in its technology and proving beyond doubt that it was, in fact, a worthless, obsolete device. During the three weeks it took to prepare this report, Diana kept rising and rising. Shorts were feeling the pain. Finally, on October 15, we were ready to release the report.

Up until this day, we had released all our reports via the PR Newswire. PR Newswire publishes releases about stock opinions from firms in good standing with the National Association of Securities Dealers (NASD). These releases can then be picked up by the other wire services. This report needed to be handled differently, however. For one thing, it isn't practical to issue a 16-page press release, especially not one of such a technical nature. For another, our report had been leaked. Before it was published, we were getting calls about it from retail and institutional investors and brokers, and we knew this would continue.

We needed to release the report simultaneously and democratically. I didn't want to give it to one person and then have that person characterize it to others rather than passing on the actual document. If we were to fax the document separately to individuals, our fax machine and personnel would be tied up; it would be time-consuming and expensive.

We wanted no one to control the report. It is what it is. Come and get it, draw your own conclusions, form your own opinion. Thus, we decided to publish the report on the Internet after putting out a brief release announcing its existence and Web location. That was the genesis of our policy of free and open dissemination of our information. No fee, no commitment, no need to open an account. Get it and read it anonymously.

We announced the location of our report over the PR Newswire at 7:01 A.M. and again at 9:10 A.M. Both releases were picked up by the major wire services. On the first day, the report was downloaded over 300 times.

I had barely been home the night before our release. I hadn't slept much that entire week—because of work, not because of tension. For me, researching and preparing a report is relaxing. We were discovering information that added to our conviction about Diana's stock and business at deep levels. We were talking to people who were involved in the design of products competitive to Diana's. They knew this design, and they knew how it compared to others. We could describe not just the functionality of Diana's equipment but also the genesis of its design, how it was designed, and its flaws. We were confident of the accuracy, completeness, and fairness of our report. From that does not come anxiety or nervousness. From that comes peace, satisfaction, conviction. Regardless of the price action. Regardless of the "squeeze."

The tension would come later, when Diana's insiders successfully manipulated the stock, and New York Stock Exchange officials failed to stop them. Not that anyone should ever count on any official—Exchange or otherwise—to stop stock promoters from going about their business.

Diana had recently trumpeted a "deal" it had made with a company called Concentric Network Corporation that we discovered to be a sham. Concentric was a real company, but this turned out to be a false deal. Diana had simply enlisted a legitimate but needy third party to help simulate "sales." I thought our report would undermine any credibility Diana would receive from this announcement. On the other hand, several major institutions were still issuing *buy* recommendations on Diana and holding its stock. All I had was faith in the efficient pricing mechanism, despite what I knew these institutions could do to Diana's stock price in the short term.

I got to work early that day, concerned about our first foray onto the Internet. My office, which was at 555 Madison Avenue at the time, was a 12-by-12-foot room with force-fed air. We had to put in a big fan that sounded like an airplane engine. It was hot and noisy all year round. Coming out of that room was like stepping out of a steam cooker. We had three work areas in that tiny room, with a fax machine, a printer, four computers, and six phones with seven lines.

SOLD SHORT

It was like being in the cockpit of a 747. When a phone rang, you had to pick it up quickly, because it *hurt* if you didn't.

The morning of October 15, 1996, Asensio & Company's tiny broker-dealer trading fund was short 43,000 shares at an average price of $38, a $1.6 million position. Diana had closed the previous day at $30.95, down $0.47, which made our unrealized profit before the opening 43,000 shares × ($38 − $30.95) = $303,150. That's small potatoes to a Wall Street hot shot. To us it represented a big chunk of our trading capital.

The stock opened at $32, but there was palpable tension in the trading. Few buyers. No sellers. Traders were standing to the side and observing. The stock slowly sank over the first hour of trading. It hit $28.63 at 10:26 A.M. We were comfortable, looking forward to further trading. We had a high degree of certainty that this stock promotion was finished. People had to realize, we reasoned, that there was no realistic possibility of Diana ever creating value, of having sales or gross profit margins with this product. This stock had a long way to fall.

And then came the halt.

I gazed incredulously at my ADP quote machine. Trading in Diana had been halted by the New York Stock Exchange. What?! Why? How was the order flow going right before the halt? Who halted it? When was it going to open again? I phoned our superb floor brokers, the twins Larry and Howard Helfant. Throughout the morning they had been giving me "looks": how many buyers were in the crowd, how many sellers. What the specialist had on the books: how much was on the bid, how much was on the offer. Who was on the bid, who was on the offer, who was in the crowd. This is the type of information that can be obtained only from Johnny-on-the-spot traders in a listed market.

Meanwhile, it seemed like every short seller in the game was calling me. Even diehard longs were phoning. This was only our second hostile, adversarial short sell, but the first had been nothing like this.

I had too many calls to return. People with connections to the promote were trying to get through to tell me what the company was up to. But I didn't speak to them, either. I was focused on what was happening at the New York Stock Exchange. When I tried to reach Richard A. Grasso, its chairman, I was shunted down the chain of command to the general counsel, who referred me even further down the chain. I finally got a callback from Tom Viet, the Exchange's vice president of client services—the man in charge of keeping Diana, the NYSE's paying customer, happy. I asked him about the Exchange's halt policies, who had requested Diana's halt, and the reasons the Exchange had allowed it.

Trading halts arise from significant order imbalances or when a company has news to release that is expected to impact its stock price. In theory this allows investors to digest the news and make informed trading decisions.

Under the listing agreement, companies listed on the NYSE are asked to call the Exchange 10 minutes before making a material statement. Client Services then calls the trading floor to recommend that trading on the security be halted. A floor governor makes the ultimate decision whether to halt the stock. It takes the say-so of two floor officials to override this recommendation.

Legitimate trading halts occur often; they're a useful way to maintain a fair and orderly market. But what was up with Diana? What did the company all of a sudden claim was so important? What possibly could have occurred? If it had something to announce, one would think it should have been announced before the stock opened. Suddenly at ten o'clock, on the morning we release our report, the company makes representations to the New York Stock Exchange that something has occurred. My initial impression was that there had been no legitimate reason for Diana's request to halt trading.

Nevertheless, the stock continued to be held. It was now past noon. This was no ordinary halt. Where was Diana's immediately pending, big market-moving news? If the halt was a reaction to our report, then it had nothing to do with any internal Diana news. If the company wanted to comment on our report, it could, but that was no reason to halt the stock. I already knew of the scarcely concealed contempt the Street has for short sellers, but now I sensed a palpable and dangerous prejudice that favored paying customers of the New York Stock Exchange over the public. Along with other short sellers and the integrity of the markets in general, I was a victim of that prejudice.

At 2:34 P.M., almost four hours after the trading halt, Diana issued a press release. The "news," which supposedly refuted my report, cited nothing specific. It referred to me as "a short seller posing as a securities analyst of Diana's stock." In fact, I was an analyst—the *only* securities analyst doing independent, objective, and, most important, uncompromised work on Diana.

James Fiedler was the head of a small company called Sattel Communications Corp., a division of Diana that had supposedly created the would-be wonder switch. Fiedler claimed to possess a letter from an engineering analyst alleging that I solicited a negatively biased technical report from him in exchange for $5,000 plus a percentage of my short-selling profits. In fact, I had never solicited from anyone anything but unbiased, truthful information on Sattel's products. Within 24 hours I served a demand on Diana to produce this letter, but to this day it has never surfaced.

The only other piece of "news" in this release was an incredibly premature, ridiculously trivial, and ultimately untrue announcement. Only 15 days into the new fiscal quarter, Sattel was supposedly expecting to report a modest profit in the quarter as opposed to a forecasted loss. (We already knew that the only deal it had going was with Concentric. There would be no additional income from any other source.) Sattel also announced it had added new personnel in sales and research and development, and a new chief financial officer. Good reason for a trading halt—not.

Well, that was the big news. No transaction had occurred, let alone one that would be expected to have a significant impact on the stock price. Furthermore, nothing in this release was of such an abstruse or confusing nature that it would necessitate the continued halt of trading in the stock.

All that had happened was that James Fiedler, a man who seemed more and more to be the architect of an overblown stock promotion, had been involved in a fabricated attack on my integrity. But I can absorb a personal attack. What made me truly livid was the way that Fiedler abused the procedures of New York Stock Exchange in order to halt trading in Diana.

Americans have a collective sense of entitlement that extends to justice. When fairness is denied, when those in power change the rules without explanation simply because they can, we react with frustration and anger. I know that I certainly do. But there was no time for that now. There was work to be done, facts to uncover. I had to decide: What if the stock reopens higher? Do I stay in if it's going back to $50? It had been at $29—that's $21 of losses times tens of thousands of shares. And if the market could so easily shrug off the cold truths in our report, will it continue on back to $100? Why not? Crazier things happen all the time. I had to deliberate these questions seriously.

At any rate, the Diana release had no substance. A securities analyst would not be able to look at it and say "Yes, here's something to buy on." So why did the company issue it? It needed to show that the game was still on. In effect, they were signaling the promoters that Diana was ready, willing, and able to take the scam to the next higher level of deception: "Yes, people, the cat's out of the bag. But we're in it together, and for the long run. If you liked our stock when you didn't know the truth about it, you gotta *love* it now."

And then there are those investors who perceive a company's statements as authoritative because they want to. They're hopeful; they refuse to take their losses. They blame the stock's decline on a short seller. They may think, "Okay, he's taken his shot, the worst is over . . . it's going back to $120!"

The so-called news was out. There was nothing that required thoughtful assimilation. So the next question was: Why isn't the stock trading now? There was a good answer to this from a stock manipulator's point of view, which I would soon learn, but I never learned the NYSE-sanctioned answer—the possible justification for *continuing* to halt the stock for yet another hour *after* the Diana press release. Only a few minutes were left in the trading day.

Okay, I thought, the stock will stay closed until tomorrow. Let investors read our report and Diana's vapid press release tonight. It's good to allow everyone to think things through overnight. But that didn't happen. Instead, trading resumed at 3:51:56, more than five hours after the halt. Again, there was no expressed reason why the NYSE reopened the stock a mere eight minutes before the close. Why not wait till the next morning? We quickly learned the sinister strategy behind allowing only eight minutes of trading.

When trading resumed, a 32,100-share block immediately crossed the tape at $33.50, almost $4 above where the stock had last traded before the halt. The run-up ravaged our tiny trading account. In the few remaining minutes before 4 P.M., 188,200 shares traded, closing at the high of the day, $35.75. Incredibly, the Dianites had tacked 5 points onto the price since the stock was halted, costing the tiny Asensio trading fund $244,750. This represented a disastrous 50 percent of the net regulatory capital of our brokerage operation. More significantly, on a day when the most lethal possible news had been released—a report that definitively refuted any possibility that this company's product possessed the virtues it had been claiming—the stock actually closed more than 2 points *above* the previous day's close.

Diana Day Afternoon

It appeared that the promoters' spin had carried the day. We had taken our best shot and the market shrugged it off. According to the script Diana's promoters concocted that day, the pall cast upon the company would now lift, and the stock could rise back where it belonged, over $100. I didn't know specifically who had been buying the stock in those eight minutes, but I did know that someone had done a helluva job rallying the troops. I figured that during the five-hour halt, some or all of the major institutions supporting the stock had scrounged up buyers to pile into Diana.

Things looked grim. And we had no way of knowing what was actually going on.

It wasn't until a Securities and Exchange Commission (SEC) filing a few weeks later that the story became clear. What happened was, that morning the followers of Diana's institutional backers who were already stuck bought even more shares while the broader Diana market sold off. The tide had turned before the halt. Those who could get out had started doing just that. It appeared that major holders, unable to unwind their large, concentrated positions, had tried to create market action to keep the followers in. But the followers elected to take the opportunity created by the institutions buying more of what they already owned and sold to *them*. The institutions couldn't prop up the stock if their own followers were selling to them. Despite what had looked early on to be a rout for the manipulators, the credibility of the facts had overpowered them, foiling their strategy and necessitating more drastic action. We'll probably never know exactly what went on behind the scenes. We can, however, indulge in some informed speculation.

In those five hours, Team Diana strategized its defense. Calls would have to have been made from the real inside promoters to the people they had put into the stock. The call was simple. Here's what might have been said: "We have looked at Asensio's report. We view this as a buying opportunity and are going to do just that—buy." Those people would have to have made determinations, in the face of my report, whether to buy along with the orders from the big perma-bull holders or to abandon the promote.

This is what I believed happened during the unjustified five-hour trading halt. Of course, these calls should have occurred while the market in Diana was open and flowing, but they didn't. That's a very important distinction. In a football game, if a running back has broken into the clear and is charging toward the goal line, the defense isn't allowed to suddenly call a time out in the middle of the play to foil the touchdown. All they can do is chase after him.

Companies have many weapons to counteract the market effect of short sellers. Their corporate communications departments can publicly refute any reports or rumors that they feel are damaging their share price. They can make new announcements that might appear to have the potential to increase shareholder value. If they feel their share price has been battered unfairly, they can use cash reserves to repurchase their own stock—or at least announce plans to do so—shoring up the price as well as banking this "bargain" stock. And they can attempt to attract new buyers through vigorous promotion and solicitation by complicit financial institutions. All of this is standard corporate procedure—these are perfectly legitimate attempts to support the price of a stock. I say, let them support their stock, but don't let them manipulate it.

If Diana supporters could concentrate their buying at the end of the day and cause the stock to close up, they could score a significant propaganda victory. Many people might not even realize it had been halted a large part of the day. The promoters could never sustain this kind of manipulation over five hours—there was too great a risk of rebellion in the ranks, as had happened that morning; in a mere eight minutes, however, a bogus buying frenzy could be better simulated.

During the five-hour trading halt, Diana surely disclosed its "news" to individuals who then helped arrange large and aggressive stock purchases immediately upon the resumption of trading. This buying volume was intended to make it appear that Diana's press release had generated interest in the stock and had successfully discredited our report—to create the illusion that Asensio & Company had artificially depressed its stock and that it would now recover and rise. It was also to serve as a cover story that gave institutional buyers an excuse for their buying.

For whatever reason, Dawson Samberg Capital Management, Inc., a large, well-known, and highly respected institutional investor specializing in technology stocks, owned a shameful 7.8 percent of Diana. What was happening here? Based on the per-share price disclosed in the SEC filing, during the last eight minutes of that day, Dawson Samberg apparently purchased for its clients 35,000 shares of Diana at an average cost of $34.31.

Consider what this means. Dawson Samberg probably spent as much as $1.2 million of its investors' money in order to support a company whose lead product had that morning been debunked in exacting detail. Representatives of Dawson Samberg would have been seriously malfeasant to further invest substantial sums in the company without having read the report. If they saw the report and believed it, they should have sold the stock, or at least stopped to think a little: "Hmm, maybe we should wait a quarter or two. Why rush out and buy a stock on the very day that serious questions are being raised about it? If we really believe in this company, and we already own almost 8 percent, why rush in now?" Instead, knowing that Diana had neither denied the report nor offered any specific rebuttal for any single point made in it, Dawson Samberg bought more.

In this case, we thought Dawson Samberg's action went beyond simply being irresponsible. Arthur Samberg, the president of Dawson Samberg, had in fact purchased 20,000 Diana shares for his own private account months earlier in a negotiated transaction at a per-share price of $20.50. Now, this is a supposedly shrewd guy. Why would a shrewd guy buy this stock?

Samberg held those shares on October 15. Although there are no laws or Exchange rules against such dealings, he faced an awkward conflict of interest, or at least the appearance of such a conflict. He had to decide whether to use investors' funds to buy and therefore help prop up the stock price or to exit before it collapsed completely. Who goes first?

Such maneuvers aren't just harmless little zero-sum games that cigar-chomping tycoons play to one-up other tycoons. These machinations have real victims. Small investors were drawn into the Diana promote as cannon fodder. To many of them and their brokers, Dawson Samberg's purchases were an endorsement of Diana. To them, Dawson Samberg's actions meant a hell of a lot more than the advice of some Cuban from a firm they'd never heard of. Followers left in this stock until the bitter end saw their investment shrink 99 percent. There are other victims, too: legitimate companies that honestly state their risks and potential. They shouldn't lose out on funding to the Dianas of their industries.

The Asensio & Company trading account held only $500,000 in net equity in October 1996. I didn't know about the heavy Dawson Samberg purchasing at the time. What I did know was that we were facing a potential killer: The short interest was so gargantuan that it was like rocket fuel. Short sellers forced to cover might end up tussling over shares like bargain shoppers elbowing each other over discounted Versace. In the short run, this could juice up the stock price into the stratosphere. And last time Diana ran up it had gone all the way to $120.

Although I had taken some profits that morning, I was still short a lot of shares.

We have to manage our risk. Back then, unbelievably, we paid our monthly operating expenses with our monthly trading profits.

Diana Day Afternoon

We are also technically sensitive to price action and volume. Wall Street is not a place for martyrs. We don't sit on a stock and take losses. We believe the only right thing to do is to manage the risk, preserve our capital, continue the work, and come back again with a more profitable position. Winning the war doesn't require winning every battle.

I know this is not at all the way that short sellers are perceived. Because of the theoretically unlimited downside risk we take, we are considered buccaneers. And because of the aggressive, public brand of short selling we do at Asensio & Company, I know that we in particular are perceived as stubborn and combative.

I have seen too many short sellers, especially in the bull market of the late 1990s, stand firm in the face of mounting losses. We did not want to become another bull market casualty. Even if a company is ultimately doomed, a great promote and a tight rig can temporarily shoot its stock into the stratosphere. Short sellers who, like us, have limited amounts of capital and who refuse to cut their losses are often not there at the end for the collapse.

I stayed in the office very late on the night of October fifteenth wondering whom I had spoken to who had spoken to Diana. I tried to discover who had provided Diana with the letters that said I had solicited a negative report. That's not as hopeless as it sounds. Whenever you break an industry down to its lowest common denominator, you will always find a small group of people who know each other. That's an important concept when you're dealing with the sort of esoteric products we usually find at the center of a stock promote. Only so many people are truly informed on any abstruse technology, even fewer on the specific application being touted. If you dig deep enough, usually you will find someone knowledgeable who is willing to discuss it. That said, I wasn't able to trace the alleged letter, and to this day a copy has never surfaced. Either Fiedler fabricated the letter's very existence, or whoever had been coerced into concocting such a letter managed to save his or her own reputation in the end by suppressing its release.

The uncertainty that night was beyond frustrating. After all the work that went into Diana, after all the millions of dollars I had generated for our clients, our little trading fund faced a potentially crippling depletion of capital. Future campaigns—research and reporting on the many, many other frauds that were thriving in a raging, ravenous market—might have to be sidetracked by the more immediate need to generate operating capital.

What's worse, a terrible injustice would have been perpetrated. The bad guys were standing on the other side of the river, laughing, with their saddlebags full of loot. And as the stock rose higher and higher, the short sellers, despite being on the correct side of the Diana fraud, would have been squeezed out of the market, sending the stock ever higher and "justifying" the institutional support for this no-product company. October 16 would truly be a day of reckoning.

A little of my own background and the firm's early short-selling history might be helpful before I write about how things turned out for the mighty Diana team and its hagridden short sellers.

CHAPTER TWO

MAKING OF THE SHORT SELLER

Over the past five years, Asensio & Company has found itself embroiled in many tense, high-stakes shoot-outs with a rogues' gallery of thugs, schemers, and goofballs. You'll be reading about some of these brutal battles and colorful villains in the pages to come. But first, in order to help you understand why, of all the short sellers in the world, I have become one of the few publicly admitted practitioners of the art—why I have voluntarily chosen to become the lightning rod, as it were, for all that the go-go-go Wall Street majority finds distasteful in the process of selling rather than buy-buy-buying stock—I thought it might be helpful to tell you where I'm coming from, in both senses of the phrase.

In 1958, when I was three years old, Fidel Castro overthrew the corrupt Cuban dictator Fulgencio Batista and introduced communism into America's immediate "sphere of influence." China, the Soviet Union, and the Soviet satellites became Cuba's trading partners and ideological comrades. Castro's ascension was not merely some political power play—it was truly a revolution, violent and deadly. There were ongoing street battles, and people were being imprisoned or executed by firing squads. Thousands of anticommunist

17

SOLD SHORT

Cubans and their families fled the country. The vast majority of these refugees emigrated to the United States. I was one of them.

On January 3, 1961, just weeks before John F. Kennedy's inauguration, President Eisenhower broke off diplomatic relations with Cuba. On April 17, 1961, 1,500 CIA-supported Cuban exiles landed at the Bay of Pigs, 90 miles from Havana, in a mismanaged attempt to overthrow Castro's regime. The invasion failed, and over 1,100 of the exiles were taken prisoner. You can imagine how this must have worsened the already tattered relationship between Cuba and the United States—though it was nothing compared to the nerve-wracking showdown President Kennedy would face in October 1962, when the United States learned that Castro had allowed the Soviets to place nuclear missiles in Cuba.

I don't recall those days as particularly unsettling. Children tend to thrive on excitement, and those were exciting times. Armed men marching in uniform, armored military vehicles rumbling down the avenues, people making impassioned speeches on street corners, grown-ups being so occupied by the events of the day that discipline is relaxed . . . It can be downright fun for a six-year-old. But with upheaval comes uncertainty, and my family had decided to send me away for my own safety.

Five days prior to the Bay of Pigs invasion, my parents obtained a passport for me with a visa to enter Spain. On May 15, 1961, my mother packed my clothes in a suitcase and took me to the docks, where I was to board a large ship with my aunt and uncle, leaving my parents and sister behind.

My father, Manuel Sr., was reluctant to accompany my mother and me to the docks to see me off. He disagreed with my being sent away. He felt the danger was exaggerated. A few months later he was jailed briefly due to a misunderstanding over an offense so minor it would under most other circumstances be comical fodder for a treasured family anecdote. But there was nothing funny about what was

18

happening in Cuba at the time. After this incident, my father changed his tune about the level of everyday danger in Havana.

Although my aunt and uncle and I were on a ship bound for Spain, that was not in fact our intended destination. On May 21 we disembarked at a port of call in Caracas, Venezuela. This was our true destination. We moved in with friends there. I still have the Cuban passport that was stamped "illegal entrance into Venezuela." I was six years old and had left my parents and sister behind in Havana.

On August 15, 1961, I was put on a plane, all alone, to New York. I settled with an aunt in Brooklyn who had moved to the United States before the revolution. To my six-year-old eyes, Brooklyn was magic. The love of Brooklyn summers is still with me. To this day I often go there just to walk around. I can't distinguish between the romantic notion of what summertime Brooklyn is to me and the reality that others might see. I see a glorious, multihued gathering of people on their stoops in the evening, staving off the stifling heat until bedtime.

Within a few years my family reconstituted, one by one, in Brooklyn's Borough Park. I was so young that learning English was no problem. I attended St. Francis de Chantal, a strict Catholic grammar school with real-live nuns, and Bishop Ford High School, where at the time there were no other Latinos. My father eventually got a solid job at IBM, and I later worked my way through the Wharton School at Penn, anticipating a career on Wall Street.

To my chagrin, however, I didn't get hired. Now, at the time there weren't nearly so many jobs in finance as there are today. But that wasn't the only reason I failed to crack the market. I knew finance and I understood balance sheets. But back in the 1970s, there wasn't such a great interest in hiring middle-class Latinos. I remember a kid, a junior partner with Morgan Stanley, in a second-round interview, looking me up and down and telling me, "Y'know, there's only so many investment bankers in the world, and I don't think that you are . . . the type." I was so naïve; I didn't realize what he'd meant until many, many years later. I may not have been a pretty sight in my $50 brown suit, but I often wonder if anything has since awoken that pompous, pathetic little fool to the meanness of his thinking. Fortunately, I did not have a clue, so the meanness was lost on me. Or was it?

After suffering the footprints of "white shoes" on my backside, I thought of a great idea in, of all places, Caracas. You see, this was only four years after the gas crisis, when I had been caught with a gas guzzler and suffered the shortages acutely. It certainly gave me a healthy if grudging respect for OPEC, the Organization of Petroleum Exporting Countries. So it was only natural for me to turn to a Spanish-speaking OPEC country, Venezuela. It was soaked in petrodollars, and I was able to get interesting and lucrative work doing bank-loan syndications. The currency at the time was strong, so

Return to Cuba

For 38 years after leaving my homeland, I never met anyone who lived in Cuba. I had little, if any, interest in Cuban affairs or U.S.–Cuban politics. The media and fragments of discussions I picked up from family members and their friends formed my view of Cuba.

In 1999, I met Bruno Rodrigues-Padilla, the Cuban Ambassador to the United Nations. Bruno was my age, bright and candid, and he had made his life in Cuba. I was surprised by his normalcy and intelligence. But, hey, what was I expecting? After all, he was a diplomat living in New York City. I came to realize that, as a typical Cuban-American, I had become deeply biased against my own homeland. I was missing an informed and independent understanding. I decided I needed to learn about Cuba firsthand.

Throughout my life I had been told the legend of Vicente Garcia, my

Making of the Short Seller

mother's grandfather. It was all quite vague. The story went that Vicente had been a great warrior, a revolutionary hero, and president of a revolutionary government established on the island during a 10-year war against Spain. (The war that finally gave Cuba its independence came several years after the Ten-Year War.) Being a Cuban-American kid growing up in Brooklyn was tough enough. I had little interest in a nineteenth-century ancestor, and even less interest in Cuban history. As I grew, my doubting nature further discounted the seemingly embellished legend of Vicente Garcia along with all the other old-timey Cuban stories I was told.

Bruno and I developed a friendship. Bruno's wife, it turned out, had been a friend of my late Uncle Frank. To my great surprise, Bruno was aware that my Uncle Frank's grandfather was Vicente; he told me of Vicente's important place in Cuban history. My interest in Cuba was current, not historical. With Bruno's help I planned a trip to my homeland in September 2000. Unenthusiastically, I tacked on a side trip from La Havana to Las Tunas, to visit Vicente's birthplace.

Things in La Havana were completely different from what I'd expected. Americans are blitzed with propaganda that will have us believe Cuba is some overly regimented, broken-down backwater, with dogs lazing about to a soundtrack of buzzing flies in the middle of La Havana's main intersection. On the contrary, upon arrival I swiftly got a truer picture. I was able to hire a taxi, had complete freedom to circulate, and had a rented cellular phone within minutes of deboarding. Perhaps Americans don't realize that the United States is the only major country observing a Cuban embargo—which is not to say the embargo hasn't made a serious dent in the living standards of the common people. Nonetheless, Europeans have been making Cuba a popular holiday destination for years, and there is a respectable tourist industry to serve their needs.

Oddly, I felt at home. I fell in love with the city and its people. On the fifth day, I was scheduled to fly to Las Tunas. It meant rising at 5:30 A.M. to go to the airport and not returning to the capital until after 2:00 A.M. I didn't want to lose even a single day of the sights and feel of La Havana and thought about canceling the side trip to Las Tunas. But in the end I decided to go.

Las Tunas turned out to be as magical as La Havana. In Las Tunas

SOLD SHORT

I met with Victor Manuel Marrero, the city's historian. He was a meticulous professional, and passionate about his highly detailed work. For 20 years he had researched and documented Vicente's life. Now, this was not some family storyteller. Victor had a staff, a library, and access to the national archives. And Las Tunas had been the site of important colonial revolutionary events and battles. Las Tunas had three historical museums, including Vicente's home and a monumental Vicente Garcia memorial complex. I still did not know Vicente or what he had done, but I realized I was in the right place and with the right man to learn.

Vicente was born in Las Tunas in 1833 to a wealthy family. He was involved in revolutionary events as early as 1856. During 1868 he participated in a series of meetings to plan a nationwide revolution against Spain. He was one of five leaders to be given the title of mayor general. Vicente was the first of the national revolution army mayor generals to commence formal war preparations. He left his home and moved to the countryside near Las Tunas and soon amassed a small army of 300. On October 4, 1868, he became the first of the revolutionary leaders to declare war, announcing he would attack the Spaniards in Las Tunas. On October 13, he gained temporary control of this strategically important city before being forced to retreat.

Vicente's wife, Brigida, and four of his six children continued to live in Las Tunas. The Spaniards barracked the family in their home without food, demanding that Brigida write a letter asking Vicente to surrender. Brigida did not sign the letter. Four-month-old Maria and four-year-old Saul starved to death. A citywide revolt ensued and the Spaniards agreed to allow food into the house. Vicente gained control of Las Tunas in 1869. He knew his forces were not sufficient to hold the city against the large number of approaching Spanish troops, so he ordered the burning of over 100 buildings, starting with his own house. The town was abandoned but later rebuilt by the Spaniards.

Vicente fought the full 10 years of that war, controlling his region several times. He was made president in 1876. But other regions did not fare so well. The war was lost. Exiled to Venezuela, he left with 75 men and their families on June 7, 1877. In Venezuela he and his troops established a cocoa plantation. Vicente was planning his return to the island to continue his lifelong battle for Cuban independence when on March 4,

1886, he was poisoned by a Spanish spy. Brigida returned to Cuba and served as a nurse in the final war for Cuban independence.

Victor Manuel had a wealth of detail about Vicente's battle tactics. For instance, when Vicente attacked Spanish supply convoys he would engage the lead and trailing wagons. His troops would take those wagons, and others if possible, as soon as they could. In this fashion, regardless of the outcome of the battle, he was assured of some gain that he could use later. Victor has compiled hundreds of documents, including the Spanish orders to assassinate Vicente. As a fellow researcher, I admire Victor's fine, detailed work.

The story of my great-grandfather's life is exciting and noble. Discovering Vicente's life's story had much less impact on me personally than meeting Victor Manuel and all the other kind and fascinating people I found in Cuba.

---

my income was substantial even in dollar terms. I met and married a woman in Caracas and generally had a pretty great life there.

But after a few years I saw the handwriting on the wall—the boom was going bust. I always say that leaving Venezuela was my first good short sell. I looked at the currency, the politics, and the social organization. I said, "This thing ain't gonna stick." In 1979 when I left Venezuela I still had no value in the United States. The only job I could have gotten was at a commercial bank, lending money to the same countries I considered overleveraged and headed for trouble.

So I enrolled at Harvard Business School, with a concentration in corporate finance. As a case-study-method education, HBS proved all it was cracked up to be. But the most significant event of my two years there was, in fact, my beginner's luck with two sweet arbitrage deals. The profits from these enabled me to strike out on my own after I graduated and was again unable to crack Wall Street.

Many traders have one trade that they'll always remember. My first arbitrage deal not only changed my financial situation, it also changed my life. And it wasn't just me. This particular arbitrage has taken on legendary status. Every now and then I'll run into another trader who also has fond and indelible memories of the deal.

DuPont was in the process of buying Conoco in a two-step mega-merger. The first step was paid in cash, the second in straight-up shares of DuPont stock, then worth about $67. By offering much more in cash for the first step, DuPont had already secured over 51 percent of Conoco. For some reason Seagrams, which had lost the battle for control of Conoco, was persisting in its own bid and offering $110 cash for a limited number of shares. Seagrams would be forced to accept DuPont shares worth $67, far less than $110. Why was Seagrams doing this, knowing that DuPont already had 51 percent of the company? To this day, it's still a mystery. Seagrams' offer was confounding the market, causing Conoco's stock to trade well above $67, at over $90, while DuPont's control was already certain. Conoco's remaining shareholders were stuck with a deal worth just $67 per share.

Joe Perella from First Boston, which had conceived these two-step mergers, was recruiting at the Harvard Business School. While everyone else was kowtowing to him, I was drilling him about the two-step merger with Conoco and Seagrams.

The uncertainty about the back-end value of the DuPont shares injected by Seagrams' cash purchases may have kept Conoco's stock price in the $90s, but once the Seagrams tender offer was fulfilled, all that shareholders would be able to get for their Conoco stock would be $67. Surprisingly, I found some very short-term $90 Conoco puts selling for about $1. This meant that I had a shot to turn $1 into $23 in a few weeks. If the stock dropped to $67 after Seagrams' buying ended, those puts would be worth $23 each—a 2,300 percent return in a very short time. I was certain the stock would trade at close to $67 after the Seagrams buying ended. But here's the catch: No one knew how soon and how swiftly this would happen. Those puts might have expired before the inevitable slide occurred.

Nevertheless, I invested 100 percent of my savings into those puts. And the stock cooperated: it began to drop. When it hit $80, I could have sold the puts and had more money than ever before in my whole life. And I needed it, too! But neither my profits, large and material as they were, nor my need to pay bills caused my opinion to waver. I decided to hold until it went to $67, even though the put options were due to expire in less than one week. The stock kept slipping, soon trading below $70. What a joy; I was hooked for life. I had made my first big trade—and it was a short sell. Little did I know that 15 years later another fairy-tale deal—Diana Corp. at $120 when it was worth less than $1—would come my way.

This and another arbitrage trade, in Marathon Oil, not only made it possible for me to remain solvent when I came out of Harvard and again met frosty stares on Wall Street but actually allowed me to open my own brokerage.

Some might attribute my apparently antagonistic relationship with the established powers of Wall Street to the days when I was fresh out of Harvard Business School and Wharton and couldn't get hired. I saw that as an obstacle, not a cornerstone on which to build a career or an investment philosophy. If Wall Street wouldn't have me, I'd strike off on my own.

My bride and I moved down to Boca Raton, Florida. The minimum capital requirement to start up a small brokerage firm was $25,000. I had enough money saved from my trading to open a firm I called First Boca Raton Investment Corp. Almost as soon as I did, I got creamed in a trade where I was long the stock, long the calls, and short the puts in City Services, which Occidental Petroleum had offered to buy. What happened was, I got overconfident. In the middle of the trade, I went to Venezuela with my wife, trying to shop a business plan to get more equity into the firm. Meanwhile, the Federal Trade Commission (FTC) had had enough of these big oil mergers. It stopped the deal cold—and my winning streak along with it.

I lost everything, and then some. My account had a negative balance. I scraped bottom.

I hadn't thought much about these years until recently. When I was being deposed in a ridiculous lawsuit by a company I had researched and reported on, Hemispherx Biopharma, I was questioned extensively about my activities from when I graduated Harvard in 1982 to when I started at Bear Stearns as an investment banker in 1986. The plaintiffs pursuing this lawsuit, apparently for no good reason other than to harass me and run up my legal bills, were grasping to find threads of indecency in my life. As if that would turn their ugly, malicious 30-year-old company into a prince. It was a complete waste of time. The jabbering of the attorneys rolled over me as I mused about those days. Those four years after Harvard were tough years. They strained my mettle and my marriage, and the latter didn't survive.

Boca Raton (Spanish for "Mouth of the Rat") is a lush, palm tree–studded mecca for middle- and upper-middle-class retirees, located about 60 miles north of Miami. The typical Boca residence is in a sprawling condominium complex centered on a private golf course. The typical Boca resident is a conservative investor with a sizable portfolio.

I started in the securities business there as modestly as one possibly could, taking an office at the Atrium Financial Center, on North Federal Highway in Boca. The Atrium complex rented small offices on a month-to-month basis, with telephone, messaging, and other support services. I didn't need a fancy office. I wasn't looking for retail accounts among Boca's rich residents. I would visit companies that were looking for financing and offer my services as an investment banker.

Making of the Short Seller

At the time, Boca was just beginning to become a hotbed for speculative underwriters. All around me were firms preying on South Florida's wealthy retirees. Most notorious among these was the South Florida office of the now-defunct Greentree Securities, which took early-stage speculative companies public through a sales force of brokers calling on unsophisticated, small retail accounts. According to a 1996 article in *Time* magazine, one of the forces behind Greentree was Canadian Irving Kott, a convicted boiler-room stock fraudster whose brokerage customers, *Time* claimed, lost hundreds of millions of dollars. Greentree was run by Kott's son Michael.

Another underwriter, Stuart Coleman, was at the peak of its power when I was down there. Observing that operation was probably the best education I could have ever had in the mechanics of questionable stock promotions. This was no simple boiler-room operation. The firm's main office was in New York, and it had several branch locations. It had sales training programs. The organization had compliance consultants who were experts at dealing with state and federal securities regulators and corporate finance personnel to guide the offerings through the SEC and to structure the deals. It had relationships with financial public relations firms and ways of structuring offerings to place private stock with favored clients before the deals were registered. It also had close working relationships with SEC attorneys who knew how to keep the company from getting in trouble, at least long enough to make the principals rich.

When an underwriter registers with the SEC to sell stock in a public offering, it also has to register at the state level to allow individuals to buy and sell the stock in each state. States have what are known as blue-sky securities laws. These laws were enacted to help stop unscrupulous companies from trying to deceive investors by withholding material negative information—from painting an unrealistic financial picture, as it were, of clear blue skies. Speculative underwriters have attorneys that blue-sky their deals in certain key states. How can any state regulator watch all these deals and check every fact?

Now, Stuart Coleman was a complex organization, but it paled in sophistication and dollar amounts compared to some speculative underwriters we saw in the 1990s, such as Stratton Oakmont. The SEC eventually shuttered Stratton, and several of its principals pleaded guilty to criminal charges. Even while permanent injunctions were in place, however, Stratton was able to prolong its existence thanks to the brute force of money. It was even able to spawn new fraud factories in its dying days. Before Stratton breathed its last, it spun off into Biltmore Securities, which was located in Boca. Biltmore eventually caught the SEC's attention and was closed, as well.

Despite Boca's pervasive fast-and-loose atmosphere, I resolved to take only clients who had business plans with a legitimate chance of working out and who were willing to raise money from institutional investors, not penny-stock promoters. There weren't very many of those in Boca at that time, but the area's financial world didn't consist of *only* stock promoters. There were some companies, for example, that were involved with the IBM PC, which was booming in the early 1980s and which was manufactured at IBM plants there. There were a number of industrial parks, and some of the executives there were looking to finance their entrepreneurial plans.

There is a tremendous amount of up-front work in structuring a business plan that can attract institutional venture capitalists. Despite all the work, you never know what more the venture capitalists will require. Most start-up businesses didn't have the money to pay cash fees up front. So I had to be careful as to what I got involved in. If the venture was not ultimately financed, I'd receive little for my work. Arranging financing from a venture capitalist is a completely different process from structuring and underwriting speculative penny-stock IPOs.

Selling an IPO might involve dividing up, say, a $5 million financing with 1,000 different sales of $5,000 each. Those sales are executed in a liquid security, in which investors think, "Well, in the worst case I'll get out at the same price, because IPOs rarely drop below their offering price." The sales method of a speculative IPO is to have many brokers phoning people who already have cash in their accounts, customers they're already working with, trying to get them to buy IPO stock.

These customers have already got money on deposit with the broker. They don't have the sophistication to evaluate the risks and financial returns. And they have no influence over the terms. They can take the price, business plan, and structure they're being offered, or not. And, hey, it's only $5,000.

Compare that to trying to sell a business plan to venture capital institutions that do get involved, want board participation, want control over cash disbursements, want to have budget discussions, want to assess risks, want a bigger percentage of the company than you're offering, and maybe for less money—and are making large investments, which gives them the power to make these demands. These are dramatically different processes. Nobody could argue that funding through venture capital isn't vastly more difficult.

I was offered several chances to turn some of my deals into shaky IPOs, but I refused. Why did I refuse? I don't know. Lots and lots of people do it all the time. To this day, I have never been involved in taking stock in a private company that has gone public through a promotion. Not only do these stock promotions almost always cause unsophisticated investors to lose money, they also divert funds from legitimate companies.

One time it got ugly. I created a business plan for Therapeutic Technologies, a medical company that served paraplegics. I believed that public funds shouldn't be solicited. It was too soon for an IPO, although I thought it might be a good investment for a professional venture capitalist who could negotiate fairly with management to get the right price, based on the risk and opportunity. But no, Therapeutic wanted an IPO.

Because I was against the IPO, Therapeutic cut the deal to go public behind my back—and with guess who: Greentree Securities. Greentree was willing to do the deed. Then, after the deal closed, Therapeutic didn't want to pay me. But my contract was written so that I'd get paid no matter where it got financing. I sued and won a $127,906 judgment. Therapeutic still refused to pay. Two days before Christmas 1986, my attorney and a deputy sheriff marched into Therapeutic's corporate headquarters in Fort Lauderdale and threatened to have everything inside carted away. The then-public company abandoned the office and relocated to a Miami-area condominium, leaving the sheriff's office with corporate records and $25,000 worth of office equipment. The company's officers then had the nerve to boast that most of the office equipment was rented and that its plant in Columbus, Ohio, was still operating.

A lighthearted January 21, 1987, *Wall Street Journal* article titled "Next This Company Will Move to a Phone Booth in Key West" described my struggles in trying to collect. In this business you dream of your first appearance in the *Wall Street Journal*. Will it be a chronicle, perhaps, of my shrewd trading? An uplifting portrait of a Cuban immigrant's success in the white-shoed investment world? No, it's a mocking sidebar about an impoverished, unknown investment banker's attempts to collect money from a deadbeat.

Had I been involved with the Therapeutic public offering, I could have been paid, and paid large. Easily. No problema. And I was in dire need of funds. But I drew the line, a line I didn't cross then and haven't crossed since: the thin line from investor to stock promoter.

I finally left Boca in 1986, when I was offered a position at Bear Stearns in New York. Bear Stearns apparently hired me because the firm was looking for entrepreneurial bankers who "didn't fit the mold." In my case, a bad idea.

Making of the Short Seller

I lasted only a year at Bear Stearns. Here's what I think happened: If I were to wake up one morning and see a mountain to my right that I think would look a whole lot better to my left, and all I had was a small shovel, but it was something I really wanted to do, I would take that shovel, go to that mountain, pick up a shovelful of dirt, and not stop until that mountain was moved. It'd be stupid, and I may not like the job after it's done, but it would get done. But if someone were to give me a bulldozer and a crew, and ordered me to go move that mountain, I just couldn't get into it. What can I say? Nature. Don't ever try to betray it.

In 1993 I finally hung out my Asensio & Company shingle. I've always kept a small staff and maintained low overhead, but in the early days things were really tight. Our first work was government jobs that were being bid out to minority-owned companies. It's generally acknowledged that there's a bit of politics involved in the awarding of these contracts. But although we have never given political contributions to anybody, we scored two of the choicest government contracts in the country.

The first was to be comanaging underwriter of New York City's general obligation debt. In addition to our proposal for the job, we submitted a comprehensive, detailed research report on New York City's budget, revenues, and income—and I'm proud to say that Asensio & Company was the youngest brokerage ever to be awarded that job. We learned a whole lot about government financing and the way that the city pays its bills. I look at that report every now and then to remind me how difficult it is to get started in business.

We were also hired by the state of Wisconsin—a sought-after, competitive, $200,000 contract. There were no politics involved in getting this job. These were pragmatic, independent-thinking mid-westerners. They would have nothing to do with a broker unless that broker had some good research to offer them for their commission dollars.

SOLD SHORT

In 1993, the year we began, our income came from enormously leveraged trades. We had less than $25,000 in equity and made more than $200,000 in trading income in the three months we operated. This was before the popularization of day trading would create wild volatility. You can imagine the stuff that was going on with that account. In fact, the number of trades we did that year was so high, we got fined for trading too much too soon. It was a violation of our restriction agreement as a recently admitted broker-dealer. Later, when our target companies would seek material with which to besmirch us, these technical infractions would come back to haunt us.

In 1994 and 1995 we did research on the long side. We did an analysis of Coca-Cola when most Wall Street gurus thought the stock was going down. We looked at it and disagreed. The issues we raised were printed in *Barron's*. You can find it posted on our website. Now, people point to these reports from the long side and say it's nothing like what we do today—but it is. Every report, long or short, is a fundamental and independent analysis of the value of the underlying business both today and in the future.

As I've already explained, we got into short selling because we were fundamental analysts coping with a raging bull market. Experienced and reputable technical and fundamental analysts often state that they are concerned with the market because of its valuations. I have never felt that way. I looked to the fall of the Berlin Wall, the democratization of capital markets, and the decline in government regulation and intervention in the private sector as highly bullish.

But even before the tech bubble burst, in spring 2000, I had for the first time in my entire 20-year career on Wall Street begun to feel bearish because of the low cost of equity. The last time I had felt we had reached such an extreme was in 1982, when we saw 18 percent short-term interest rates. I believed then that the bottom had been reached. In 2000 I believe the opposite was true. As stock prices rise, equity becomes cheaper for companies: It costs them fewer shares to raise capital. Investors demand less and less for their money, certain that an even less discerning investor will come along and bail them out. But equity must have a cost. I believe that investors pushing up share prices to the point where there are negative or zero returns on capital ultimately must lead to economic difficulties.

I don't believe a capitalist society based on free enterprise can function with excessively low-cost equity capital. It is no different from when short-term rates were extremely high at 18 percent. Stock prices must reflect risk and future growth potential. When they don't, shams and frauds and even the honest are encouraged and enter the market and try to siphon off some of the largesse. So in a sense, a bull market is fertile ground for short sellers—but only if they really, really do their homework.

And what about the future? I'd like short sellers to be free to work, win or lose, independently of sometimes compromised regulators and sleazy lawyers. That's all.

CHAPTER THREE

THE FIRST SHORT: GENERAL NUTRITION TAKES ILL

We've encountered some perpetrators of deception in the markets who were truly malevolent characters, possibly even psychotic geniuses. We've come up against fraudsters so slick and professional that if they'd poured all that talent and energy into legitimate businesses they might have become actual corporate titans rather than playing at it for a few years before disappearing in disgrace (though not necessarily without the loot). But our first short did not pit us against some fiendish Dr. Evil. Our first short, in fact, was not only a legitimate business but a well-known household brand. What made it an interesting transaction—and a quintessential short sell—was that this company was involved in lucrative transactions with the investment banking sides of eight major Wall Street financial houses. And the stock-analysis departments of those firms, ostensibly independent of the investment banking side, ostensibly shielded by a so-called Chinese Wall, was releasing glowing appraisals of this company's stock while its business was deteriorating and the personally held shares of the company's top executives were being dumped faster than a Dennis Rodman bride.

SOLD SHORT

One question I am regularly asked: "When, why, and how did you become this aggressive, hostile *thing* that destroys companies?" The short answer is "I'm not, and I don't." The long answer is a bit more complicated.

By now you know my opinion on companies that sell stock to the public. If you're public, it's all about debate and disclosures. The short seller is vital in making the opaque transparent and insuring an orderly market. You also know that I believe that there are few unfairly *under*valued stocks in bull markets such as the one that began in the mid-1990s. However, an inflated market valuation based on irrational exuberance or investor sentiment is one thing. Overvaluation as a result of corporate deceit, fraud, or trickery is another.

So I suppose it was inevitable that by January 1996, with my humble investment bank in search of places to grow our money and that of our clients, I would finally put my market views into trading action. A confluence of events brought me to the realization that General Nutrition Corp. (GNC) had become grossly overvalued. The company was the unqualified darling of eight top-bracket Wall Street analysts, had rock-solid institutional investor support, was a runaway leader in its flourishing category, had a $1.8 billion market capitalization, and had grown in a short time like a St. Bernard puppy. The company had over 2,500 retail stores at the end of 1995, around 60 percent of them company owned, and planned to open 475 new stores in 1996.

While this growth seemed impressive, it camouflaged the real story. What I saw was heavy, rapid, and aggressive insider stock selling. I saw weak same-store sales growth, attained through excessive and costly promotions and mass-market discounts. I saw extremely low average annual store sales of $450,000. This made me wonder how GNC could pay overhead and still deliver anything more than illusions to their customers. Not that illusion sales aren't profitable, but this company's ugly balance sheet certainly was no illusion. I saw $200 million of bank debt and a tangible net worth of just $2 million. And all this before I found out that a vitamin scare was just around the corner.

During the week of November 9–15, 1995, Bill Watts, GNC's president and CEO, sold 80 percent of his holdings in the company, and two vice presidents sold 100 percent of their holdings. Altogether, five top executives sold a total of 283,000 shares that week. This was not a lot of stock, but these guys didn't hold a lot to begin with. Now, insider sales aren't in and of themselves an indication of trouble. When corporate executives sell a portion of their company's shares but continue to maintain a large holding in the company, they might simply be generating some cash. Sometimes people need money, want to spread their risk, or simply feel the time is right to cash in some of their chips.

When James Q. Crowe, president and CEO of Level 3 Communications, Inc. (Nasdaq: LVLT) decided to pull some cash from his LVLT holdings so he and his family could begin enjoying the fruits of his success, he issued a letter to shareholders. He announced on May 17, 1999, that he would be selling through a trustee 4,000 shares a day, no matter what the market price that day, for the next 250 trading days. The sales would execute automatically. At the end of the year he would still retain over 10 million shares of LVLT. To me this was a shrewd move, showing both integrity and business sense. Crowe was straightforward enough to disclose his intent openly in a press release rather than forcing investors to pore over a series of insider-trading reports as they speculate about his intent. He made provisions for his sales to have minimal impact on the market. And, most important, he retained a massive stake in his company even after the sale.

This is not what was happening at GNC. At the same time that analysts were pushing the stock to investors as a *buy*, insiders were clearing the shelves. It looked to us like they weren't scaring up a few bucks to redo the rec room and they weren't making personal judgments that the overall market had peaked. We believed this showed that the insiders had advance knowledge, not yet publicly disclosed, that serious problems were coming. If this was true, the executives should have waited to inform the stock's analysts or disseminate information to this effect before selling. Instead, they elected to unload their stock and then file statements disclosing their sales with the minimum of disclosure. Let's see if we were right.

Through December 1995, GNC stock held steady in the low-to-mid 20s. Institutional holders included at least 21 major funds with over 1 million shares each and dozens more with over 100,000 shares each. Whom could these guys sell to? It would have been beyond unlikely, beyond shocking even, for an analyst to have been bold enough to step forward and publicly question the value of this stock.

PaineWebber, Bear Stearns, Morgan Stanley, Alex. Brown, Smith Barney, and other heavy hitters were all bullish on GNC. And the stock might have held together, except that the company's problems coincided with an abrupt turnabout in the zeitgeist. After a consumer love affair with herbal remedies and other nutritional supplements, medical researchers were beginning to question their safety and efficacy. People started to realize that just because they bought something in a health food store, just because it was labeled "natural," it didn't necessarily mean the product would be good for them. Whether significant or not, these doubts came at the worst possible time for a company with such shaky financials.

GNC's business depended on store traffic, which was usually at the mercy of current health fads. For example, when melatonin was being hailed as a cure for jet lag and other sleep disorders, new customers crossed the GNC threshold in search of melatonin—and as long as they were there, maybe they'd pick up a few other things. And maybe they'd come back. In January 1996 beta carotene was the fad generating store traffic. But there were doubts. Nutrition experts started to question the value of powdered supplements, such as beta carotene, as opposed to live sources, such as fresh vegetables. At any rate, the medicinal benefit of any packaged vitamin or supplement has never been proven conclusively.

Other hot products generating store traffic were diet aids and energy boosters containing ephedra, also known as ephedrine or ma huang. Ephedra, particularly in combination with caffeine, can elevate blood pressure, an obvious danger to those who already have high blood pressure. This stimulant was implicated in more than two dozen deaths.

Some diet aids contained senna (also known as locust plant, or *Cassia angustifolia*), a potent laxative, or *Uva ursi*, a diuretic. Senna can flush electrolytes from the body, including potassium, which helps regulate the heartbeat.

In August 1995 the Food and Drug Administration recommended that a number of diet aids, including Super Ultra Slim Tea and Dieter's Tea, be labeled to warn consumers that the products contain laxatives, can cause adverse effects, do not significantly reduce the absorption of food calories, and can lead, with continued use, to serious injury or death.

Some states moved to ban ephedrine from over-the-counter products. Several scientists questioned whether the products had any value at all. Purdue University herb specialist Varro Tyler, Ph.D., was quoted as saying "The only way ephedra might work is by causing your hand to become so jittery you can't get food to your mouth." Seven percent of GNC's products contained ephedrine.

I had been looking for our first target. There seemed to be great promise in the changing public sentiment against nutritional supplements. At this point, I wasn't focusing on GNC and hadn't seen its dreadful financials. I was looking at herb companies doing pyramid-selling schemes.

A public relations guy at one of these companies inadvertently indicated to me that he was ultra busy battening down the hatches for a very nasty upcoming vitamin scare. Naturally I was interested, but he could or would reveal no more. So I had a kernel of knowledge needing follow-up. I found a big pharmaceutical company that owned a vitamin manufacturer and tried to sound them out. This led me to more people, and I got more color, and more color, until finally I was led to an ongoing National Cancer Institute (NCI) study. Was the rumored vitamin scare the blow-back from the soon-to-be-released findings of the NCI study? But the study was ongoing; interim results were not scheduled to be released.

We called a list of NCI phone numbers and eventually found the person in charge of the study. I called, and an associate in his office gave me the whole story. The NCI had conducted a large, long-term study on the effects of vitamins on smokers and nonsmokers. While I couldn't get precise results from the doctors doing the study, the situation looked awful. The tests had been halted prematurely because the subjects in the placebo group were getting along better than the people taking the vitamins. How screwy is that? The study had been large and well administered, and I was certain that the results would be damaging to some sector or company in the vitamin industry—perhaps a certain retailer with less-than-enthusiastic shareholders on its management team.

At this point, I came upon GNC, learned of its problems, and began my due diligence. I discovered that in the early 1990s, a far less momentous vitamin scare in Finland had slowed traffic in GNC and caused earnings to fall significantly the following quarter. Plus, GNC had some past run-ins with the Federal Trade Commission (FTC). According to GNC's SEC filings, the FTC in 1984 instituted an investigation of GNC, alleging deceptive acts and practices in connection with the advertising and marketing of certain GNC products. GNC accepted a proposed consent order, finalized in 1989, under which the company agreed to refrain from, among other things, making certain claims with respect to its products unless the claims were based on and substantiated by reliable and competent scientific evidence. The FTC also chastised GNC regarding its "iron deficiency anemia" products in 1970—GNC paid a civil penalty of $2.4 million for this infraction.

On January 3, 1996, GNC announced lower fourth-quarter earnings, and the stock dipped. The next day Bruce Missett, an analyst from Morgan Stanley, declared that the market had overreacted; he maintained his *strong buy* recommendation. Morgan Stanley held 1,679,506 shares of GNC in two accounts as of September 1995—a $35 million investment. To me, these were 35 million reasons to ignore the recommendation of Mr. Bruce Missett. In fact, I shorted GNC and began to assemble Asensio & Company's first *strong sell* advisory.

One of the principles that allows us to sell short and publicly disseminate opinions comes from the Supreme Court decision *Ray Dirks v. the SEC* in the early 1980s. The SEC had censured Dirks in 1973 for issuing reports to his clients about an incipient scandal at Equity Funding—a scandal that Dirks is credited with uncovering. That's right. The SEC sided with the then almighty NYSE, which didn't want its members uncovering fraud. The Supreme Court overturned this censure.

Dirks is better known today, however, as a champion of speculative stocks. He and his John Muir Company in the early 1980s and Short Busters Club in the 1990s were allied with a slew of dodgy securities. In 1994 Dirks was accused in *Business Week* of the misleading promotion of stocks in which his company held an undisclosed position. (The article contains an amusing bit of Dirks-speak. When an incomplete disclosure is brought to his attention, he replies, "When you do industry reports on 20, 30, 40 companies, you make mistakes—not that I'm saying this was a mistake.") Ironically, the legislation Dirks helped bring into being can now be used to protect short sellers who might publish negative information about the companies Dirks himself promotes.

As we prepared our report, we learned through a January 16 media alert that the NCI would be announcing results of the two beta carotene studies at a January 18 press conference. Usually the results of such studies are first published in peer-reviewed medical journals, then publicized. A press conference was unusual. We decided to write as much of our report as we could, then finish it with results of the studies when announced and publish a *strong sell* that same day, January 18.

As the buzz commenced, GNC's institutional armies went on full alert. In coverage issued January 17, Janet Kloppenburg of Robertson Stephens & Co. preemptively discounted the potential effect of the study on GNC sales and reiterated her *buy*. As of September 1995, Robertson Stephens held 800,000 shares of GNC in one portfolio and 400,000 shares in a mutual fund—it was a $25 million fan club.

At 6:00 A.M. on January 18, I had someone at La Guardia set to fly to D.C. for the National Cancer Institute press conference. But these best-laid plans went awry: His flight, all flights, had been fogged in. So we had to try to reach a law firm in D.C. and find someone there who could attend the conference in our stead. Of course, we couldn't rouse any lawyers at that time of the morning. We reached security guards and receptionists. I was almost frantic. Even though I had a strong inkling of the contents of the two reports, based on past experience I knew that anything can happen between an inkling and the printed page.

Fortunately, we got a representative to the National Cancer Institute who obtained and faxed us a copy of the press release. Once I read it, I knew everything would be all right. The NCI's Beta Carotene and Retinal Efficacy trials (known as CARET), a large, long-term study of the effects of the combination of beta carotene and vitamin A as preventive agents for lung cancer, had terminated the week before, after its 18,314 participants were instructed to stop taking their vitamins. "Interim study results indicate the supplements provide no benefit, and may be causing harm," according to the synopsis.

The other trial, the Physician's Health Study, had contacted 22,071 male physicians nationwide over 12 years. The result: "The study showed no significant evidence of benefit or harm from beta carotene on cancer or cardiovascular disease." Peter Greenwald, M.D., director of the NCI's Division of Cancer Prevention and Control, stated, "The National Cancer Institute has never had a recommendation for Americans to take supplements. . . . These studies show nothing to suggest that smokers or nonsmokers might benefit from beta carotene supplements."

Could anything have been more damaging to a company specializing in nutritional supplements? As soon as the press conference ended, we were ready to roll. We placed our *strong sell* advisory on the news wires, highlighting the two studies, the deteriorating fundamentals, and the key officers aggressively selling their stock.

This was the first time we or anyone else in our business had issued a short-sell recommendation over the news wires. It was also new to the securities industry to have one of its very own member firms speak out against a company that had been its darling.

Today we continue to issue reports through the news wires, but ever since GNC, investors also have been able to check for our latest reports at www.asensio.com. Although in early 1996 the day-trading phenomenon was still a few years away, in terms of accessing corporate information on the Internet, the revolution was on. The Internet had become an empowering tool, and the wall between insiders and outsiders was showing cracks. As someone who believes in total transparency of information about publicly traded companies, I couldn't be more pleased.

Please understand the situation and my mind-set at the time. Not only was I a complete unknown, but I was also a neophyte in the world of short selling. While today we field hundreds of calls a month from an international array of short sellers, back then I didn't know a single trader who sold short on a regular basis.

Plus we were hopelessly naïve. We felt the materiality of our information would speak for itself. We had found a distortion of the facts and were setting the record straight. Our perception was that even without a widely disseminated report exposing the company's omissions and misstatements of fact, the stock was overvalued and sure to decline.

Yeah, right. What we didn't know was that we were stumbling toward a pair of spinning buzz saws, one powered by the institutions backing GNC and the other by an upcoming public offering that would require a robust share price and an optimistic outlook.

We blithely hit the wires. Anyone clicking NEWS for GNC found something they might never have seen before. Remember now, this was my first *strong sell*. The overall reaction can be characterized as "Who the hell is Asensio?" Portfolio managers called, though none out of true diligence. A few called out of curiosity, some irate, some just plain comical. "Oh, yeah?" said one. "Well, we know what's going on. Just wait till you see what we're gonna do to you." Thugs. It was just what I would get later from some bought-and-paid-for retail broker calling me with glee on some other stock scam, telling me he was going to buy more, in the face of the plain, negative facts, and would bury the shorts with his awesomely macho power and might.

But that day the stock didn't move. The media consensus: "General Nutrition carries the day." A national business paper opined what a great, leading-edge company GNC was, such a great marketing company—not even a vitamin company, just a genius marketing company. "They're selling the sizzle," they gushed, "not the steak." Only *The New York Times* had a clue. On January 19 the paper reported, "Federal health officials said they hoped this would spell the end of the beta carotene fad." God bless the *New York Times*.

On January 19, in the face of market intransigence, we published a follow-up report titled "The Closing Bell Falls on Deaf Ears." After summarizing the grievous import of the previous day's news, we took on the institutions: "This morning's market action shows the unwillingness of large institutional holders to sell their stock. Investors continue to listen to analysts who have no choice but to continue to recite the Company's position. We believe that there is no reason to hold these shares. . . ."

In response to this, GNC's general counsel called me and threatened litigation. And the institutions, like good soldiers, reinforced the battle lines for GNC.

Dana Telsey of Bear Stearns published an analysis on January 19, maintaining her *attractive* rating on GNC stock, arguing there are always studies coming out and the impact of those studies is always short-lived. Bear Stearns held at least 10,380 GNC shares as of September 1995 and had been involved as an underwriter in a public offering for the company. A Smith Barney report of January 19 discounted the NCI studies as "irrelevant to GNCI" and advised investors to "buy on weakness." Smith Barney was also involved in underwriting the upcoming GNC offering.

All the analysts pointed out that beta carotene represented only 0.3 percent of GNC's sales, but they neglected the huge impact beta carotene had been providing in drawing new customers into the stores and the negative impact of the smaller, less publicized Finnish study. Now U.S. government officials were telling consumers that beta carotene was just a fad.

The analysts' view was based on earnings per share. They weren't going to decrease those earnings per share because of an event that I viewed as a negative for future earnings. The way Wall Street adjusts earnings is to take direction from the company, and GNC's professed direction was clearly up, up, and away—even though, up in the boardroom, guys who knew more than anyone about the company were flinging their personal shares onto the trading floor.

Remember, this was our first deal. We felt we were providing a service to professional investors. To me, GNC's problems were obvious and too numerous to ignore. I phoned a large portfolio manager who had an enormous GNC holding to try to convince him to let me sell the stock for him. It would have been a nice commission for us, and it would have helped him to exit a deteriorating situation. The conversation went nowhere—but I learned my first lesson about how little some big investors really know about their holdings. But he held on with a white-knuckled grip, like a water skier refusing to let go while being dragged to the seabed by a sinking motorboat.

On January 22, 1996, just four days after the attack of the killer press conference, GNC announced a secondary offering of 16.4 million shares. None of the shares was sold to raise capital for the company; all were from insiders cashing out. This was a bailout of massive proportions. The sellers were telling the Street, "You like it so much, here, you can have it."

The offering was to be underwritten by Morgan Stanley, Alex. Brown, Donaldson Lufkin & Jenrette Securities Corp., PaineWebber, and Smith Barney—the core of the GNC fan club. The firms could not have been sanguine about the timing, whether coincidental or deliberate, but the offering proceeded nonetheless. Despite the tsunami of negative developments, the bankers had decided to continue to furnish GNC its seawall of support.

Alex. Brown underwrote 2,261,674 shares in connection with the offering, and its analyst Marcia Aaron rated GNC a *strong buy*. Morgan Stanley underwrote 2,261,674 GNC shares in connection with the public offering, and its analyst Bruce Missett rated GNC a *strong buy*. Donaldson Lufkin & Jenrette underwrote 2,261,674 shares, and its analyst Gary Balter was recommending GNC. PaineWebber underwrote 2,261,674 shares, and its analyst Mark Hanratty rated GNC *attractive* on September 20, 1995, with a $50 price target. Smith Barney underwrote 2,261,674 shares, and its analyst Gary Giblen rated GNC a *buy*. Smith Barney added GNC to its emerging growth mid-cap focus list on February 28, 1996.

Fortunately, although the market was initially defiant, it was not insane. From January 16 on, GNC stock slowly, steadily drifted downward from $22. Too many sell orders were coming in, and despite the institutional support, the stock price sagged to $19 in a few days. We were a small company with a significant paper profit, so we covered. For us this was an insta deal—in and out before the month was over. We had made our largest one-trade, short-term profit to date. Unlike some of our later targets, this stock wasn't a complete zero; it just needed to move down to find its true value. It would eventually drop as low as $9; for three years, until the 1999 buyout offer of $25, it never again climbed back into the mid-20s.

On February 7, 1996, the GNC public offering hit the market. Why wasn't it delayed until more information was available about the study's impact? Perhaps because the underwriters wanted their payday and because the primary seller, GNC board member Thomas H. Lee, understood only too well the company's declining situation.

The firm of Thomas H. Lee is a large leveraged-buyout outfit. Lee's most famous coup was in Snapple, which was sold at substantial profit to Quaker Oats at its very peak of value. (Today it's obvious that Quaker Oats overpaid for Snapple, and the acquisition cost shareholders dearly.) A director of GNC, Lee controlled an enormous block of its stock. Thomas H. Lee Equity Partners, L.P., would realize gross proceeds of $202 million from the offering. The ML-Lee Acquisition Fund would rake in $105 million, and the Lee Trust (beneficiary: Thomas H. Lee), $29 million. In other words, almost all of the February 7 public offering was Thomas Lee–controlled stock, and, as with Snapple, Lee was unloading his stock at the ideal time. The balance of the offering's proceeds went to another GNC director, Thomas Shepherd, who sold 87,686 shares in the offering for $1.8 million.

Commenting on Thomas Lee's cashing out $336 million of GNC stock, Bear Stearns, in a January 23 report, lamely claimed that "the timing of this transaction coincides with business opportunities that are available to the Thomas H. Lee Company, rather than any issues related to [GNC]." What are these business opportunities? And, hey, if Lee likes those better, maybe I should too? I have often been accused of being an astute observer of the obvious.

On March 5 GNC announced that its year-end earnings per share would be up 44 percent over the previous year. Still, the insiders continued to bail out. GNC chairman Jerry Horn, president and CEO William Watts (who had already sold 80 percent of his holdings the past November), Louis Mancini (president of GNC's retail division, senior VP for production, and general manager), and Edwin Kozlowski (senior VP, CFO, and treasurer) all sold stock.

On May 28, after the close of trading, GNC announced that comparable same-store sales in the second quarter for company-owned stores would be 3 to 6 percent below the previous year's. The next day the stock dropped from $18.50 to $14. After this announcement, the friendly analysts started acting like it was General Nausea Corporation: Alex. Brown cut GNC to *buy* from *strong buy*, PaineWebber cut it to *neutral* from *attractive*, and Smith Barney moved to *underperform* from *buy*.

GNC, unlike the tech pretend-to-bes on which Asensio & Company later focused, had intrinsic value and muddled through. In July 1999 GNC accepted a buyout offer of $25 per share from Numico NV, a Dutch company.

Asensio & Company's primary focus before we started our adversarial short-selling was risk arbitrage. And at around the same time that the GNC deal was closing we were very fortunate to find two great arbitrage trades involving Bally. A Bally takeover deal had been on the Street for more than 18 months and had been just about left for dead. No one believed the deal was going to close until the day it actually did. It's a tribute to the people of Alliance Gaming that they actually pulled it off in the end. The deal was valued at over $12 a share, but two weeks before it closed, Bally stock was at $6—that's how little confidence the market had in the deal's consummation.

The First Short: General Nutrition Takes III

I call this type of investing high-risk, wide-spread arbitrage. We were in this deal large. The price would narrow when people thought it was going to close, then the deal would fail to close, and boom, the price would widen again. It was like a dysfunctional seduction, where one day one party is keen and the other isn't, then the next day things are reversed—more like a show-biz wedding than a corporate merger.

I was on that deal every working hour of every day for six months, nonstop. That's what some arbs do and what we did in the wild short sales to follow. But this deal was about generating lots of capital, fast. We were invested to the limit and leveraged to the max. A quarter of a point meant a great deal to us. I phoned lawyers and court officials involved in some related litigation; spoke to regulators, financiers, back-office personnel, secretaries, neighbors, and, for good measure, other gaming companies. I had a call list that went on forever. I looked at the deal on the table and bet that this was the one that was finally going to get financed. And it did.

The year 1996 was the first big year for Asensio & Company. GNC was not only our first aggressive short sale but also the beginning of our long-fought-for prosperity. We would need the bankroll, because we were about to enter the fray in one of the most notorious and risky short plays of recent times: the glamorous, high-flying, and indubitably dubious Diana Corporation.

Sadly, just as my business was beginning to thrive, I was stung by the death of my uncle Francisco, who insisted on being called Uncle Frank. Uncle Frank was the very proud grandson of Vicente Garcia, the highly regarded warrior and general who fought against Spanish oppression.

Uncle Frank, who wrote several books about his grandfather and Latin American art, migrated to the United States long before the rest of the family. He was a classic New Yorker, unassuming,

SOLD SHORT

Gene Marcial: The Promoter's Pal

Hey, sports fans! Wouldn't it be great if there were some weekly sports magazine that had a column where some guy tried to pick winning teams—and, on a regular basis, the guy was spectacularly *wrong*? You could use his picks as a negative indicator. Whenever he said one team was going to win, you would bet on the other team.

Well, the business world has such a person, and his name is Generoso "Gene" Marcial. He writes a column in *Business Week* called "Inside Wall Street," but apparently he has crawled so deep inside the Street that he can no longer see the light of day. Marcial swallows the hype of the hypesters, regurgitates the pump of the pump-and-dumpsters. No other pundit has come out on the *buy* side of so many stocks identified by Asensio & Company as grossly overvalued.

Once you learn to look for Marcial's cues—unsubstantiated enthusiasm, dark hints that short sellers have oversold a stock—you, too, can profit by shorting his picks. A survey by TheStreet.com found that Marcial's picks tend to burp up briefly on the Friday mornings they appear, then slowly sink, sink, sink.

Perhaps Marcial's most egregious lack of quality control came on January 27, 1997, when he devoted precious column inches to the pronouncements of Michael Schonberg, a Dreyfus fund manager whom you will meet later. The performance of Schonberg's penny-stock portfolio was about as stiff as Keanu Reeves playing Hamlet. Still, Marcial allowed Schonberg to pump his fund's million-plus-share holding in the ridiculous Ultrafem, which soon went bankrupt quicker than you can say "He shills shocking sham stocks." The SEC finally fined and suspended Schonberg in 2000. Marcial still has his column.

Here's the scorecard for Marcial vs. Asensio:

June 21, 1993: Gene Marcial plugs General Nutrition. "The stock has more distance to go on the upside, says one [unnamed] analyst, who is impressed by its continued fast sales growth." Better not make it a longer-term holding then that Friday morning blip, Mr./Ms. Unnamed Analyst.

The First Short: General Nutrition Takes III

November 27, 1995: Gene Marcial has discovered a new remedy for impotence! And it's called Viagr- . . . oops, no, it's something called MUSE, made by Vivus (Nasdaq: VVUS). We reported on December 10, 1997, that MUSE inflamed and enlarged the penis but did not actually cause it to become erect. The stock trades today at a very limp $4.

September 2, 1996: The short sellers have pummeled drug maker Biovail (NYSE: BVF), but they can just shut up, because Gene Marcial knows better. His sources say the shorts haven't done their research. On September 13, 1996, we issued a *strong sell* on Biovail after extensive research correctly foretold that, contrary to bullish expectations, the company didn't have a generic copy of the block-buster drug Procardia. (Okay, the stock did well, anyway.)

March 17, 1997: "What's so hot about Hemispherx?" asks Gene Marcial, waxing rhetorical and just a wee bit alliterative. Phase III trials for its drug Ampligen, he whispers, "are under way in 30 sites." In reality, the FDA had approved Phase III trials for Ampligen way back in 1992, and even now, nine years later, Phase III has not been completed. But Marcial is still so enthusiastic about Hemispherx (AMEX: HEB) that on November 23, 1998, two months after Asensio & Company—not to mention Marcial's *BW* colleague Gary Weiss—have laid out the devastating case against the Hemispherx promotion, Marcial offers "shortbuster" Ray Dirks a turn at the podium. Dirks tries to promote the safety of Ampligen with O.J.'s-glove-don't-fit logic: "If the drug was unsafe, the FDA wouldn't have permitted its use in this manner"—this shortly after the FDA told Hemispherx to stop claiming its drug was safe. May we suggest the snappier "If it's in Phase III, it ain't so dead-ly"?

August 25, 1997: Gene Marcial takes "a second look" at Sterling Vision (Nasdaq: ISEE), in which "smart-money investors" are "snapping up shares." According to "one money manager" (no names, please), the $6 stock is due for a $20 buyout. "One analyst" (anonymous) is predicting $1-per-share earnings in 1998. In fact, our August 19, 1997, report showed that insiders were selling millions of shares on the heels of these false takeover rumors, spread by hacky financial columnists (no names). The stock, now called Emerging Vision, trades around 50 cents.

September 29, 1997: Gene Marcial has discovered a new remedy for impotence! And it's called Viagr- . . . oops, no, it's something called Vasomax, the third loser stock promotion from Zonagen, Inc. (Nasdaq: ZONA). Too bad. Marcial backs the wrong horse once again. He quotes the very enthusiastic Jacqueline Siegel of Raymond James & Associates (comanager of a Zonagen stock offering) and Drs. Ray Rosen and Irwin Goldstein (Zonagen corporate consultants) and claims that Vasomax "helps restore a man's natural ability to achieve an erection—without resorting to artificial means." Since FDA trials showed that this is in fact *not* true, perhaps Marcial was relying on firsthand information.

August 16, 1999: Gene Marcial makes a pun of sorts in asking "Time for Biotime?" In 1998 Asensio & Company reported on the inflated claims and limited market for Biotime (AMEX: BTX). Marcial must have missed that, because here he is allowing "investment pro" Al Kingsley to promote the 7 percent stake in BTX held by his Greenway Partners money management firm. Biotime received the expected FDA approval for its blood extender, Hextend, but what Marcial, despite his tireless investigative work, fails to disclose is that the product is barely selling for less than $30 per liter. So? So Biotime, in its earlier promotional material, had been promising a $100-plus price tag. Not to mention a little overzealous faux pas in their SEC filing that mistakenly called their water-based plasma extender a blood substitute. Not to mention that, as of early 2001, sales of the product have been described in filings as "immaterial." If I were Gene Marcial, I might describe these as "bloody large discrepancies."

matter-of-fact, but very sophisticated, a highly intelligent man who greatly enjoyed the city's wealth of culture.

Uncle Frank established and ran *Noticias de Arte*, a Spanish-language arts newspaper, for over 25 years. It was a free handout that he distributed himself; he would sell ads to Goya Foods and the like. He filled the paper with wonderfully rich critiques of Hispanic art activities and New York arts and cultural events. Uncle Frank was a renowned critic of modern Latin American painting. When he was young he'd had a gallery in Cuba where he socialized with the great Cuban painters of his time: Wilfredo Lam, Mario Carreno, Amelia Pelaez, René Portocarrero. He had left Cuba with sadness but never spoke badly of Castro's regime, something that infuriated his Miami comrades.

My father had come up from Florida to be with Uncle Frank in his last days. The morning Uncle Frank passed away, I had stayed home with my father. We were watching a man involved in one of the scams Asensio & Company had focused on being interviewed on CNBC. The call from the hospital came while the man was telling viewers about his extraordinary (not) new (not) product.

I was very close to Uncle Frank. I often think of the coincidence of these events and of the enormous good fortune the firm has had since he passed away.

CHAPTER FOUR

DIANA:
"THE SWITCH WORKS!"

Chapter 1 described the events of October 15, 1996—the day the Diana promoters tried to "get shorty." Now the complete Diana Story. It's the tale of a big clunky rusting hunk of metal that was being fobbed off as a glossy new sports car. And when a promoter named James Fiedler saw that old jalopy, he figured it might just be capable of carrying him and his associates into a land of bilk and money.

I was not the first to note Diana's preposterous overvaluation. Diana's rise had been ridiculed in *Barron's*, by Dan Dorfman on CNBC, and by Floyd Norris in the *New York Times* long before we kicked in our two cents. But at that point there had been no public discussion of specific technical problems; we figured that was the reason the stock was able to keep sloughing off the negative press. This was one of those deals where the shorts were too outraged by the ridiculousness of it all to stop and explain the deal to anyone without getting emotional.

Diana had been a Milwaukee-based holding company for various low-tech ventures. Its chairman and CEO was Richard Fisher. Eighty-eight percent of Diana's sales derived from its unprofitable

SOLD SHORT

Atlanta Provision Company subsidiary, a distributor of meat and seafood. Diana had been trying to sell this unit but found no takers.

In December 1994 Diana entered into a joint venture with Sattel Technologies, Inc., a small San Fernando Valley–based telecom firm, to form Sattel Communications Corp., which would be 50 percent owned by Diana. (Diana's stake soon grew to 80 percent.) Prior to this deal, Diana stock had been selling at around $3.50 a share. Soon after, however, Fisher met James Fiedler, an experienced telecom promoter. Fiedler had been fired a year earlier after presiding over the rise and fall of a would-be cutting-edge telecom called Summa Four Network Systems, Inc. Fisher put Fiedler in charge of Sattel in September 1995, and a high-tech promotion was born.

Sattel's engineers had designed a telephone switch that Diana dubbed "DataNet," intended for remote territories of Southeast Asia. Despite its inapplicability to modern, first-world needs, DataNet was to become the centerpiece of a massive promote. According to an SEC 8K-A filing dated January 16, 1996, Sattel's total investment in equipment had been only $43,962. During the 166 days between Diana's purchase of Sattel and the announcement of the conclusion of its "development" of DataNet, Sattel's total expenditures were only $124,000. Sattel didn't even hire managers until a year after it developed DataNet. Somehow the market had missed these details. More obvious observations.

Despite having spent so little on R&D, Diana was ready to unleash the mighty DataNet. In 16 press releases and a promotional Internet site, Diana claimed that the primitive DataNet would revolutionize and economize the data switching capabilities of Internet Service Providers (ISPs). Diana's 5.3 million shares rocketed from a pre–Sattel $3.50 to well over $100, beefing up the company's market capitalization from $20 million to over $600 million.

The Diana promotion played out in four sequential phases spanning several years. Each time the stock crashed through the floor, it would come bounding back on a fresh blizzard of "new" information. The first and most successful phase, which took Diana into the public eye, was begun by retail brokers and Jonathan Steinberg, who bought the stock for a hedge fund he was managing called Wisdom Tree, L.P.

Jonathan Steinberg's father, Saul Steinberg, is a legendary corporate raider, best known for his Reliance Insurance Company. Jonathan Steinberg's wife is CNBC's cult icon Maria Bartiromo. In 1988 the younger Steinberg bought the *Penny Stock Journal* and remade it into a glossy monthly, *Individual Investor*, which focused on small stocks. In 1997 the SEC began to investigate a conflict of interest in his running a hedge fund that held many of the stocks recommended in his magazine. Steinberg shut down the fund. (In September 2000, reportedly starved for capital, Steinberg sold *Individual Investor's* website, InsiderInvestor, to EDGAR Online.) Later, when I spoke to Russell Amuth, portfolio manager at Wisdom Tree, and Eric Singer, a Wisdom Tree analyst, I would gain insight into Steinberg's early investment in and promotion of Diana. But Diana soon grew way beyond just one modest fund and rag sheet.

Also early in Phase 1, Joe Noel, a telecommunications-equipment analyst at Hambrecht & Quist, a white-shoed San Francisco–based investment house specializing in technology stocks, had been privately giving Diana a hearty thumbs-up, ostensibly only to his best clients. These recommendations were widely leaked, which led me to believe they'd been intended for broader consumption all along. Noel continued to rate the stock a *buy* even after it rose to its improbable heights. He had made a few successful calls in early 1996, notably PairGain Technologies and Cascade Communications, so his credibility at the time was riding high.

Mind you, this was a 1996 Internet/telecom promotion. The Street was ill-equipped to evaluate these product claims, and Sattel had found fertile ground to cultivate its fairy tales. Individual investors and large institutions piled in. None had any knowledge of the switch and its functionality. They couldn't have, because it wasn't at all what it was supposed to be.

Likewise, as the shorts began sniffing around and taking short positions, they, too, risked great sums of money without taking a good, deliberate look at that switch. The fact that Diana had paid so little for the switch or its development was publicly available in footnotes to Diana's SEC 10-K filings, but nobody had brought out that simple fact. To many seasoned short sellers, this case was just too obvious and offensive for them to bother with serious research. While I respect the intuition of certain short sellers and have seen some of them profit from such "vibe-based" investing, Asensio & Company didn't take the plunge without methodical fact checking.

We found that the few telecom consultants who knew the switch referred to it as a "boat anchor," the only use they could think of for that hunk of metal. It had been designed years earlier for installation in small islands in Southeast Asia with minimal switching needs. Wags in the press, referring to Diana's main source of income, called it a "meat switch." Bethany McLean of *Fortune*, in mentioning our report, would in November 1996 dub it a "dubious switch."

Although it would be months before we were able to compile an exhaustive engineering report on the switch's software and hardware, we felt its low creation cost and nonexistent development costs were important issues—not to mention Fiedler's history of overpromoting telecom products. We decided to prepare a report on the company. It would be our second public short.

Our previous success with General Nutrition would have no impact on the way our Diana report would be received. It's no different today, 25 shorts later. We don't expect a stock to trade down simply because of the performance of our past reports, no matter how consistently accurate our calls. But this time around, as opposed to GNC, we were more insistent. We firmly believed that Diana was nothing but a scam. Period. Terminal value: Zero. Our battle with Diana would become a steady, public, and at times vicious conflict.

Our reports would add important information to the public discussion. We were the first to disclose the low cost for the switch's creation; Diana's lack of R&D, technical research, and manufacturing capability; the fact that management had been issuing misleading statements; and past questionable dealings of James Fiedler and others at the company. We were the first to attack the product's technology and utility. The other shorts had gone no further than saying "Hey, it's a decades-old, low-tech stock promote run by Fisher that's turned into a high-tech promote now. It used to be based on sausages; now it's based on an Internet switch. Ha ha ha, isn't that funny." They were right to scoff, but Diana's shortcomings were still meat related—its public relations department was manufacturing bologna, and management's product claims were what is known in the meat business as "all fat, no beef."

No one had challenged Fiedler's promotional declarations the way we did. When he issued a statement, we would respond, "No, that's not true. Here are the facts." Nobody else examined Fiedler's background and that of his cronies, Mel Ethem and Tony Squeglia. This was the third telecom promote to be launched by that ignoble triumvirate. Fiedler was the tech guy and the leader, Ethem the marketing maven, and Squeglia handled corporate communications—the spin doctor. They knew enough to promote the type of breakthrough telecom product that could ignite widespread interest, but they never actually bothered to produce and market such a product for real.

Their first concentrated effort was at Timeplex Inc., where Fiedler was the executive VP and chief operating officer, Squeglia was in charge of corporate communications, and Ethem was VP for worldwide sales. Timeplex had been a leading supplier of T1 multiplexers, but with T1 business stagnating, Fiedler announced in October 1991 that the company had produced breakthroughs that everyone else in the industry had wanted to accomplish but none had. Or so he said. In fact, it was one of Fiedler's trademark maneuvers to grasp onto the rear bumper of a bandwagon and portray himself as the driver. That "breakthrough" promotion was soon forgotten.

The three moved on to Summa Four. Fiedler served as Summa Four's president from June 1993 until July 1994. His promotional exertions there were typical. During Fiedler's first eight months, the stock rose steeply, as high as $42.25. By the end of his tenure, Summa shares had plummeted. After a string of positive news, a surprise July 5, 1994, announcement blaming delayed contract negotiations for disappointing earnings caused the stock to drop to $12. Fiedler was fired not long after this earnings announcement.

The tricky telecompadres insinuated themselves in whatever was hot at the moment. They went from multiplexing and routers at Timeplex to scaleable, small, computerized switches at Summa Four. Now it was the mid-'90s—time to move on to the Internet, to Diana.

In September 1995 Fiedler was made chairman and CEO of Diana's Sattel subsidiary. Squeglia came aboard as Sattel's director of corporate communications, and Ethem as vice president and general manager of North American operations. While in the past they had been involved in promising blue-sky telecom promotes at legitimate companies, this time they were climbing into a total shell, a nontech company whose primary revenue source was a money-bleeding meat distributor. Perhaps not coincidentally, Diana's stock rose from $7 to $12 the month Fiedler signed on.

At the time of Fiedler's appointment, Diana was claiming that Sattel's DataNet switch could provide 75 percent savings to ISPs on dial-up transportation costs as well as eliminating the need for costly equipment, providing greater security, and delivering all-digital transmission for improved error-corrected data. According to our analysis, these claims were simply untrue. Nonetheless, by December 1995 the stock had spiked up from $12 to $25.

Diana was one of the first shorts vs. longs battles to be fought on Internet message boards. An anonymous poster who turned out to be one Alan Wolman disparaged Diana's short sellers, stated that a painful short squeeze was likely, and claimed to have knowledge that "several large funds may be initiating long positions." Pretty standard message-board bravado, right? Except that, without disclosing it, Wolman was at the time a broker at Bear Stearns. The New York Stock Exchange disciplined Wolman for improperly circulating rumors and fined him $10,000. Such were the passions incited by Diana.

With the bad press sloughed off, with more institutions hopping aboard, and with nobody doing serious research on the company, Diana's stock nearly doubled again in April 1996, up to $51. But Team Diana wasn't nearly ready to cash out. For them, the month of May would be merry, merry indeed.

The company needed to start posting some sales agreements for the DataNet, but naturally there were no takers. The pièce de résistance to the promotion would be a "customer" to provide the appearance of sales and income.

Concentric Network Corporation was then an ISP with an acute cash-flow problem. Concentric's wealthy venture capitalist had cut the firm off, and it needed money to meet payroll and operating expenses. Diana, its coffers swollen from offshore placements that capitalized on the stock promote, offered Concentric a $5 million cash loan, convertible into Concentric stock. At the same time, Concentric signed a sales agreement for the DataNet that, in the end, was never honored.

On May 8 a Memorandum of Understanding between Concentric and Sattel was announced. This jolt of credibility, as artificial and absurd as a pink plastic lawn flamingo, propelled Diana into the stratosphere. In words he must have choked on, Hank Nothhaft, Concentric's CEO, allowed Diana to quote him in a press release as stating "The Sattel agreement is key to Concentric Network improving its coverage and dramatically reducing its cost of providing services." On May 10 Diana published a release valuing the Concentric deal at $42 million, stating that Concentric had ordered 21 switches at an average cost of $2 million each.

Thanks to the Concentric "deal," the institutional support, and the absence of serious analysis, the stock shot up as high as $120 on May 24. I look back and wonder about the people who paid that much. Obviously they were thinking that someone else would soon be offering more for the stock, and more and more and more. But no—$120 would be the apogee of the Diana rocket. When did those buyers finally realize there would be no "greater fool" to bail them out?

Our *strong sell* report was issued on May 29, 1996.

We followed up with another report on June 4. The stock began tumbling downward. The short interest in Diana rose to 1.2 million shares, representing almost 25 percent of the total stock in the float. Among other things, the stock suffered from the fact that finally someone had begun releasing truthful information about the company. For example, we cited Diana's ludicrous description of itself as a "leader" and "manufacturer" in the telecommunications industry, when in fact it was most emphatically neither.

On June 14 Diana published two press releases claiming that its first DataNet switch was now "up and running" for Concentric. The following week we published a report that debunked Diana's DataNet claims and explained the unbearable lightness of the Concentric deal. Fiedler shot back the following day with a bold declaration that Diana would be shipping the remaining 19 switches of its 21-switch, $42 million Concentric deal within four *days*. Over four *years* later, those switches have yet to be shipped. The damaging dis-

closures, along with the way the company's meat division was clog-
ging its cash arteries, dragged Diana's stock down as low as $34 a
mere month after its $120 peak. It is hard for me to fathom how in-
vestors and institutional buyers could note this company's wildly er-
ratic price behavior and stream of damaging revelations yet continue
to purchase or hold this stock.

On June 28, 1996, Diana filed its annual SEC 10-K statement
for the year ended April 1, 1996. The company's 10-K contradicted
most of its own DataNet product claims and stated flat out: "The
Company had no significant research and development activities
during the last three fiscal years." The smoking-gun 10-K also disclosed that Sattel Technologies, Diana's joint-venture partner, was
unloading its Diana stock. Sattel Technologies had reduced its interest in Sattel Communications Corp. from the original 50 percent
down to 4 percent and had surrendered 15 percent of Sattel and
50,000 Diana shares in exchange for being released from product
development obligations and further capital contributions to the
DataNet. Diana also agreed to help Sattel sell up to 100,000 shares
of Diana common stock. Please note: This information is not the
proprietary research of a connected, seasoned analyst. It is based on
astute observation of the obvious.

Many SEC filings since at least 1996 are available for free at
www.sec.gov as well as on such sites as www.FreeEdgar.com and
www.10kWizard.com. I cannot urge investors strongly enough to
examine these filings and compare them to a company's claims before investing. On the surface these filings might seem intimidating,
perhaps deadly dull, but I assure you that the more you examine SEC
filings, the more you can see in them and the faster you can zero in
on the truth about a company. SEC filings are truly the window to
the corporate soul. Certainly, if every Diana shareholder or potential
investor had read and understood the contents of this 10-K, there
would have been less demand for the stock.

Around this time, Diana was able to put Phase 2 into motion. Apparently it figured that not many investors would read the 10-K. And it was right.

On July 26, 1996, Diana hired investment house Hambrecht & Quist to help it "evaluate strategic alternatives," including separating its units—essentially meaning a divorce of Sattel from the unsellable meat division that was providing most of the company's revenue. (Or, as described so felicitously in Diana press releases, "Diana also has an indirect subsidiary that distributes beef and other food protein.")

Now, you may recall that Hambrecht & Quist's telecommunications-equipment analyst, Joe Noel, had been the only major analyst publicly talking up Diana, which made him a valuable asset to Phase 1 of the Diana promote. Knowing little about him, I decided to speak to him, clue him in to the truth about the switch, and see if we could reconcile our very different perceptions. I'm sure he knew who I was and what I had been saying about Diana, but still I felt that any legitimate analyst could be persuaded by the truth. But his shield was up; the conversation went nowhere.

Our analysis of Diana's business model led us to believe the company possessed little or no assets, cash flow, technology, or even any debt that could be restructured in such a way as to enhance or create shareholder value. The hiring of Hambrecht & Quist looked to us like an attempt at damage control. Diana stock ended the month at $24, slowly finding its way down to its proper level, which I estimated at below $5.

On September 6 we published a report based on an SEC filing that disclosed that Arthur J. Samberg, the president of Dawson Samberg Capital Management, had purchased 20,000 Diana shares for his own account in a privately negotiated transaction at a cost of only $20.50 per share. Dawson Samberg owned 323,000 shares of Diana at an average price of $31.73. Later, on October 15, after we reported the direst of all possible facts, Dawson Samberg would commit even more investor funds to the sinking Diana, helping to temporarily shore up the stock.

But Diana was like a monster in a long-running series of horror films: Think Jason in *Friday the 13th*. No matter how many times the Diana monster was killed, it would not stay dead. In September 1996 its stock came back to life, creeping up near $50 a share. At about this time we began our deep, fundamental analysis of the DataNet switch, from both a hardware and a software point of view. Among many other contacts, I spoke to Steven Allen at Flextronics, the nominal subcontractor for the Sattel switch. Allen told me that even if Diana were to find a buyer for this unsellable switch, it would be difficult to construct, because the blueprints were all wrong. Flextronics, he said, refused to build the switch because of this lack of documentation.

Our detailed, 16-page October 15 technical report set off a morning selling binge that led to an unjustified five-hour New York Stock Exchange trading halt. As described in Chapter 1, trading resumed with only eight minutes remaining in the trading day. By that time the institutions had galvanized enough buyers to run up the stock, and Diana's stock closed that day more than 2 points *above* the previous day's close. It was more than just contradictory behavior; it was downright nauseating.

It was gut-check time for all short sellers. We'd seen Phase 1, in which the Dianites were able to run the stock to $120. Could they do it again in Phase 2? Could any short seller justify maintaining a short during the ride up? Many, including us, could close out their positions profitably, but now that the truth about the DataNet had been entered into the public record, the very thought of having to go out and cover the short by purchasing this penny stock at a price somewhere in the $30s was wrenching. The next day's action would help us to know whether the unthinkable would become the inevitable.

SOLD SHORT

The morning of October 16 would be a turning point for both the Diana promotion (for the worse) and for Asensio & Company (for the better). It began dismally, however, as buyers bid up shares in a Hail Mary effort to stem the tide of reality. We sat tight, trusting the market to act rationally. The price held, but we could see that there would be no second run over $100 a share. There were simply not enough takers in the broader investment community.

Nonetheless, we were a fledgling among wildcats; we had to trade responsibly and preserve capital. That day we decided to close out almost half of our public broker–dealer's 38,000-share short position.

On October 18 Diana issued a petulant release in which Fiedler referred to our "so-called report" and suggested that we "should ask for a refund from the 'consultant' that wrote the report." Three days later the false claims continued, with an allegation by Diana that I had solicited yet another consultant to produce a negatively biased report. The unidentified consultant was quoted thus: "Although he didn't outright say he wanted negative information, he did very strongly imply such." Now Diana was issuing blockbuster statements about what some consultant, who may or may not have existed, inferred from statements I may or may not have made. The company truly was scraping the bottom. In the release, Fiedler reiterated what must have seemed to him a witty bon mot suggesting I ask my consultant for a refund. He also made technical claims about the switch that our experts had determined to be untrue. Figuring I had nothing to lose, I attempted to contact some of the institutional backers to gain some insight into their continued support for Diana.

For a long time I would go in to work and make a ritual daily phone call to Dan Benton, a portfolio manager who worked with Arthur Samberg at Dawson Samberg. He never called me back, but for whatever reason—whether perseverance or perversity, I'm not quite sure—I continued to phone every day.

Diana: "The Switch Works!"

I phoned Fred Stein of Neuberger Berman, another Diana shareholder. To my surprise, he came on the line, if only to inform me that I was the most despicable person he had ever known. He said he had been co-investing with Arthur Samberg for 25 years and didn't think there was much of a contest between Mr. Arthur Samberg and "some Cuban short seller named Asensio" as to whom he should trust.

I spoke to Kip Sheeline, a banker at Hambrecht & Quist, about their "work" on the Sattel spin-off. The investment banking activity at Hambrecht & Quist meant, in theory, that there was now a so-called Chinese wall between the bankers and the firm's analyst Joe Noel. Noel was legally restricted from speaking on Diana. H&Q had, however, hired an industry analyst to counterbalance my report.

Anyone can look back at Diana now and see it for what it was. But back then, as in the heat of all exciting claims, you had to be a dedicated and independent investor to have a clear grasp of the truth and to make proper judgments. You had to seek out and understand the gist of our technical report, which required serious deliberation. You had to see through Diana's disinformation campaign against me, and you had to have a healthy skepticism that not all corporate information was honest, complete, and accurate. You had to understand that it wasn't short sellers who caused this high-flying glamour stock to collapse, but in fact it was the company's lack of a marketable product despite claiming otherwise. All this to gain an ounce of credibility on the short side. And all the longs needed was: "The switch works!"

This wasn't as easy a call as it may sound. Think of the credibility Diana had. It had such major institutional holders as Putnam and Dawson Samberg. It had Hambrecht & Quist, a respected firm that had not only privately released glowing reports on the company but was also structuring some sort of deal that looked like it was going to add value. It also had an independent consultant apparently contradicting my report: "The switch works!"

67

SOLD SHORT

I never said the switch didn't work. They were playing a stupid semantic game. What I said was the switch wouldn't sell. As it was designed for areas with minimal communications needs, it was, among many other fatal shortcomings, incapable of ringing more than a small number of lines, and that wasn't one of its big problems. *Whatever they paid for that consultant, they should ask for a refund.*

October wound down, and Diana was pushed into the $27 range. After another rise in November, we decided to short our first Diana shares in over a month. These additional 9,600 shares sold short in the upper $30s would prove to be, on a percentage basis, our best trade yet, because a nasty storm was brewing, and Diana stock was heading for the cellar.

On November 27 Diana reported the second-quarter results that had been so breathlessly and portentously leaked back on October 15, allegedly "forcing" the five-hour trading halt. The company reported a loss; Sattel's only reported income was from the apocryphal sale of two switches to Concentric. Of course, this was not income; it was merely the creation of a receivable that was instantly doubtful. Concentric didn't have any money to pay for the two switches—the transaction was just for show. Eventually Diana would sue Concentric for payment and, as part of the settlement, agreed to be paid from the proceeds of a Concentric public offering. This would help kick off Phase 3, but more on that later. (Note: Phase 3 came after the stock had been kicked off the NYSE and traded on the lowly pink sheets for less than $2 per share.)

At the same time, it was announced that Richard Fisher was stepping down and James Fiedler would be taking over the entire enchilada. When one is an officer or a director of a company, as Fisher had been with Diana, one is subject to certain SEC restrictions on the buying and selling of that company's stock. Now that Fisher had resigned, he could sell his Diana stock without restriction. He was allowed to bow out with millions, but there is some

The Technology Knowledge Gap

Investing was, for most of capitalism's history, predominately an accounting endeavor. Investors focused on past results and the immediate future. They studied statements and performed calculations on operating margins, and working and fixed capital requirements. Investing in today's technology stocks involves a very different process.

Technology investors assess the value of products that do something new or very different from the way it's been done. The investor must therefore learn about a new drug, or a new semiconductor microchip, or a new software program. The investor has to learn about it and form an opinion about whether it will work and whether it will sell. And the investor then has to decide whether the technology is worth more than the value implied in its current market value.

The process of learning about a new thing is almost the exact opposite of analyzing the financial performance of an existing, mature business. Projecting earnings of an established business in a competitive market takes work and talent. Learning about a new thing, even if you are an expert in the field, and then projecting its earnings, is a far more difficult process.

Wall Street is not about long-drawn-out, reflective thought processes. Wall Street is about selling. Talking more than listening. Convincing the other guy to do what you want him to do. Now.

This forms the first part of The Technology Knowledge Gap: the lack of incentive to devote the time to getting it right.

In any industry there are grassroots workers like salespeople and field engineers who know who's got the hot product. These are the people on the ground. Often we find an information gap between them and management. Management may know, but it may not be in their interest to tell. Management is often the information gatekeeper for investors. Wall Street analysts obtain much of their data from conversations with management and materials supplied by management.

The gap between the grassroots workers and the Wall Street analysts, and the gap between the time required to learn a new thing and the time Wall Street devotes to research versus sales, create the space where short sellers operate: The Technology Knowledge Gap.

69

SOLD SHORT

The technology gap helps explain why, for instance, Diana could ever have traded at a $600 million valuation when grassroots workers correctly believed that Diana was a ridiculous scam. Even those who knew questioned their judgment when they saw Diana's stock price. How could this be happening on Wall Street? Management talked to analysts. Analysts talked to brokers. Brokers talked to investors. Investors believed they were learning about a great new thing. Investors were certain Diana had a product that would sell and sell big. It did. But the product was Diana's stock held by insiders and Wall Street sold it while it was hot, thanks to The Technology Knowledge Gap.

---

small consolation in knowing that, had he cashed out at $100+ a share, he would have walked away with a far, far greater fortune. Fiedler had always been the engine driving the Diana promote, and now he had been handed the steering wheel, too. (Or had he simply been left holding the bag?)

Diana opened 1997 at $27, but by the end of January it traded down to $14, with no floor in sight. On February 4 the company was finally able to unload its meat division, Atlanta Provision Company. But even this nonevent had an interesting and sleazy sidelight.

According to the *New York Times*, at least $135,000 of the purchaser's funds came from the booty of $2.85 million allegedly stolen from a New York City foster care agency by Michael Pope, a board member of the center. The money was supposed to pay for foster care and medical expenses for the center's 493 foster children. The center lost its foster care contract with the city when these allegations came to light. When the city canceled the contract, 120 employees lost their jobs, and the foster children were transferred to other agencies. Pope's broker at Merrill Lynch, Richard Ross, was paid $25,000 to keep quiet about the unusual withdrawals, prosecutors said. Ross, who was also charged in connection with the embezzlement, pleaded guilty to possession of stolen property.

Unloading Atlanta Provision was good news for Diana in that the company might generate some quick cash and would no longer suffer that subsidiary's inevitable quarterly losses. But it was bad news in that now the promote no longer had much in the way of sales to help cloud its overall picture.

By February 20, 1997, the inevitable collapse was at hand. The New York Stock Exchange halted trading in Diana for the entire day—this time, no complaints from us—amid rumors the company would soon be delisted. In anticipation of this event, Diana had already applied for a Nasdaq listing. It would soon resume trading there, like a villain switching getaway cars in the heat of a chase.

This was the beginning of the end—the end of Phase 2, that is. Phase 1 had taken Diana from $5 to $120. Phase 2 had pushed the already discredited stock from $20 to $50. The stakes were getting lower, but as long as there was still money to be squeezed out of Diana, we knew we hadn't heard the last of Fiedler and his band of switchsters. They didn't need some fancy telecom switch to communicate *this* message: time for Phase 3.

Diana's stock, now listed along with all the other penny stocks on the over-the-counter "pink sheets," fell below $2 in April 1997. By summer, however, rumors of positive blowback from the Concentric deal, a misrepresented private placement fire sale, and a dearth of timely financial disclosures were raising hopes—and Diana's stock price—again.

By July 17, 1997, Phase 3 was in full swing, and Diana's stock was up fivefold, to $10. Can you believe it? Investors had been bidding up shares in the belief that Diana's ownership of Concentric stock was going to generate huge profits after Concentric's initial public offering. (Diana owned this stock as a result of the $5 million convertible loan arranged at the time that Concentric signed the DataNet sales agreement.)

Because Diana had yet to release its long-delayed annual SEC filing due to a "significant liquidity shortfall" that had impacted its ability to continue as a going concern, buyers were unaware of a crucial fact. Phase 3, based on the Concentric windfall, simply multiplied the number of Concentric shares originally given to Diana by the planned offering's per share price. But what promoters were neglecting to factor in were a series of reverse splits that had reduced Diana's actual share holding by a factor of 15. In other words, buyers were expecting a cash influx 15 times greater than that which Diana would actually be receiving. Gee, I wonder what gave them that idea.

On August 7, 1997, we burst the Concentric bubble and reported the truth on Diana's ballyhooed private placement bonanza. Although its value had been well obfuscated, we cut through the balderdash and determined that any significant Diana price rise at that point would be utterly logic-defying.

Furthermore, Diana had become a defendant in nine separate shareholder lawsuits accusing its managers of stock fraud. Phase 3 had run into some problems. Phase 4 would require some adjustments.

In December 1997, after selling off everything but the original Sattel "assets," Diana was renamed Coyote Network Systems, Inc. (Nasdaq: CYOE). Fiedler was ready to jump into this new vehicle and to take Squeglia along for the ride.

You can't keep a bad man down. By December 1998 Fiedler was able to run Coyote stock up from $4 to $16 by finding another pliant telecom analyst and inventing a customer. Yes, this would be Phase 4.

Vik Grover of Kaufman Bros. took the baton from Hambrecht & Quist's Joe Noel. Vik would bring us a lot of laughs later when he became the key supporting analyst behind Able Telcom (Nasdaq: ABTE), a messy stock promotion with which I became deeply involved. On November 9, 1998, he initiated coverage of Coyote with a *strong buy*. It's interesting to see the same people popping up time and again aiding and abetting completely different promotions.

On December 3, 1998, a Coyote SEC S-3 was filed for insiders to sell large blocks of stock. Coyote applied for Fiedler to register 183,750 shares, approximately one-third of his position, including stock obtained through warrants that were priced under $3 per share when issued in mid-1997. Squeglia was given the ability to sell about 16,000 of his 42,000 shares, some obtained also through warrants priced under $3 per share.

In a September 24, 1998, press release, Coyote claimed to have signed a three-year, $37 million contract with one Crescent Communications. Supposedly Coyote had booked $11 million in sales—of its $15 million quarterly total—to Crescent in fall 1998. On December 8, 1998, Fiedler's longtime henchman, Tony Squeglia, told TheStreet.com reporter Kevin Petrie that Crescent chairman Gene Curcio had an office in Long Beach, California. The Long Beach address turned out to be a post office box, and the company's operations appeared to be nonexistent. On December 9 the stock tumbled from $14.25 to $6.44 with an uncommonly high volume of 2.4 million shares, and the next day saw an all-day trading halt in Coyote shares.

After all this, Fiedler was still allowed to run a corporation that the stock market said was worth $80 million. In May 1999 Coyote settled a class action suit with an undisclosed cash payment. In March 2000, soon after a nauseating piece in the *Wall Street Journal* that glorified Fiedler and his executive siblings but inexcusably neglected to mention the Diana fiasco, Fiedler stepped down as chairman and director of Coyote.

SOLD SHORT

In July 2000 Coyote, under new management except for Squeglia, underwent yet another name change, this time to Quentra Networks (Nasdaq NMS: QTRA). Strangely enough, as with Coyote, you'll find no mention of the name "Diana" anywhere on the company's website or in its promotional materials. On December 15, 2000, Quentra filed for Chapter 11 bankruptcy protection and now trades on the ignomious pink sheets.

As for Fiedler, we'll be watching to see if and when he resurfaces. If he does, it's a safe bet he'll be pitching some sexy new telecom gadget that sounds too good to be true: another coyote in sheep's clothing.

CHAPTER FIVE

SOLV-EX:
SOMETHING OILY

Solv-Ex. If you followed stocks in 1996 and 1997, you probably remember the name. At first Solv-Ex Corp. (OTC: SOLVQ) was extolled for what it brassily proclaimed itself to be: an environmentally friendly innovator capable of reducing North America's dependence on imported oil. Later it achieved dubious fame for being a key player in a widespread and colorful British mutual fund scandal. Finally it became notorious for what we exposed it to be: a convoluted, international scam of epic proportions.

The 17-year perpetuation of the Solv-Ex promotion was not unlike the reign of a cruel and corrupt dictator over a divided people. Both retain power despite all evidence against them simply because there is no faction strong enough to depose them. Both carry on in their later years despite being hobbled and hounded by whatever means justice authorities are able to use to pierce their protective insulation. Why do they persist? Well, of course there is arrogance and self-righteousness; after a while they come to believe their own propaganda. And then there is greed. As long as they are in power, they are able to siphon off cash and perks from public accounts while maintaining that they are in fact servants of the public. The final decline of Solv-Ex was like a slow-motion coup d'etat of a tin-pot tyrant.

The oily fingers of the Solv-Ex debacle soiled participants both willing and unwitting from the United States and Canada overseas to the United Kingdom, Luxembourg, Liechtenstein, Switzerland, Scandinavia, and the Caribbean. The cofounder, CEO, and chairman of Solv-Ex, John S. Rendall, besides dispatching goons to harass me and my associates, might have spent more company funds on the production of litigation and anti-Asensio press than on the production of oil. It brings me great pleasure to relate the story of the Solv-Ex scam in all its depraved, twisted, and often amusing detail.

Solv-Ex Corp. was formed in July 1980 in Albuquerque, New Mexico, when Samuel A. Francis, who would later be convicted of securities fraud for a different stock swindle, teamed with Rendall to arrange financing to commercialize certain patents allegedly owned by Rendall. The name Solv-Ex was based on the "solvent extraction" process that Rendall claimed to possess for separating low-grade oil from New Mexico shale or Canadian tar sands. Later, when Rendall decided it would be a nice touch to pitch the Solv-Ex process as solvent-free and thus environmentally friendly, the name "Solv-Ex" would become the absolute antithesis of what the company supposedly represented, but nobody bothered to change it. And really, what did it matter?

In Solv-Ex's 1981 IPO, Francis was issued 1,750,000 Solv-Ex shares for approximately five cents per share and Rendall was granted 2,700,000 shares in payment for rights to his "patents." In 1983 Solv-Ex sponsored the Santa Rosa (New Mexico) Tar Sands Project, claiming it could set up a $24 million plant and extract 4,000 barrels of bitumen per day from the sands. This bitumen could then be refined into oil. The scheme was tentatively offered $42.6 million in federal aid.

On the promise of this money shower direct from the U.S.

Solv-Ex: Something Oily

Treasury, Rendall and Francis went straight out and sold $4 million of stock to the public at $4.25 a share. But in December 1983 Solv-Ex abruptly announced it was abandoning the Santa Rosa venture. Odd behavior?

No. One week earlier, a House Government Operations sub-committee had lowered the boom. Representative Mike Synar, the committee chairman, blasted Solv-Ex for not disclosing that one month prior to the $4 million sale, an independent report stated that Solv-Ex had overestimated the potential amount of bitumen in Santa Rosa by a factor of 2 or 3. Oops! Solv-Ex's stock plunged from $4.25 to $1.75.

Despite what would seem like a huge, red, garish, permanent STOP sign to any half-informed investor, the Solv-Ex scheme chugged along for another 14 years. It based its promotion on the delightful notion of being able to extract a valuable commodity from what would seem a harsh and worthless landscape and also on a warped appeal to the patriotic (read: anti-Arab) instincts of Americans and Canadians.

The process of separating bitumen from tar sands is common and long established. It involves agitating the sands with steam and hot water in some sort of cleansing apparatus. The bitumen is then refined into oil. Syncrude Canada Ltd., a giant, 36-year-old extractor of bitumen from tar sands, actually used a standard washing machine to test its process at first. Syncrude and its competitor, Suncor, use caustic soda as a solvent in the extraction process for greater efficiency. Both spent decades and billions of dollars getting started.

Solv-Ex, much smaller than either of these industry leaders and incapable of matching their know-how or capital commitments, argued that its process, which dispenses with the caustic soda, would be cheaper because of lower disposal costs for its nontoxic tailings, or waste products. As if that weren't enough of a miracle, Solv-Ex claimed to be able to extract from the same sands alumina, the raw material of aluminum production, and TiO_2S, a substitute for titanium dioxide as a pigment or filler for the paper, paint, and plastics industries. Oh, and maybe a little gold on the side.

New Mexico sands are not rich in hydrocarbons; Rendall turned next to the tar-sand Promised Land: northern Alberta, Canada. (Rendall had served from 1977 to 1979 as the plant manager of RTR Oil Sands Alberta, in Fort McMurray, Alberta.) In 1988 Solv-Ex acquired for next to nothing the Bitumont lease in Alberta's remote Athabasca oil sands region. The place is so far north, in fact—so far from prying eyes—that in at least one Rand McNally atlas it is not even included. In 1995 Solv-Ex acquired the Fort Hills lease, which is adjacent to the Bitumont lease. The territory does in fact possess rich tar sands, but neither of these leases was considered a great enough prize to be snapped up by the big boys. Nearby, Syncrude was producing 200,000 barrels a day; Suncor, 80,000 barrels.

In the mid-1980s, the province of Alberta, eager for industrial development, invested $3.3 million in Solv-Ex's New Mexico pilot plant. In 1995 the province approved a plan for Solv-Ex to build a $100 million plant in Alberta capable of producing 14,000 barrels a day. (Although the plant never produced a single barrel of oil at anything approaching an economical cost, Rendall would shamelessly appeal for an additional $600 million—in order, he said, to ramp up to 80,000 barrels a day.)

I believe that just as stock investors lose their objectivity, Alberta's optimistic provision of seed capital, along with its longing for the jobs that Solv-Ex was promising, caused its watchdogs to become emotionally invested in the company's success, blinding them to the reality of this enormous scam. After we were short we tried to contact authorities and media in Alberta to inform them about Solv-Ex. Initially Asensio & Company represented to Alberta a malevolent force that was challenging the integrity of the entire province and threatening to take away jobs. Once again the question

Solv-Ex: Something Oily

was: *Whom do we trust?* A businessman promising jobs and prosperity and eco-friendly oil and love—okay, maybe not love—or a Cuban short seller, whatever *that* is, who seems to be calling us a bunch of suckers and rubes?

Only when the truth emerged, when Solv-Ex treated its labor force so shabbily that its own workers ended up providing the most damaging testimony of all, did the Alberta government take notice. Albertans weren't the only ones to be sucked in. In 1987 Shell Oil, after a substantial investment in Solv-Ex, decided it wanted nothing further to do with the company.

In 1990 Samuel Francis, Solv-Ex's original secretary-treasurer and still a large shareholder, was indicted by a New Mexico grand jury for racketeering in connection with the promotion and sale of penny stocks. Francis also had ties to Thomas Quinn and Arnold Kimmes, stock manipulators whose connections to Solv-Ex, when exposed a few years later, would cause a hellaciously "bad hair day" for the stock. In 1992 Francis was convicted of securities fraud and was sentenced to a year and a day at Club Fed.

Attempting to distance the company from the crook, Jack Butler, Solv-Ex's president, claimed that Francis had left the company in 1985. Nonetheless, an October 27, 1994, SEC filing discloses Francis's holding of 1.05 million Solv-Ex shares, or 5.38 percent of the total outstanding. Too bad they couldn't squeeze enough shares from Francis to push him below 5 percent, at which point his interest would not have to be disclosed in an SEC filing.

I first learned of Solv-Ex from a *Business Week* article titled "The Secret World of Short Sellers." I was interviewed for the article because of my work on Diana Corp. and was the only identified short seller in the piece. Solv-Ex was prominently mentioned as a target of those "anonymous" short sellers, and I was intrigued. Asensio & Company put SOLV on our "watch list." At any given time we have perhaps 100 stocks on that list. We keep an eye on news and trading developments in those stocks, and every now and then one leaps off the list and becomes our next target.

The Solv-Ex promotion hit its stride around December 1995, when the company was authorized by the province of Alberta to proceed with construction of its plant. By that time Rendall had assembled a board of directors with impressive resumes. One thing was strange about this board, however: Many of the members were in their late 60s or 70s and long retired. W. Jack Butler, 74, the president of Solv-Ex and a director, had been with Mobil Oil Corp. from 1951 to 1985, including a stint as the Middle East regional director.

Next, like all long-term scams, Solv-Ex sought some impressive-sounding third-party verification. It commissioned Pace Consultants, a legitimate energy-research firm, to independently "audit" its extraction process. Solv-Ex never made the actual Pace documents available. The company did, however, hold an Alberta "love-in" in which it quoted a Pace manager's endorsement and touted the Pace Report as confirmation of its impressive $5.21-per-barrel projected production cost.

Our inquiries, however, uncovered that the alleged Pace manager was no longer employed at the company. Furthermore, Pace engineers then came forward to describe Solv-Ex's characterization of its report as blatant misrepresentation. It was Solv-Ex, they said, that provided the cost projections; Pace was concerned only with the feasibility of the project. In other words: Can they get oil from the sands? Well, sure. Big deal. It was Diana Corp.'s "The switch works!" all over again. The $800 million question: Can they do it in a way that's economically feasible? On March 16, 1996, Pace vice president Dan Foley told Canada's *Financial Post*, "Throwing a number out without backup on what those numbers mean can be misleading to the public."

Speaking of throwing out misleading numbers without backup, on January 23, 1996, oil-industry analyst David Snow released one of the most hyperbolic stock reports ever issued by any stock promoter. His *major buy* recommendation included projected earnings per share in 1997 of $2.50, $20 in 1998, and, in due course, $98 a share—sustainable for 40 years! Snow put a two-year price target on Solv-Ex of $200, asserting it would reach $1,000 within 10 years. Ah yes, another one of those $1,000-a-share stocks.

Three days later the second half of Solv-Ex's one-two sucker punch was delivered. Believe it or not, it actually connected with quite a few suckers. On January 26, 1996, Morgan Grenfell's senior oil analyst, Charlie Maxwell, "unofficially" sent a positive recommendation on Solv-Ex, labeling it the "Classic Growth Stock of Our Generation," to selected recipients via his office fax machine. Maxwell had attained renown in the 1970s for coining the term "energy crisis." (You don't think these terms just coin themselves, do you?) Maxwell talked up Solv-Ex to, among others, financial pundit Bob Metz, who reported these comments in newspaper pieces.

So what was in it for "Energy Crisis" Maxwell? Maxwell owned 100,000 shares of Solv-Ex at the time and was an old cohort of Rendall and Butler, having worked under Butler at Mobil for 11 years before becoming an analyst. When confronted, he described what he did as "kind of a cheerleading piece, not an analysis." Oh. "If this works out the way we expect," he wrote, "Solv-Ex, between now and the year 2008, will be the fastest growing oil company in the world." Bemoaning the undeserved "attacks" on the company, Maxwell said, "The short sellers have taken a pure white wall and thrown a lot of black mud at it."

The Solv-Ex promotion was perhaps the greatest blizzard of way-over-the-top pumpery I have ever witnessed. A newsletter writer, Richard Geist, in October 1995 predicted a share price above $50. In April 1996 he painted the gloomiest of all possible pictures but blamed it on the shorts, reiterating against all reason his *strong buy*. In August 1996 Geist again reissued a *strong buy* while ludicrously spinning Solv-Ex's crippling labor predicament into a positive: "Fortuitously, this situation has led to lower costs and a more efficient construction process."

Xenophobic scare tactics abounded. An April 1, 1996, release on something called PRExpress cited Geist's comments and insinuated that "sheiks with billions of dollars" were in league with the short sellers and that major oil companies were fighting to suppress Solv-Ex's superior technology. (No one seemed to point out that Suncor and Syncrude were *already* quietly doing what flag-waving Solv-Ex would never accomplish.) Geist upped his price target to $70 to $80 and asserted that Solv-Ex would make the United States and Canada "independent of any reliance on Arab oil." Now, I am not one to lightly dismiss claims of conspiracy, having seen many in reality, but I was on the front lines of the Solv-Ex battle, and I don't recall any sheiks or oil company execs covering my back at any point during this fight. Coincidentally or not, the stock rose on April 1 from $10.50 to $12.88.

Solv-Ex rose to $38 in February 1996 (a peak market cap of $800 million) on the strength of an overseas supporter whom you'll soon meet. It dropped to $22 a month later. On March 25, 1996, the stock collapsed from $22.50 to $7.38 in a single day amid stories of a grand jury investigation of possible stock manipulation involving two mobsters with Solv-Ex connections, the aforementioned Samuel Francis associates Thomas Quinn and Arnold Kimmes. Kimmes had pleaded guilty to racketeering and securities fraud in 1992. Quinn, Kimmes's partner and a disbarred mob lawyer, was an alleged member of the Genovese crime family. Quinn and Kimmes were bucket shop masters who capitalized on the Regulation S loophole that allowed unregistered stock to be flipped to U.S. investors. Solv-Ex, which placed almost all its shares in this manner, would have been a perfect vehicle for them.

Regulation S

Let's say a company listed on an American stock exchange wants to issue stock privately to an investor. Perhaps it is trying to raise some cash; perhaps it wants to compensate someone for services rendered. Under SEC rules, in order for that investor to sell that stock freely, he or she either has to wait one year or the company first has to make a filing with the SEC to register that stock for that investor. Until that stock is registered with the SEC, the investor is not free to sell.

Theoretically, these registration regulations are in place to ensure that investors have access to a prospectus when they buy and sell stock in a company. A prospectus tells them how much stock is being sold, who's selling it, and where the money's going. Filed by the company with the SEC, it contains information and risk factors about that company.

But in an effort to encourage foreign investment in American companies, for several years the SEC permitted, under certain circumstances, an exception to these registration rules. This exception was spelled out in a directive called Regulation S.

Under Reg S, a bona fide non-U.S. investor could buy stock privately from a public company in the United States and then after 40 days sell it without the company ever having to file with the SEC to register the stock. The person who bought that stock from the private buyer might have thought he or she had purchased publicly traded, registered stock, but in fact the stock was never registered. Reg S offered the seller anonymity, less hassle, and a quick turnaround. It offered the company a quick and easy way to create new public shares.

Reg S was abused by companies like Solv-Ex and eventually was stricken from the books. Before the regulation was withdrawn, however, Solv-Ex sold at least 18 million shares through private placements and offshore Reg S offerings without ever registering a single one of these shares with the SEC. By July 1997 we calculated that Solv-Ex had obligations to issue shares to convertible security holders that far exceeded the 30 million shares it was authorized to issue. This was one of the Solv-Ex scam's final acts before its collapse.

An odd by-product of the Reg S offerings was that investors buying stock at below-market prices but forced to wait 40 days before selling often locked in a profit by simultaneously shorting the stock. For example, let's say a stock is trading for $25, but you are offered 1,000 shares at $20. That's a $5,000 profit if the price holds. But if the price drops, your profit drops; if it drops below $20 before you can sell, you actually lose money. If, however, you simultaneously short the stock at $25, you don't care what happens. If it drops to, say, $20 a share, you break even on the long side but net $5,000 on the short side. If it rises to $30, you make $10,000 on the long side and lose $5,000 on the short side, again netting $5,000. No matter what numbers I plug in, you net $5,000, guaranteed.

Investors "connected" enough to get in on below-market offerings—and savvy enough to know that the underlying stocks were often garbage—simultaneously shorted their Reg S stock. So at any time within 40 days of a Reg S sale, it was a safe assumption that a portion of the short interest in the stock was attributable to the Reg S stockholders—ostensibly the "friends" of the company.

Why would characters like this be attracted to such an abstruse and distant venture? The October 3, 1996, *Albuquerque Journal* tells the reason in stark and sickening detail. A list of New Mexico's wealthiest residents spots John S. Rendall, oil tycoon, at #10. His estimated worth: $52 million. Proof that you don't have to be involved in some famous corporation—hell, you don't even have to be involved in a corporation with an actual *product!*—to become stinking rich.

Bad guys were being tied to the stock, but Solv-Ex maintained a body of support. A former elected official named Danny Dalla-Longa criticized Solv-Ex in the Alberta legislature in April 1996. His deadeye denunciations, unfortunately, were premature. Albertans were still enthralled by the Solv-Ex dream and all the beautiful jobs and pretty-pretty tax dollars it promised. Not until Solv-Ex stiffed its workers and contractors would the province turn against Rendall. Dalla-Longa was blasted by the local press, which had also bought big time into the Solv-Ex promise of cheap oil in the sands. The pitifully unobjective local media never really comprehended the truth behind the Solv-Ex fantasy.

I wasn't the first short seller to sniff something amiss here. Before I even got into the fray, a hedge fund hired consultants to evaluate Solv-Ex. Quilcap Corp. hired Vancouver-based Weir-Jones Engineering Consultants, which, according to newspaper reports, concluded: "We do not consider that the bitumen extraction procedure is . . . particularly unique. . . . For these reasons, we do not attach much credence to the Solv-Ex claim that they would be able to license their technology to the owners of other [oil sands] leases. . . . The suggestion that Solv-Ex could become a significant producer of aluminum is at best highly questionable."

This was like waving a red flag at a charging bullshit artist. Solv-Ex hired the firm of Cleary, Gottlieb, Steen & Hamilton to sue both Quilcap and Weir-Jones for "breach of contract, fraud, tortious interference with prospective economic advantage, and unjust enrichment," claiming they had signed confidentiality agreements and then blabbed. Ed Mishkin, the lead attorney in the suit, became an adversary of Asensio & Company a year later; according to a press release, he was allegedly going to represent a scam called Crystallex (AMEX: KRY) against us in a suit as misguided and preposterous as this one.

In September 1996 Solv-Ex hired another Mobil Oil retread, Herb Schmertz, the author of *Goodbye to the Low Profile*, a memoir of his years flacking for Mobil. Schmertz was involved in the sponsorship of Mobil Masterpiece Theater, a response to the public anger over the 1970s "energy crisis"—if I may call it that without owing residuals to Charlie Maxwell. He oversaw a mendacious advertisement Solv-Ex placed in the *Wall Street Journal* headlined "You've Probably Never Heard of Us. You Soon Will Because Our Technology Will Reduce American Dependence on Middle East Oil."

Audaciously, the company included this ad in its promotional kit with the tag "Reprinted from The Wall Street Journal," as if this had originally been editorial copy produced by hard-hitting journalists.

Meanwhile, as the Solv-Ex promotion reached outrageous proportions, as more and more "respectable" names joined its family of fraudsters, the company quietly sold millions of unregistered shares overseas. These shares went primarily through a Swedish investment bank and a well-born young Englishman who was a rising star at Deutsche Bank Morgan Grenfell in London. This budding über-banker had apparently developed a false sense of invincibility, and in the tradition of Nick Leeson and Barings Bank, his reckless and illegal trading in Solv-Ex shares for a DB mutual fund would lead to one of the most destructive, most gleefully documented banking scandals the English press has ever seen.

Enter Peter W. Young.

Like many recently minted investment professionals, Peter Young, a whippet-thin whippersnapper with a degree in mathematics from Oxford University, had a taste for the finer things in life. Young, a rising star at Morgan Grenfell, was already pulling down a £300,000 ($450,000) salary with bonuses as the fund manager of Morgan Grenfell's European Growth Unit Trust. This mutual fund, which held £788 million ($1.2 billion) as of September 3, 1996, was meant to be invested in European companies. Young, however, ignored his European-only mandate when the chance arose to abet the Solv-Ex scam. In the end, it would cost his managers their jobs, it would damage Morgan Grenfell's reputation and cost it hundreds of millions of pounds, and, if Young's defense lawyers were to be believed, it would drive the talented young man to madness.

Young was a wizard at weaving a hazy international web of accounts and front companies. As early as spring 1995, he approached employees in the U.K. office of Fiba Nordic Securities, a Swedish brokerage, for help in setting up some Luxembourg front companies to hide his activities. Fiba Nordic did far more than that. It introduced Young to two savvy Swiss attorneys, Marco Wolf and Juerg Wyler, who set up a series of holding companies for him. For at least five of these holding companies, including Young's most active account, Russ Oil & Technology SA, the pair served personally as company directors. Fiba Nordic had also been conducting Reg S offerings for Solv-Ex. Young was to become Solv-Ex's best and most insatiable Reg S customer.

On January 23, 1996, Solv-Ex placed 489,474 shares with Russ Oil at $17 to $18 a share. The stock closed that day at $20.31, yielding a paper profit of approximately $1.4 million. In a September 1996 Morgan Grenfell SEC 13D filing, the company stated its belief that "Russ Oil was . . . a device used by Young to divert money and opportunities of the [funds] for his own benefit. . . . The shares of common stock of Solv-Ex held by Russ Oil are held in a personal account of Young." In other words, according to his own employer, Peter Young paid for Russ Oil's Solv-Ex shares with money from his fund, then kept the shares for himself. Hey, that's one way to cut out the middleman.

Young continued to soak up Solv-Ex shares as fast as they could be printed. On March 8, 1996, Solv-Ex announced that "a group of diversified European investors" had paid $30.7 million for a private placement of 1,081,967 shares—an average price of $28.37, which was an extremely baffling $2 premium to the market. The "group of diversified investors" was, of course, an undiversified individual named Peter Young, acting through two of his Luxembourg shell companies, Alulux Mining SA and Sandvest Petroleum SA, both of which were predominantly vehicles for investing in Solv-Ex.

It's difficult to say how much Young's bosses at Morgan Grenfell knew of his illicit dealings. I arrived early at the office every day for two weeks to phone them in London but never received a return call. The Leeson case and others have demonstrated that successful young traders are often given extraordinary sums to put into play with only a modicum of supervision. Even if the amounts and concentrations of Young's Solv-Ex purchases sounded no alarms, however, it wouldn't take a Sherlock Holmes to deduce that Solv-Ex was in no way, shape, or form a European company. Also, Young moved his family from their modest house into a far grander £350,000 ($525,000), five-bedroom residence in Amersham. When asked where he obtained the money for the move, he explained that the Swiss lawyers, Wolf and Wyler, had loaned him £350,000.

Young bought almost all the shares of three different Solv-Ex Reg S offerings. He acquired 750,000 shares through the Cayman Islands–based Silva Investments Ltd., from unknown sellers. Another Young entity, Phemex Establishment, of Liechtenstein, in 1996 made a $33 million loan to Solv-Ex—a loan for which Morgan Grenfell would end up holding the bag when we later uncovered the transaction and highlighted its default status. Morgan Grenfell itself owned 40,100 Solv-Ex shares. Altogether, Young invested an astounding $70 million in Solv-Ex in 1996. After 16 years of drilling for small retail investors, Rendall & Co. had struck a gusher. The penny stock scam was now an epic international swindle.

This was the first half of what I call the Solv-Ex "double steal." Part 1 involved squeezing millions out of investors. Peter Young accomplished this beyond anyone's wildest imaginings. No wonder John Rendall stated, shortly before Young's fall, "I think he's a hero. And for my money, I owe him a lot." The second half of the double steal, funneling those millions out of the public corporation and making them disappear, would require the pretense of some large and expensive enterprise—the supposed construction of a secret, "revolutionary" plant in remote northern Canada.

By the summer of 1996, spurred by a U.S. federal investigation into Solv-Ex trading, British market authorities had begun to examine Young's dealings. Young didn't take the intrusion well at all. Calculated or not, his behavior became eccentric and weird. In an oft-cited anecdote, his wife sent him shopping and he came home with 30 jars of gherkins. Reportedly he often sat in silence with his children in a darkened room, chatted to colleagues about his patent on a rocket launcher design, and developed a mathematical model to mimic the burrowing of termites.

In September 1996 Young's world blew apart. The assets of Russ Oil were frozen after Morgan Grenfell discovered that 25,000 Russ Oil shares were placed in Young's private account in Jersey in exchange for a bond convertible into shares in Sensonor, a Norwegian high-tech firm that is whatever the equivalent of a penny stock would be in Norwegian currency. Morgan Grenfell discovered that Young had used a Russ Oil dividend payment totaling £350,000, not a loan from Swiss lawyers, to purchase his house. Young was dismissed for cause on September 23, 1996, and his assets were frozen. The British tabloids, always eager for a how-the-mighty-have-fallen tale, salivated over Young like a wolf pack over a lamb chop.

As Young's stricken face became as familiar to Britons as Princess Di's or Michael Jackson's, Young's lawyers obtained a bizarre emergency injunction against a woman known only as "Sandra." Sandra was barred from publishing a Polaroid photograph she took of Young in October 1995 and was also restricted from divulging "particulars of anything said or done" by Young. It later emerged that the Polaroid depicted Young with two prostitutes named Tracy and Sandra, and the "particulars" being hawked by Sandra were details of his visits to them. But Young still had a sensational photo op in store for the tabloids.

On September 28, 1996, the Serious Fraud Office raided Young's home but made no arrest. (I phoned one of Young's neighbors for an eyewitness report.) Under pressure from U.S. authorities, Morgan Grenfell was forced to call in the Fraud Office to investigate what was described as a £180 million ($270 million) "black hole" at three of its supposedly top-performing investment funds. Morgan Grenfell promised to compensate investors after its review.

In October 1996 Eric Langaker, a founding director of Fiba Nordic, was forced to step down because of his involvement with Young. Five senior managers of Morgan Grenfell, including Keith Percy, its CEO, Mike Wheatley, its chief compliance officer, and Glyn Owen, Young's direct boss, were released for inadequately supervising Young.

The company determined that Young had purchased 12.4 percent of Solv-Ex for Morgan Grenfell and its funds. Of course, he could have bought the whole company for a heck of a lot less. Solv-Ex shares were at around $1 before Young had bid 'em up. If he hadn't raised the stock price, he could not have spent $70 million for all of Solv-Ex's stock. Morgan Grenfell announced that it planned to lower its Solv-Ex holding to 5 percent. Rendall, shameless about his part in bringing a great bank to its knees and ruining so many careers, proudly shot back that the Morgan Grenfell shares were restricted and couldn't be sold! Well, wait till you hear what he was doing with his own restricted shares.

The Morgan Grenfell scandal, which had remarkable staying power in the British media, wasn't over yet. On March 25, 1997, Sir John Craven, the chairman of Morgan Grenfell, resigned, reportedly in part because of disappointment over the Peter Young debacle. In the end, it was estimated that Young's misdeeds cost Morgan Grenfell an estimated £400 million ($600 million).

Meanwhile, Young declared himself mentally and legally incompetent to defend against either a civil lawsuit by Morgan Grenfell or criminal prosecution by the Serious Fraud Office. But we're not talking about 30 jars of gherkins anymore. Young attempted to accentuate his "mental incompetence" in a November 10, 1998, London court appearance. Much to the delight of the British press, Young showed up to the halls of justice garbed in a beige skirt, red lipstick, and high heels, clutching a pink handbag. He may have been dressed like a woman, but Peter Young was no lady.

Amazingly, the Morgan Grenfell scandal did little to tarnish Solv-Ex. At this point, the fraud was so evident that we could no longer resist. On October 7, 1996, Asensio & Company released its first report and *strong sell* recommendation on Solv-Ex. We focused on the American roots of the Morgan Grenfell scandal. U.S. federal investigators searching for Solv-Ex's "European investors" had largely uncovered the scandal. After discovering documentation of the $33 million loan, it was hard for us to believe that Solv-Ex officers could have been unaware of Young's illegitimate activities. We also suspected that Solv-Ex still needed to complete the double steal. We figured the company would attempt to filter the money through a bogus construction operation and that the obviousness of the sham would soon cause the entire scheme to unravel.

Unfortunately, though the writing was on the wall, Rendall had abundant stores of misguided energy remaining and could still find believers. Given our absolute certainty about Solv-Ex, this would lead to lots of great trading opportunities. On November 8, 1996, Solv-Ex announced it would seek to raise $30 million in yet another European Reg S offering.

Solv-Ex was undeterred by the fall of Peter Young. The company went out once again in search of a complicit partner to simulate the appearance of sales. It was reminiscent of Diana Corp.'s deal with Concentric when on November 27, 1996, Solv-Ex announced an output deal with Raisio Chemicals Oy, a Finnish company, to supply synthetic titanium dioxide, one of the miracle process's by-products, as paper pigment. Was the deal ever consummated? Let's just say that had the printer of this book been awaiting shipment from Solv-Ex for its paper pigment, you would not be reading this today.

December brought more strife to Solv-Ex. *Business Week* published an article that included Solv-Ex as a stock that had allegedly been affected by "mob manipulation." The Boilermakers Union filed 12 actions with the Alberta Labor Relations Board about safety concerns at the Solv-Ex construction site. And the Alberta Labor Department began investigations into the firings of 23 Solv-Ex employees.

Meanwhile, hired goons, apparently dispatched by Solv-Ex, questioned my doorman and garage man in an attempt to intimidate me. They tried to get my estranged second wife to say bad things about me. Do scamsters think they can attract investors and add value to their company by smearing their detractors?

The harassment continued. Some retired New York cop or something showed up at our office in a trench coat. He had a fake-looking portfolio and fake business card, and said he wanted to open up an account. They thought we were a retail brokerage firm. We aren't. He was dismissed. But then I realized it would be more interesting to toy with him, to check him out. As he was leaving, I chased after him: "Come back, come back, we *want* you to open an account!" But the elevator doors had closed. I called and called. My hot prospect got away!

I started receiving disturbing e-mail, far more vicious and violent than in previous and subsequent campaigns:

> Thiefs [*sic*] and liars like you should be in jail. I hape [*sic*] they nail your balls up!

> How was your testimony for the Grand Jury? We Know [*sic*] a lot anout [*sic*] you now.

> Be sure and let me know which prison will be your new home. I'll send you some pictures of the Miami docks to remind you of home.

Even today I am slammed online. The Assman. Ass-ensio. Clever. Most of these posters are "bombers"—professionals, if you can call it that, hired by scam companies to lend them the appearance of having legitimate followers. I do not follow the message boards; they're rife with lies and obfuscation. I'm told that the bombers accuse anybody on these boards who questions the honesty of company statements of being in my employ.

A warped mind on the Yahoo Hemispherx message board refers to me disparagingly as "the Cuban refugee," as if my origins are somehow proof of mendacity. To me, hearing that someone who's achieved something was a refugee—the poorer the better—is a mark in his favor. If you asked what has contributed more to my small success, Harvard or my very wet back, I'd be hard pressed not to say the latter.

I can understand investors being upset that I am the messenger informing them that their investment isn't what it appears to be, but I have zero patience with ignorant, racist jibes that have nothing to do with the content of my reports—or with anything at all. But I also got gratifying e-mail, in greater numbers, in fact, than the vicious stuff.

> I am a new investor in Solv-Ex as a result of my broker's recommendation. My broker, at Roney [sic] and Company, claims you are putting out false information to devalue the stock. Frankly, your reports appear well written and genuine. I am confused.

A good first step. At least this investor's mind has been opened to the possibility that his broker isn't fully informed. Denishia Martin, a columnist for something called the *Bull & Bear Financial Report*, wrote a glowing blurb about Solv-Ex, calling it "a company with a vision, managed by visionaries." But after reading my reports, she e-mailed me and admitted that she hadn't really done her homework, regretted her plug, and was planning a retraction. Not all shills are paid; some are honestly hoodwinked by these master con men. And they're especially susceptible knowing that the predominant desire on the Street and in the media is to discover stocks that are going up, not down.

By February 1997 we knew that the cash from the bogus-but-real Young debt was almost spent and that Solv-Ex was now, finally, a "terminal short"—that is, soon to be trading for pennies. But a misleading new Solv-Ex promotion had shot the stock up as high as $16. The company was stating that it was "extremely pleased that a Federal Grand Jury empanelled for the United States District Court for the Southern District of New York is investigating short selling in Solv-Ex stock" and that Solv-Ex "is not the subject or a target of the investigation."

Department of Justice regulations make all proceedings of any federal grand jury secret until publicly disclosed by the government. Violators, including the court's own employees, can be imprisoned for disclosing information about grand jury proceedings. We contacted Marvin Smilon, the Public Information Officer of the Office of the U.S. Attorney of the U.S. Circuit Court of the Southern District of New York, and he confirmed that there existed absolutely no information to support Solv-Ex's claims in the court's public record.

The following week Rendall reported that Solv-Ex's "whole plant is now ready" and that he gets "goose bumps" when "applying for permits for 100,000 barrels per day production."

We needed to find out what was going on inside the plant. We wanted pictures. But security was tight, and you couldn't see anything from the outside. So a plane was hired to fly over the plant and snap photos.

The reconnaissance mission was a success. Aerial photographs of Solv-Ex's plant coincidentally taken on the very same day as Rendall's announcement showed that not even the plant's walls and roof had been fully erected. Rendall's lame response: "He must have been looking at old photos."

Solv-Ex: Something Oily

Ultimately, Rendall's Achilles' heel would be Solv-Ex's dismissive treatment—and nonpayment—of its construction workers. When five different unions filed papers to organize Solv-Ex workers, the company fired 240 employees—half its workforce. Rendall claimed the construction was basically complete and that the company needed to raise more money, was focusing on producing oil for investors, and needed only those workers involved in that part of the business.

One disgruntled union official, in the wake of these layoffs, claimed that Solv-Ex was "bringing bitumen up to the extraction plant and installing a phony conveyor system to show investors they're nearing completion." Another said, "The plant is nowhere near finished. I think this is another way of Rendall fooling his investors."

I had a wonderful source of information in disgruntled ex-employees. These hardened, no-nonsense men from the Great White North didn't need much persuasion. Unlike the weasels we find in the financial world who, even when unintentionally complicit in fraudulent schemes, would never think of blowing the whistle on a fraudster, these men were not afraid to speak out when crossed. Besides their being such a great source of specific, factual information, I liked these guys enormously. A union organizer named Campbell Stillwell read my name on a Yahoo board and phoned me on a cellular phone from a pickup truck in the middle of the Canadian wilderness. Incredibly competent, he helped me identify the best laborers in all the unions. So, sharing a common enemy, I befriended all the union heads, and through them I was able to speak to the fellows who were actually working on various parts of the plant. That's how I was able to create an astonishing document called "Nothing Works in Solv-Ex's Plant."

They had no blueprint for the plant. Foremen and supervisors for pipe fitters, ironworkers, and laborers at the plant reported to us that absolutely no electrical, fresh water, steam, or gas connections of any kind necessary to operate the plant had been made. The giant trucks used to haul the raw sands had to be cut in half to move over what they laughingly called "roads," and they hadn't been reassembled properly. So they were just left in place for decor. Some of the buildings didn't have proper drainage—once the summer thaw came they might just float away.

Several workers we spoke to claimed that management told them "all we need is to somehow produce one truck tanker of bitumen to send to Albuquerque." Geez, I can't remember exactly, but is *that* what shareholders were expecting from this company? One lousy truck tanker of oil costing tens of millions of dollars? Wouldn't it have been a whole lot easier just to have gone down to the local gas station and pumped some premium straight into a truck? The stuff wouldn't even need to be refined, and you'd save those tens of millions of dollars. Now *that's* a great idea for a company. I'll call it Pump-and-Dump-Ex.

We confirmed reports that Solv-Ex was laying off essential employees, including the process planner and his crew, the carpentry supervisor, the chief of security, the warehouse manager, the special projects superintendent, and the heads of contracting, camp maintenance, and the warehouse. The pipe-fitter foreman was laid off while Solv-Ex admitted that the plant's piping work had not even begun. A spokesman for the plumbers and pipe fitters said, "We've built Syncrude and Suncor, and we can see nowhere any foresight or planning done on this." But really, none was to be expected. Don't forget that Solv-Ex's expertise for 17 years was stock promotion and nothing more. At best, the company's attempts to build a plant were the flailings of a fish out of water. At worst, it was a necessary cover to steal the loot.

You gotta wonder. It takes a long time to burn through $70 million. Did it ever occur to them that once they had all that capital, they had a chance to actually go legit? Apparently not. This wasn't just "take the money and run," this was "take the money and on the way out the door try to take a little bit more."

We had specifics; we had Solv-Ex cold. It was hard to see how even the staunchest Solv-Ex supporter could continue to hold the stock and defend the company after this.

On February 27 Rendall announced that he possessed evidence of illegal short selling in Solv-Ex, by Asensio & Company, among others. Trading was halted on the Nasdaq, where an official said that trading would not resume until Rendall produced evidence. Rendall's "evidence"? Documents showing that certain short sellers communicated with one another, the media, and regulators—all perfectly legal acts. One member of the media who received Rendall's package phoned me; he'd reviewed the material and found nothing to write about except the foolishness of Solv-Ex.

By March 13, 1997, Solv-Ex had been in default for 67 days on the $33 million loan arranged by Peter Young from Morgan Grenfell. According to our analysis—which we told Deutsche Bank about, of course—the default allowed the bank to immediately sell 1,016,000 Solv-Ex shares. I believe the bank had been unaware of the default. This might have been the first time a flyspeck of a short seller ever notified a huge international bank that one of its loans was in default.

The Fort McKay Metis Corp., which had not been paid and was suing Solv-Ex for CAN $3 million, set up pickets and a blockade outside the Solv-Ex plant. Later five Alberta construction companies filed builders' liens worth nearly CAN $700,000 against Solv-Ex for unpaid supplies and services. The company had worn out its welcome in Alberta.

Rendall arranged a demonstration of converting a small amount of tar sands to bitumen. At best, he merely boiled the tar sands in a temporarily rigged gravel washer. At worst, according to some reports, he trucked the bitumen in. We were told that trucks entered the high-security compound full and left empty. These reports, from picketing plant workers, were based on the height of the trucks' springs; the trucks rode considerably higher coming out. Unsophisticated investors and media, apparently unaware that the practice of washing tar sands and producing bitumen was common and long standing, were impressed by the demonstration and began a buzz: "Asensio is wrong—the plant works!" Oh no, not this. The plant and the switch work.

Reality check #1: The Solv-Ex promotion had been based on Rendall's claim that he could produce bitumen for $5 a barrel. Bitumen production has to be a continuous process, not a barrel at a time deal. While it's impossible to divine exactly how much money had been spent on the "plant" and how much had been siphoned away, it's probably safe to say that the single barrel Rendall produced for this audience had cost upward of $40 million. That's pretty pricey oil, even in an energy crisis.

Reality check #2: The unfinished plant did not employ any of Solv-Ex's proposed methods. Any bitumen produced in this manner would not validate the "patented Solv-Ex technology."

Reality check #3: Y'know that bitumen that was "produced"? According to one of Solv-Ex's own chemists, it sucked.

In May 1997 three officials from the SEC and two from the British Serious Fraud Office conducted an on-site investigation of the Solv-Ex plant. As required by its regulations, the SEC disclosed to some of the workers that its investigation concerned possible Solv-Ex violations of antifraud laws, misrepresentations, failure to disclose material information, and certain transactions involving unregistered stock.

In late May Merrill Lynch, facing a declining stock price, sold off 470,000 Solv-Ex shares that Rendall had deposited in a private account to secure a loan. Apparently unable to face the latest grim

Solv-Ex: Something Oily

reality, Solv-Ex asserted that it did not consent to the transaction and that Rendall was "reviewing his legal options" against the broker who sold the shares to meet a margin call. By this action Rendall conveyed the impression that he didn't want to sell those shares— even though he in fact benefited from the sale, as the shares would soon be worth far, far less.

Solv-Ex attempted to assuage panicked shareholders by claiming that those shares would be sold "in a manner which will not adversely impact the market." Is it possible to dump 470,000 shares without causing a ripple? The first sale of these shares, on May 28, executed at $7.63. The final sale, on May 30, was at $6.56, a drop of 14 percent, which, under such fire-sale circumstances, seems incredibly modest. Who bought them and why is as interesting a question as why Merrill Lynch made the loan in the first place.

In June 1997 Rendall, the Oz of Alberta, in effect told shareholders to "ignore the man behind the curtain" as he started dumping his own stock. The rush to the exits was on. Rendall was extremely lucky (smart) to sell 634,100 shares for $4.24 million, around $7 a share. Within the month, the price dropped to $3. Rendall's response: Issue more stock!

Even as Rendall cashed out his shares, he readied yet another Reg S offering. This time, however, he was selling convertible securities that, if converted at the current, rapidly falling stock price, would cause Solv-Ex to come perilously close to issuing more shares of stock than the 30 million shares authorized. There were 24.3 million shares already outstanding. With the share price so low, it was quite possible Solv-Ex would need to exceed the 30 million-share limit to generate enough cash. Things were grim and getting grimmer.

Robert Gill, the Solv-Ex plant's laboratory coordinator, provided a written statement and highly detailed account of the company's attempt to fake the production of bitumen. Gill had been hired by Solv-Ex on April 6, 1997, shortly after its alleged plant start-up, and was dismissed on June 13 of that year. He had been charged with testing the quality of the plant's production and tailings. Gill told me he believed that the only possible purpose for attempting to "produce" bitumen at Solv-Ex's "scrap yard" plant was to defraud investors. A miffed Jack Butler, in a not-classy move, told the *Edmonton Sun* that Gill had been fired for missing work due to alcoholism.

Butler's disgusting "damage control" did nothing to alter the inevitable. On July 14, 1997, trading in Solv-Ex's stock was halted; it was held for 65 days. Its final trade was executed at $4.25. On July 15, facing claims of $10.8 million in U.S. funds, mostly to local businesses, Solv-Ex sought bankruptcy protection.

On July 29 the *Edmonton Journal* reported that Steve Lane, the general manager who had built the Solv-Ex "plant," described it as "worthless with its current technology." Rendall, apparently still living in a magical world where Solv-Ex was going to end forever North American dependence on foreign oil, snippily replied, "The plant works well and will work better without Steve's involvement."

On August 2 another inevitable development: A class action suit was filed against Rendall, Butler, Solv-Ex senior VP, secretary and director Herbert M. Campbell, and Deutsche Bank Morgan Grenfell. The defendants were accused of preparing and approving public and shareholder reports of a materially false and misleading nature. Charlie Maxwell was mentioned in the suit, accused of authoring false and misleading research analyses and participating in Solv-Ex investor conference calls that added to the artificial inflation of its stock price.

On August 27 the Fort McKay Metis Corp. threatened to blockade the Solv-Ex oil sands leases until all bills were paid. *Fort McMurray Today*, a local paper, showed locals were cynical, angry, and themselves teetering on the brink of bankruptcy thanks to Rendall. "To me what is happening is that they are trying to liquidate everything they can, and officers of the company are going to pocket as much as they can," said Glen Fleming of Trivax, a small, local vacuum trucking company that was owed $140,000.

On September 17, 1997, the Nasdaq delisted Solv-Ex. Rendall continued his deceptions, claiming a farcical bailout deal with Geopetrol Resources Ltd. In reality, the company had no valuable assets whatsoever. Trading resumed in Solv-Ex, now relegated to over-the-counter "pink sheet" status. The Geopetrol scam somehow helped push up the stock price. Surely there wasn't one investor anywhere on earth dim enough to sink money into this stock! Yet there was, and there continued to be.

In 1998 the *really* bad news began. On July 20 the SEC filed a complaint against Solv-Ex, Rendall, and Campbell for disseminating fraudulent information, plus a couple of other little matters, such as understating the company's outstanding common shares by 3 million. Corroborating our on-the-spot correspondents, the indictment accused Solv-Ex of purchasing materials, transporting them to the site, and using them to augment their actual extractions. It accused Solv-Ex of distributing the David Snow and Charlie Maxwell reports to investors even though they knew the reports contained misinformation. Scorecard: three claims of fraud, one of false SEC filings, one of aiding and abetting false filings.

In response to SEC charges, on August 2, 1999, David Snow admitted taking payments and stock options from Naxos, a Canadian public company, and issuing a positive "analyst" report about the company without disclosing his interest. He was also nailed for owning 2,300 shares of Solv-Ex, which of course he also recommended without disclosing his interest. (Had Solv-Ex shares reached Snow's $1,000 prediction, his holding would have been worth $2.3 million. Instead, they're now worth barely enough to buy a tank of gas.) Snow settled the case for $15,000 plus agreeing to a cease-and-desist order and accepting a censure.

In April 2000 U.S. District Judge Bruce Black found that John Rendall and Herb Campbell ignored negative test results and cautions from consultants and created "a misleadingly optimistic picture" of the company with press releases and statements to shareholders. The judge also found that the company and its officers made false filings with the SEC. According to Kit Addleman, assistant regional director for the SEC's Denver office, which filed the lawsuit, the judge "found there was fraud in all of the technologies." Still, there was no financial remuneration for investors who were sucked into this swindle, no compensation to Deutsche Bank Morgan Grenfell. Where did all that money go?

In May 2000 the Solv-Ex suit against Asensio & Company and other short sellers was dismissed. Once again our fledgling little firm had to endure, at great cost, the misguided legal scuds of a $100+ million scam.

In December 2000, a British crown court dismissed charges against Peter Young, declaring him mentally unfit to stand trial. He had appeared in court dressed in a cerise top, gray-flecked skirt, and high-heeled shoes, carrying a purple shoulder bag. The court was told that Young had used a craft knife, fishing line, and scissors in an attempt to castrate himself, and was now calling himself "Elizabeth."

Solv-Ex was an ugly, ugly transaction, but for all the trouble it was immensely satisfying. The Asensio & Company trading fund did well. And we helped expose a 17-year-old swindle. In this business, you can't ask for more.

CHAPTER SIX

SCHONBERG'S LIST

I'm not a fan of mutual funds. I recognize the advantages, such as the chance for a small investor to own a diversified portfolio, to track a market index, or to focus on a particular sector. I just can't see turning over investment decisions to someone whose motivations are unknown to me.

Still, even in my darkest scenario, I would never expect a fund manager to load up so eagerly on the pathetic stocks that the Dreyfus Corporation's Michael Schonberg bought with the $250 million entrusted to him by his funds' investors. Nor would I have imagined the way Dreyfus would market these funds. I would not expect a system of internal safeguards and regulations to break down as devastatingly as it did when Dreyfus failed to oversee Schonberg's purchases. And if not for our exposing a two-bit scam called Chromatics Color Sciences (OTC: CCSI), it's possible Schonberg would still be at his desk today.

Chromatics Color Sciences claimed to have developed a noninvasive bilirubinometer, which is a device used to test for infant jaundice. CCSI's Colormate III supposedly offered certain unique advantages in a market it estimated to be between $330 and $510 million. In fact, by the time we began to short CCSI, the Colormate III itself was over 10 years old. It had been FDA-approved for marketing for almost a year and had yet to register a single sale. Furthermore, the market research firm Frost & Sullivan estimated that the entire world market for bilirubinometers was not $330 million to $510 million but actually less than $2.5 million per year. CCSI's promotional literature was rife with misrepresentation. This was just one of them. This was nothing more than a low-level stock promotion pretending to be a medical stock. But despite a storied past riddled with disgrace and regulatory actions, CCSI managed a brief moment in the sun.

The Chromatics scam is merely a backdrop, though, for a much larger scandal: a big investment house trying to cover for a fund manager's portfolio so wretched that Jesse Eisinger of TheStreet.com would describe it as "a short seller's candy store."

This is the story of how Michael Schonberg came to sink millions of other people's money into one of the most irresponsibly promoted stocks in the market.

Chromatics' 4.1 million share IPO was underwritten in February 1993 by New Jersey–based Investors Associates, Inc. After that IPO, Investors Associates initiated coverage of Chromatics with a *buy* rating, listing Herman Epstein as their CCSI-related contact person. After years of government actions against it, Investors Associates was finally expelled in 1997 from the securities business and charged with fraud for using high-pressure boiler-room tactics to sell penny stocks.

In 1999 the SEC settled proceedings against three Investors Associates directors: Lawrence Penna, Douglas Mangan, and CCSI *buy*-guy Herman Epstein. The SEC alleged these three participated in fraudulent public offerings during September 1995 and February 1997 and subsequently manipulated the market in those stocks, garnering an estimated $33 million in illegal profits. The trio is now banned from the brokerage industry. To the informed investor, a *buy* from Investors Associates, particularly of a stock it had underwritten, was tantamount to a *strong sell*. But apparently not to Schonberg or Dreyfus.

Dreyfus wasn't the only titan to accept an invitation from Investors Associates (IA) to play musical stocks. (The way this game works is that the loser is the one still holding the garbage stock when it finally collapses. Of course, usually this means some small-time investor, not the big boys.) The powerful New Jersey senator Robert Torricelli chose to have his blind trust managed by Matthew Gohd, a managing director of Whale Securities. Whale, a specialist in low-cap IPOs, has a long-term record so abysmal it was the subject of a feature in the *Wall Street Journal*. In 1996, Gohd managed to score a one-day profit of over $50,000 for Torricelli in the IPO of a manipulated IA stock called Compare Generiks—a stock that became within months nearly worthless.

Furthermore, IA's Lawrence Penna pleaded guilty to illegally funneling $20,000 into Torricelli's 1996 election campaign. Investors Associates brokers from the Long Island office were forcibly bused to a Hackensack, New Jersey, fund-raiser for Torricelli and instructed to contribute the maximum of $1,000 each. Most of those brokers didn't even live in New Jersey, but that was okay—Penna and Douglas Mangan reimbursed them for the donations. Did IA honchos really think they could buy political influence this way? Is the political process so easily and cheaply corrupted? I'd like to think not.

Subsequent to its IPO, Chromatics, through private stock sales and public promotions, would sell an additional 10.7 million shares at an average private price of $2. These shares would then be resold to public investors at prices as high as $17. The following explains how this was achieved. Let's call it "Anatomy of a Chop Stock."

SOLD SHORT

On September 27, 1994, Chromatics entered into a deal with Janssen-Meyers Associates, a low-grade "chop shop," to sell up to 2,700,000 shares of its common stock at a price up to 50 percent below the market. A chop shop takes control of a block of virtually unsellable stock at a fire-sale price and then sells it to the public at market prices. To really juice the margin, the chop shop and the company will work to raise the public price by "boxing" the stock—that is, controlling the market. This allows the "chop." The chop shop then sends out its foot soldiers and cold callers to unload its cheap stock at these artificially jacked up prices onto unsophisticated, small, retail investors. The fictional firm featured in the movie *Boiler Room* was a textbook chop shop. The *New York Times* invited me to accompany New York City law enforcement legend Robert Morganthal to preview *Boiler Room*. Our comments on the movie were used in a *Times* article about the film.

The net proceeds to CCSI from this offering were $3.3 million. However, CCSI had to pay a total of $1.3 million in expenses, including $770,200 in offering costs and a $75,000 consulting fee, to Janssen-Meyers. CCSI management also received $262,400 in cash, and Janssen-Meyers took an additional $150,000 fee. Another $30,000 of demand registration expenses was paid from the net proceeds of the offering. Altogether, these payments consumed 39.5 percent of the net proceeds. And that was before the investors incurred the dilution caused by buying their shares at the inflated market price. Nice deal. An institutional-quality *buy* if ever there was one. P.S. That was sarcasm.

But that's not all. In addition to the cash payments, CCSI also granted Janssen-Meyers a warrant to purchase one share of CCSI stock for every share it sold. In other words, the deal was "That's ten for me, one for me, three for . . . me. Oh, and here's a crumb for you. Now, where were we? Five for me . . ." This is the kind of fire sale that short sellers love to see. A company would agree to such onerous terms only if there were no willing buyers for its stock based on its economic value. So, it agreed to all these concessions in order to raise less than $3.3 million . . . *Voilà!* A chop stock was born. Now, we can certainly see why Janssen-Meyers did it. And we can even see why CCSI did it. But who would be dumb enough to buy this stock from Janssen-Meyers?

Normal Janssen-Meyers procedure would be to pass this chop stock on to small, unwitting investors. In the Chromatics case, however, Janssen-Meyers found another outlet—one that was truly a stunner.

In August 1995 Michael Schonberg joined the Dreyfus Corporation to become the lead portfolio manager of the Dreyfus Aggressive Growth Fund and the Dreyfus Premier Aggressive Growth Fund. Both the $200 million Premier Fund and the $53.3 million Aggressive Fund had been flagging under the stewardship of Dreyfus CEO Howard Stein.

Schonberg's appointment to head these high-profile funds is a bit of a head-scratcher. In his previous post as a partner of prestigious Omega Advisors Inc., he purchased 615,000 shares—a 6.5 percent stake—in a suspect penny stock called Home Theater Products International Inc. After three of Home Theater's top executives pleaded guilty to securities fraud and insider trading, Schonberg's boss, Leon G. Cooperman, swiftly dumped the stock—reportedly over Schonberg's objections.

Over the course of his term as a Dreyfus fund manager, Schonberg purchased a staggering total of 1,875,000 CCSI shares for his funds. Bruce Meyers of Janssen-Meyers disclosed to TheStreet.com that Schonberg and Dreyfus funds had opened accounts with Janssen-Meyers. All of these shares were acquired for Dreyfus after CCSI had been converted from a failed Investors Associates IPO into a Janssen-Meyers in-house chop stock. Even the most clueless fund manager in Dopeyville would understand that a stock that had been passed from a fraudulent underwriter to such a low-end chop shop must have been deeply troubled. And Michael Schonberg was supposedly no dummy. (See Figure 6.1.)

SOLD SHORT

FIGURE 6.1 Chromatics Color Sciences International, Inc.: Analysis of Transactions by Dreyfus Corporation and Janssen-Meyers Associates, L.P.[1]

Date	Document Source	Number of Shares Held by Dreyfus Corporation[2]	Number of Warrants Held by Janssen-Meyers Associates, L.P.[3]
1/6/95 to 6/8/95[4]	Private placement sold		
6/8/95[5]	Private placement warrants issued to agent		2,700,000
8/14/95[6]	Dreyfus appoints Schonberg		
3/28/96	1995 Form 10-K	390,000	2,650,500
4/10/96	13-G	712,500	
5/6/96	Proxy	712,500	
3/25/97	1996 Form 10-K	1,552,500	2,461,650
4/15/97	Proxy	1,552,500	2,461,650
1/12/98	13-G	1,875,000	
1/14/98	Proxy	1,875,000	1,824,285
3/26/98	1997 Form 10-K	1,875,000	1,442,427
4/8/98	13-G	1,519,938	

[1]All figures adjusted for a 3:2 stock split effected on February 13, 1998.
[2]These shares were purchased at market prices. They may have been purchased directly from Janssen-Meyers. Mr. Meyers, a named principal in Janssen-Meyers, acknowledges that Schonberg's Dreyfus Funds were clients of Peter Janssen.
[3]Janssen-Meyers exercised the warrants they received at no cost to buy CCSI shares at $1.67 and then sold these shares. These shares may have been purchased directly by Dreyfus or sold in the open market.
[4]Michael Schonberg bought 30,000 CCSI shares at $1.67 in the CCSI private placement sold by Janssen-Meyers.
[5]The private placement warrants were issued to Janssen-Meyers at no cost as compensation for selling 2.7 million CCSI shares at $1.38 net to the company. The warrants are exercisable at $1.67 for five years.
[6]Michael Schonberg was appointed senior equity portfolio manager at the Dreyfus Corporation.
Source: SEC filings.

Schonberg's List

Schonberg's funds flourished at first, thanks to the short-lived run-up of several speculative IPOs. The promoters who unloaded their stocks on Schonberg had at least given him the courtesy of participating in the initial promotion-backed rise of their securities. Was this courtesy in fact, as the drill sergeant in *Full Metal Jacket* so memorably phrased it, "the courtesy of a reach-around"? Or was it just a good way to suck more investors into the fund? In his first eight months at Dreyfus, the Dreyfus Aggressive Growth Fund returned a phenomenal 120 percent. During that time Schonberg took the "aggressive" part of the Aggressive Growth Fund seriously. Unfortunately, he held so many shares of these thinly traded companies that he couldn't cash in on the pumped-up shares without hurting his own performance. So if you can't beat them, join them again. He bought more. And of course, après le pump . . . le dump.

Chromatics' device received FDA marketing clearance on July 31, 1997. It was time for the CCSI promote to bloom. Chromatics CEO Darby Macfarlane, a former actress who claims to have appeared on the soap opera *The Guiding Light*, gave a splendid recital of "The Infinite Possibilities of Color Chromatics" in a September 17 conference call. She said:

> Our patented technology and instrumentation has many potential commercial applications, including the beauty industry for cosmetics, hair color and custom blended foundation makeup, the dental industry for matching the exact color of teeth, caps, bonding and dentures for both dentist's office and dental laboratories.
>
> Other markets exist for detection of soil and grain contamination, such as for oil and gas spills, or the printing industry, including cross medium color matching. And broader consumer applications we are working on where a person has a pocket-size color computer like a calculator they can take shopping and use to flash on a shirt or a dress to select

correctly coordinated colors for their wardrobe. Or the consumer can use it for interior design purposes to match paint to carpet, towels to sheets, et cetera.

The Company has identified what we call "chromogenic diseases." While technically this is not a defined medical term, it describes diseases which currently are or the Company believes can be diagnosed or monitored by the coloration of human skin, tissue or fluids. There are many of these diseases, such as anemia, hepatitis, tuberculosis, forms of malignancy evaluated through biopsy tissue and different fluid laboratory analyses.

As for the principal promote, bilirubin infant jaundice:

This disease affects over half of all babies born, and nearly 100% of all premature children. . . . We are currently in various stages of discussion, negotiations or due diligence with a number of large international medical companies very interested in obtaining the marketing and distribution rights for the Colormate bilirubin monitoring device. . . . Please understand the scope of worldwide distribution we are structuring here.

The potential contract we are dealing with may be a once in a corporate lifetime opportunity, and the process of evaluating which company or companies to structure agreements with involves many principals and professionals working and meeting in many locations in the world. We have identified a number of candidates who would make excellent medical partners, and hope to decide which of these we will proceed with as rapidly as possible.

The Company estimates there are approximately 15 million bilirubin blood tests currently performed annually in the United States. . . . Assuming a (conservative) $22 fee, the Company estimates a current annual amount spent on monitoring bilirubin jaundice in the U.S. of $330 million.

Wow. How could anybody resist such a miraculous device? As it turned out, as with so many fishy promotes, the moment the performance claims started to become more specific was the moment they

fell apart. It's so much easier to sell pipe dreams than to try to manu-
facture a product at an economically viable price, scramble to find
actual customers, and allow outsiders to evaluate the truth of your
claims. This is why so many long-running promotes rely on products
whose claims require indefinite development periods, such as Solv-
Ex, with its endless oil sands projects.

Oh, and another thing before I forget. Just a detail, but it may be
relevant. CCSI had no proprietary color-identification technology.
All it did was buy preexisting, off-the-shelf equipment and then
promote it as something special.

On February 26, 1998, with the stock price at $14.50, Avalon
Research Group, out of Boca Raton, issued a *sell* and *short-sell* advisory. "Were it not for a series of private placements and warrant con-
versions," its report stated, "CCSI might have been long gone or
possibly a 'drill bit' (i.e., trading well below $1, say, $\frac{1}{8}$, $\frac{1}{4}$, $\frac{3}{8}$), and we
would not have had the opportunity to ever make this recommen-
dation." This "drill bit" still had some drilling power behind it, however. It would rise to over $17 within the month, partly on the heels
of a bogus imprimatur.

In a March 16, 1998, press release, Chromatics Color Sciences
announced it "received a letter from the American Medical Association (AMA) permitting third party insurance reimbursement in all
U.S. states for each use of the Company's non-invasive device." Not
only was this statement purposefully misleading and untrue, but, as
we disclosed, the AMA had no record of sending any such letter. In
fact, an AMA spokesperson we contacted had no record of sending
any letter to Chromatics. Upon review of the Chromatics press release, the AMA informed us that they believed it contained false information and improperly implied an AMA endorsement. What
impelled us to check with the AMA? Maybe it was the dubious sin-
cerity of Macfarlane's little pep talk.

The short sellers sniffed the air and picked up the stench of disaster. The short interest in CCSI rose dramatically, from 529,224 on March 15, 1998, to 2,625,664 on April 15 to 3,154,888 by May 15. This added supply didn't have the deeply depressive impact on the stock that one would have expected—a tribute to Macfarlane and Co.'s promotional abilities. As the price rose, shorts were "scaling it up," or continuing to sell at increasingly higher prices. This is an open market at its best: the hot air of the believers providing loft, the weighty doubts of the naysayers supplying ballast. The stock price peaked at $17 in early March 1998. Fortunately the shorts were able to borrow stock to sell. Imagine how high it might have flown if those pesky shorties hadn't been dampening the market!

Amid all this action came the sudden announcement by Dreyfus on April 13, 1998, that it had replaced Michael L. Schonberg after two and a half years as a lead portfolio manager. No explanation was offered except some sugarcoated PR that was lapped up by the *Wall Street Journal*. The same hard-hitting writer who wrote this fluff piece was put on the story after we exposed the Dreyfus scam. The title: "Short Seller Takes a Potshot at Dreyfus." Schonberg's funds, which had drawn in small investors after their initial run-ups, had begun to perform atrociously, losing tens of millions of dollars. His list enjoyed a giddy pump but suffered a hellacious dump. Premier Aggressive declined 2.4 percent in 1996, went down another 13 percent in 1997, and had sunk 15.5 percent so far in 1998. Aggressive fell 15.8 percent in 1997 and was down over 18 percent so far in 1998. It ended the year down 36.7 percent, placing it in the lowest percentile of its peer group. And don't forget, this was in the heart of a runaway bull market.

According to a shorts-bashing June 9, 1998, *buy* recommendation in Charles Biderman's *Market Trim Tabs* newsletter, the Mt. Sinai (New York City) Medical Center professor of pediatrics and chief of newborn medicine Dr. Ian Holzman was blatantly promoting the Colormate TLC-BiliTest. In May Dr. Holzman had stated authoritatively that either this device or its equivalent (which did not exist, at least as far as he claimed to know) would be in virtually every hospital, birthing facility, and pediatrician's office. Well, maybe he should have kept looking, because we found plenty that already existed all over the place. The busy doctor hadn't enough time to mention that, since November 1997, he had been the director of Chromatics' Medical Advisory Board, receiving 100,000 stock options at $7 each. With the stock trading over $16 at the time of his pronouncement, those options were worth almost $1 million.

Holzman's pronouncement helped reignite the promotion. The stock rose from its "Schonberg gets busted" $12 low of April to late-May highs in the $15 range. The company's market cap at its peak was $350 million, fully diluted. I had been watching from the sidelines as the Chromatics story unfolded, preparing research. I consulted with doctors and other medical experts to finalize my report.

As I have seen so often, the very fact that someone was seriously getting down to the work of conducting due diligence on CCSI caused the stock price to tumble well in advance of my releasing the initial report. Besides the footprints of my own investigation, writers such as Gary Weiss of *Business Week* need to verify independently information they receive from me or another short seller, and this verification process can set off a boardroom panic.

This panic is particularly likely when the information being sought is specific to a key element of the promote. In this case, the Schonberg–Dreyfus–Janssen–Meyers connection was so central to the promoters' ability to jack up the price of CCSI that its unraveling could have an explosive effect. CCSI sank like a termite-ridden rowboat, from $15 to $8, even before I went public. Only rarely do the insiders, upon hearing they are being investigated, head for the hills. They mostly respond and fight—with shareholders' money, never putting their own money where their mouths are. All react differently, but in the end, rhetoric and posturing mean nothing. Fundamentals expose a fraud and doom it.

SOLD SHORT

Often when I first report on a stock, incredibly wild accusations appear on that company's online message boards. People state with certainty that I am some master manipulator who issues false reports, front-runs those reports, then, when the stock tumbles, the story goes, I actually reverse myself and go long the stock in the knowledge that my false charges will be neatly refuted. This fictitious claim has been cultivated as a response by the companies we cover. The promoter's battle cry is never "He's wrong and here are the facts." Instead, it's "The Assman did it!"

Occasionally the ignorant compare our work to the borderline criminal acts of those who purposefully disseminate lies on the Internet by impersonating legitimate media outlets. For example, in 1999 one perpetrator designed a Web page resembling the Bloomberg News site, then created a fake "news item" damaging to PairGain Technologies. In August 2000 a college student planted a phony item on the Internet Wire that caused the stock of Emulex Corp. to crater. Both stocks recovered after the hoaxes were revealed. Now, besides our reports being completely fact based, we certainly never claim to be anyone other than who we are. Those who have come to know and trust us can make of our reports what they will. Those who refuse to accept the truth—or simply don't like our style—are free to ignore us.

I have no idea when and even if a stock I report on is going to fall. I compile my short position subject to market conditions for the individual stock and our estimation of that stock promotion's maturity. If the promotion has matured, it means the company already has:

- Disseminated the basic false claims of its promote.
- Greased up a distribution mechanism by issuing private shares or warrants to promoters and other insiders.
- Solicited analysts to cover the stock.

Schonberg's List

- Announced a bogus deal (terms are always paltry or undisclosed).
- And, usually, enjoyed at least one rapid run-up.

Because of trading rules that I consider antiquated and biased, it's far more difficult to assemble a large short position in a brief time than to purchase a long position. For one thing, it's difficult to get a "borrow" on fraudulent stocks. Fraudsters work with corrupt brokers and willing buyers to ensure that shares are placed in cash accounts or shoveled offshore and are not available to be borrowed. And even if I can get the borrow, I'm allowed to sell only on an uptick, which means that stock can be shorted only if it is going up. In full-blown frauds, it's virtually impossible to find a large block to borrow. Not that I blame promoters for this—under the current (antiquated/biased) regulations, it's a legitimate strategy at their disposal. Hey, if you're running a scam, why would you not take an assist from the SEC? More power to you.

And as for reversing myself and going long on a fraudulent stock—never. It's something I've never done. I'd never take the chance of buying a worthless stock. I don't believe that any promote can survive the bright light of factual information that has been publicly disseminated. Stocks must reflect their true value for our capitalist system to work.

On June 9, 1998, I issued a lengthy research report on Chromatics, detailing its gross overestimate of its potential market and its false technology-ownership claims. The Colormate III's principal components, we found, were a 1989 Toshiba 512K computer and a color-measurement instrument—a standard, not-invented-here instrument. The public had been led to believe that color measurement and identification was a new thing. The Colormate III did not contain any new technology and could be easily duplicated using commonly available components. Like other bilirubinometers, it could be used only to estimate the total amount of bilirubin in the blood. It did not estimate indirect or direct bilirubin levels, which are necessary and are commonly provided by blood tests.

As for Dr. Ian Holzman's claims that there were no other similar devices available, by happy coincidence we had just that month received the exact tool we needed to uncover the truth. We were evaluating an experimental, broadband, super-high-speed wireless Internet service. We were thus able to do a rapid search through the World Wide Web, where we found studies of *hundreds* of other bilirubinometers. Hundreds! All you need to make a bilirubinometer is a color meter—and they're widely available.

That day Chromatics stock fell a further 25 percent, from $8.81 to $6.64, trading as low as $4.50. But we had yet to nail the deeper scandal beneath the fraud. In order to get to the truth about Michael Schonberg, Asensio & Company investigated his other Dreyfus funds holdings. We researched a total of 19 penny-stock promotions that he owned or had owned in his portfolios.

Digging deeper, we found two instances in which Schonberg purchased shares of companies in private transactions before he used Dreyfus money to buy stock in those same companies on the open market. (Little did we know; it turned out there were *nine* such instances.) This is a variation on the concept of "front running," which is prohibited by all legitimate investment houses. Front running normally refers to floor brokers and traders with knowledge of a large institutional buy or sell order purchasing or selling that stock for their personal accounts immediately ahead of the institutional order. Schonberg's version of front running involved getting in personally before the promote, knowing with certainty that other buyers—his own funds—would be following.

We discovered that Schonberg had privately purchased 30,000 (split-adjusted) shares of CCSI. These shares had been registered for sale on May 6, 1996. At the time, he had already begun using investors' money deposited in the Dreyfus Aggressive Growth Fund and the Dreyfus Premier Aggressive Growth Fund to buy CCSI stock with no disclosure to those investors of his personal CCSI holdings. Ultimately, Schonberg bought a total of 1,875,000 (split-adjusted) CCSI shares for Dreyfus funds. From January 1996 to January 1998, Dreyfus went from owning zero CCSI shares to owning 13.6 percent of the company. Schonberg went so far as to make CCSI the largest holding in one of his funds, accounting for 12.5 percent of it. Fund managers generally avoid having any one stock make up more than 2 to 3 percent of their funds.

Have you ever examined a minor flaw in a wall or floorboard only to uncover the horror of widespread rot underneath? That was Schonberg's list: unspeakably bad companies, stocks even the most jaundiced cold caller would be ashamed to pitch.

Schonberg purchased for the Dreyfus funds 500,000 shares of Systems of Excellence, Inc. (OTC: SEXI). SEXI went bankrupt in 1996, only after, according to the SEC, it had become the most important case of Internet stock-touting fraud ever. At least five individuals pled guilty to felony charges stemming from its manipulation. Investors Associates, the underwriter of Chromatics' public offering that was barred from the securities industry in 1997, was investigated by the SEC for its connection to the sale of unregistered SEXI securities. There's a lesson here: Beware of dumb-ass ticker symbols.

As of an SEC filing dated January 28, 1997, Schonberg registered to sell 20,000 shares of American Medical Technologies, Inc., since renamed Tidel Technologies, Inc. (OTC: ATMS) for his personal account. In February 1998, Dreyfus held 350,000 shares of ATMS.

Schonberg bought for the Dreyfus funds 590,958 shares of Bentley Pharmaceuticals, Inc. (OTC: BNT), formerly known as Belmac Corp. of St. Petersburg, Florida. One of Bentley's pet projects was a hemorrhoid cure meant to be administered through the belly button. The former chairman of Belmac was Edward Vimond, who had also been a director of Chromatics since 1992 and was a paid consultant for at least its first three years as a public company.

The chairman of Bentley was James R. Murphy, a former vice president of Macrochem (OTC: MCHM). Peter Janssen and Bruce Meyers of Janssen-Meyers Associates personally held 1.6 million shares and 1.05 million shares of Macrochem respectively. Schonberg purchased for Dreyfus 1,345,000 shares of Macrochem. Macrochem was a "trend promotion," hopping aboard the Viagra craze, à la Zonagen Inc. as well as Vivus, with which we were also firmly involved.

Schonberg bought 135,000 shares of Cytoclonal Pharmaceuticals Inc. (OTC: CYPH) for the Dreyfus funds. Kinder Investments L.P., a fund established for the children and grandchildren of J. Morton "Morty" Davis, the head of much-censured D. H. Blair, controlled 9 percent of Cytoclonal's voting power as of March 19, 1997. Kinder also participated in the private placement for Chromatics. Peter Janssen controlled 8.9 percent of Cytoclonal, and Bruce Meyers controlled 9 percent of the voting rights. Both Janssen and Meyers were former employees of D. H. Blair. And, as you'll recall, Janssen-Meyers was the chop shop that provided Schonberg with much of the CCSI stock purchased by Dreyfus.

We found that Schonberg's funds owned at least four stocks with links to Lindsay Rosenwald, M.D., the son-in-law of Morty Davis and a dashing New York–based investor in biotechs. Rosenwald, a D. H. Blair managing director from 1987 to 1991, has sat simultaneously on the boards of many publicly traded biotechs. Anybody interested in exploring biotech promotions would do well to remember his name. For a medical doctor, being a stock market wheeler-dealer surely must beat managed care, whiny patients, and annoying malpractice suits.

Rosenwald's known entities include Paramount Capital, Inc.,

Schonberg's List

The Castle Group, Aries Financial Services, and the Aries Fund. The companies with which both he and Schonberg were associated include Atlantic Pharmaceuticals (OTC: ATLC), Boston Life Sciences (OTC: BLSI), Interneuron (OTC: IPIC), and VIMRX (OTC:VMRX).

Rosenwald was Interneuron's cofounder and chairman. The company floundered in 1997 when its only profitable product, a diet pill called Redux, was withdrawn by regulators when some patients using it showed signs of heart valve damage. Some shareholders and patients then sued the company. The single largest shareholder in Interneuron was D. H. Blair & Co. In August 1997 the NASD (National Association of Securities Dealers) fined Blair $2 million plus $2.4 million in restitution to customers for excessive markup of prices on new stocks. Interneuron cofounder Dr. Richard Wurtman, when asked about the connection between Blair and Interneuron, told the *Boston Herald*, "D. H. Blair has no involvement with Interneuron." When it was pointed out that Blair owned 26 percent of the company (and that it originally took IPIC public in 1990), he sputtered, "I don't know who owns Interneuron. It's been public so long now."

To the rescue came David Crossen of Montgomery Securities. Crossen stated that Blair's stake in Interneuron should not affect other investors, so long as Blair doesn't dump the stock. "I don't think Blair is planning on unloading it," said Crossen. It is not known whether Crossen is clairvoyant, or whether he understands that any company underwritten by Blair might as well adopt a skull and crossbones as its corporate logo. What is known is that we would encounter Crossen again supporting an overhyped blood-replacement stock called Biotime (AMEX: BTX). In our research we learned that Crossen wrote his Ph.D. thesis on "myth-making." We've been waiting since uncovering this nugget for the proper place to report this in a comical, raised-eyebrow manner.

As for D. H. Blair, it ceased retail operations in April 1998, but its problems didn't end there. In March 2000 Blair agreed to fund a $2.25 million escrow account to reimburse its customers for inappropriate trading. Interneuron is now marketing a cure for premenstrual syndrome (PMS).

Schonberg purchased for the Dreyfus funds 918,000 shares of CCA Companies Inc. (OTC: RIPE), a development-stage food preservative company brought public by Janssen–Meyers. Two months after going public RIPE announced its intentions to change its business and enter the Russian hotel and casino market. No chance of taint or corruption there, then.

What and when did Dreyfus know? I mean, *we* knew all this, and we didn't even work there. Was it ignoring its duty to supervise its portfolio managers, or was it aware of Schonberg's misdeeds and simply turning a blind eye in the hope of avoiding regulatory action and financial loss?

On June 12, 1998, we released a report on Schonberg's malfeasance. At this point, everything should have been clear, even in the unlikely event that Dreyfus really knew nothing about this. Then the *Wall Street Journal* article appeared, accusing me of "taking potshots" at Dreyfus, as if these weren't plain and simple facts. Was Paul Revere "taking potshots" at the British when he alerted Lexington that they were coming? Does a meteorologist get accused of "taking potshots" at the weather when he tells us a hurricane is on the way?

Dreyfus is owned by Mellon Bank. On June 16 we wrote a letter to Mellon's chairman, president, and CEO, Frank Cahouet, regarding Schonberg's trading. We received a response, as usual, not from the boss himself but from the company's general counsel. In it Michael Bleier concluded, "Mellon will not be drawn into your press campaign. Your efforts to generate publicity for Asensio & Company and its own vested interest are your agenda, not Mellon's and not Dreyfus'." Mellon then went a step further and retained a First Amendment counsel, from Rogers & Wells, to accuse us of making comments that were "false, defamatory and actionable." The attorney then asked us in the same letter to provide further information regarding Schonberg's "alleged" trading improprieties.

Let's think about this: You're Dreyfus. However you want to characterize the situation, at the very least you've got a fund manager whose trading needs to be investigated. How would you begin this investigation? Should you examine internal trading records? Should you interrogate the fund manager? No, wait, I've got it! First you should threaten and then ask a short seller for help! And until he provides you with the necessary information, you should just deny the whole thing.

Once we disclosed the facts, however, and the media picked up the story and ran with it, it took on a life of its own. Our part in the story was not mentioned, but it was still a beautiful thing for the public to get a tiny little whitewashed peek at the enormity of fidaddling that goes on within the most revered of institutions. In another case of a junk-buying fund manager, Jack Ferraro of Neuberger Berman (see sidebar on the following page), we worked with *Forbes*, *Fortune*, and the *Wall Street Journal*, but the rest of the media didn't follow up. Because those stories had no afterlife, they made less of a public impact, and Ferraro was allowed to quietly disconnect from his employer.

On June 19, 1998, a class action lawsuit was filed against Chromatics over its false and misleading statements. Officers of the company were accused of personally selling over $3.7 million in stock prior to releasing negative information. At this writing, two suits are pending, one in New York state court and one in federal court.

The company's net loss ballooned from $7.2 million in 1998 to $12.8 million in 1999. A quarterly SEC filing in June 2000 showed a

SOLD SHORT

Meet Jack Ferraro, Formerly of Neuberger Berman

Michael Schonberg wasn't the only fund manager from a prestigious white-shoed firm whom we caught, shall we say, shopping in the bargain basement. To be honest, this one was easier to spot. In our investigations into ParkerVision, Inc. (Nasdaq: PRKR), we encountered a portfolio manager of discretionary accounts at Neuberger Berman named Jack Ferraro. Ferraro was making positive comments in print and on conference calls about ParkerVision without disclosing his sizable personal interest in the company. And this was apparently without his employer's knowledge.

The Swiss-based Banco del Gottardo, Ferraro's employer prior to Neuberger Berman, acted as the agent for two ParkerVision offshore stock sales totaling 1.7 million shares for over $28 million. Ferraro brokered the Gottardo placements, for which services ParkerVision granted him 305,000 warrants.

Naturally, when we're short a stock and see a guy from such a major firm so deeply involved in it, we want to know more about him. Well, what we found was that Ferraro had a taste for speculative small-cap stock promotions.

Ferraro and Gottardo were jointly involved in at least four other stock promotions: Ferrara Food Co. Inc., which plunged in 1996 to 1 cent; Vasomedical Inc., which fell from $8.25 to $1; Intellicall, Inc., which has gone from $18.50 to $1; and Showscan Entertainment Corp., which has gone from $13 to 8 cents. Ferraro signed a consulting agreement with Showscan and received a warrant to purchase 100,000 shares. He was also involved in at least two other stock promotions: Enamelon, Inc., which has gone from $27.50 to $1; and Accumed International, Inc., which has gone from $33.75 to $1.63.

As with Schonberg, Ferraro, who had been a principal general partner at Neuberger since 1983, was placed on administrative leave while his company announced an internal investigation into the ParkerVision matter. This was on October 13, 1999. Neuberger Berman had gone public only days earlier, on October 7.

Also like Schonberg, Ferraro quietly cleaned out his desk at some point during this period of administrative leave. He is no longer employed by Neuberger Berman. However, his landing was a soft one. According to *Fortune*, he had Neuberger Berman stock worth more than $6 million.

---

loss of $3.2 million and a pitiful $41,000 in sales of bilirubin products—remember, this is *three years* after FDA approval. (This is a heck of a small share of that supposed $330+ million market. If we ever find the guys who own the remaining $329,959,000+ shares of that market, we'll want to buy a piece of them.) Three years of negligible sales, yet the company still boasted a $100 million market cap. What did people think, that after three years on the market and almost no takers, the device would suddenly catch on?

Where are they now? Janssen-Meyers is gone. In late August 2000, CCSI swooned on heavy volume, dipping under $2 with no natural floor beneath it. Darby Macfarlane, the former soap actress, was written out of the script, and a new character took over. Perhaps the CCSI technology can answer this question for Macfarlane: What color is your parachute?

Speaking of which. . . . On June 23, 1998, the New York State Attorney General's office announced it was going to examine Michael Schonberg's trading. On July 8 Dreyfus placed him on "paid administrative leave." The company suffered the financial repercussions of his dreadful stock purchases and its lack of supervision of his funds for months to come. Dreyfus quickly cut its combined CCSI holdings nearly in half, to 780,000 shares. (Hey, not fair. The pumpers became the dumpers.) But the problem with unwinding Schonberg's ghastly assemblage was that microcaps such as these have low liquidity, and the very act of unloading them in quantity depresses the price even further. (Of course, if you have sold these stocks short, this is a very good thing.)

On May 10, 2000, the SEC and New York State attorney general took an enforcement action against Schonberg and Dreyfus for failing to inform investors of the risks in Schonberg's funds and for improper and misleading allocation of IPOs to those funds. Dreyfus was also found to be deficient in its code-of-ethics policies and to have lapsed in its supervision of those policies. The company's code-of-ethics policy prohibited managers from participating in any activities that could cause or give rise to conflicts. It also required managers to periodically report holdings and transactions. These policies and procedures, the ruling found, nonetheless did not detect the conflicts of interest between Schonberg's personal trading activities and the management of his two funds.

As terms of the settlement, Dreyfus was assessed $2,950,000 in fines. Schonberg was fined $50,000 and barred from working for any investment adviser for nine months. Regrettably, neither Dreyfus nor Schonberg was forced to admit any wrongdoing.

Unlike with the Peter Young scandal, in which Deutsche Bank Morgan Grenfell accepted its responsibility and made restitution to investors, Mellon Bank/Dreyfus never reimbursed its investors for their losses. Deutsche Bank Morgan Grenfell fell on its sword, firing Peter Young's supervisors, all of them leaders of the firm. Mellon Bank never publicly acknowledged firing any supervisors as a result of the Schonberg scandal and didn't even fire Schonberg immediately after the scandal broke. But then, unlike Peter Young, Michael Schonberg didn't embarrass his bosses and enthrall the tabloids by showing up for a court appearance in a skirt, heels, and lipstick, either.

CHAPTER SEVEN

BY-THE-NUMBERS STOCK PROMOTIONS

Zonagen: What Goes Up Must Come Down

Most stock promotions zero in on some sexy product or notion that can capture the public imagination. Zonagen Inc. (Nasdaq: ZONA) took the concept of a sexy promote literally. As Pfizer's Viagra became the most talked about new product of the late 1990s, Zonagen, after two earlier failed stock promotes, dusted off a 45-year-old generic drug called phentolamine. Then, without adding any other active ingredient or even making any chemical alteration, Zonagen claimed that a phentolamine pill helped overcome male impotence. Zonagen called its pill Vasomax, and for a time, it was the prime stud in the stable, raising the firm's stock price with ease and confidence.

There are a few stories in this book that remain unresolved, in that the stock hasn't yet completely tanked or the dishonesty of the promotion hasn't been widely recognized. This is not one of those stories. We have the benefit of hindsight with Zonagen. You don't need to take my word for any of this. The events we predicted have occurred, and, despite Zonagen's denials and continued attempts to perpetuate the promote, these events have been properly reflected in the drug's failure to get FDA approval and the company's wilted stock price.

It used to amaze me that scammers just never gave up. Now I understand that a stock promotion has got just as much infrastructure, in its own way, as a real company. To a skillful stock promoter, control of a public corporate shell, no matter how discredited, is a valuable commodity. No stock promoter is going to give up control of the shell or ever admit defeat. Not only would that turn off the money tap, but it would also leave the promoter wide open to civil and criminal liability. And, as in the case of Zonagen and others in this book, third parties who, knowingly or not, get involved develop a commonality of interest in denying that anything ever went wrong.

Well before our first report on Zonagen, repeated experiments and trials had already shown that phentolamine, the only active ingredient in Vasomax, had not caused erections. Zonagen itself even admitted in a 1996 SEC registration statement that, with regard to efficacy, its German study "did not provide the Company with the necessary p-value required to prove statistical significance." One would have thought that anyone analyzing the drug's prospectus could have obtained this information easily. Right? Wrong. Despite the public information, Zonagen somehow arranged a licensing deal for Vasomax with one of the world's largest and presumably most sophisticated pharmaceutical concerns, Schering-Plough (NYSE: SGP), a company with recent annual sales of almost $9 billion.

As we were finalizing our Zonagen research and analysis of the phentolamine trials, we heard rumors from several reliable sources about the impending Schering-Plough deal. It's extremely unusual for such a giant to allow itself to become a promotional tool for such a shaky minor player. This alliance would lend credibility to the promote and could have jacked up the ZONA stock price. But we believed our research to be unassailable. The Schering-Plough deal did nothing to change our opinion of Vasomax. The facts were so evident, and negative, that we believed any excitement about the Schering-Plough deal would be short-lived. We were sufficiently confident in our work that we publicly announced our negative opinion on the same day that Zonagen announced the Schering-Plough deal. We issued our initial report the day after this amazing pact was announced.

This begs the question: If *we* believed with a high degree of certainty (and were ultimately shown correct) that Vasomax was not only ineffective but also possessed potentially dangerous side effects that made it a long shot for FDA approval, how could Schering not have known?

The Beginning: Foreplay

Let's go back to 1997. Pfizer's Viagra had captured the public imagination, from Jay Leno's wisecracks to septuagenarian sugar daddies enjoying a new lease on lovin'. It was the most exciting drug in modern medical history. Maybe Schering-Plough believed that anything could sell on Viagra's coattails. Vasomax might not have been effective, but Viagra worked, so if Vasomax was safe and the company could make any efficacy claims for it at all and it could be sold as a cheap substitute, sales were assured. Viagra was to usher in a whole industry of hope for males with erectile dysfunction (ED). Perhaps some doctors would recommend Vasomax.

This, of course, is the most benign possibility. It's also possible that Schering-Plough was simply lusting for a quickie: that is, a pop in its stock price. It's one thing to do a speculative deal and just keep quiet and hope. It's another to let your big-league Wall Street analysts pump a highly suspicious deal, which is exactly what Schering-Plough appears to have done with Vasomax.

"We believe Vasomax as an oral therapy represents a therapeutic advance in the treatment of erectile dysfunction for patients seeking effective therapy for this condition," said Thomas C. Lauda, executive vice president of global marketing for Schering-Plough. "Acquiring worldwide rights to Vasomax strengthens Schering-Plough's portfolio of compounds in late-stage development, and when approved should be a significant addition to our growing product line, building on our long-established presence in the urological therapy area. We are impressed with the quality of the work Zonagen is doing in the field of reproductive health, and we are looking forward to a long-term relationship."

According to the promote, Vasomax allegedly worked by relaxing a certain smooth muscle in the groin, thus increasing blood flow to the penis. The primary side effect was supposedly a stuffy nose due to dilation of the blood vessels. And at high doses, Zonagen cautioned, the drug could cause low blood pressure. It seems counterintuitive that a drug that can cause low blood pressure was being promoted as something that could *increase* blood pressure in the penis. Worse, our research led us to believe that phentolamine affected *all* smooth muscles in the body, not only those that control the flow of blood to the penis. One rather important smooth muscle is the heart—though, in the end, it wasn't side effects on the heart that caused the FDA to halt Vasomax's clinical trials in the United States.

Phentolamine is a generically available drug originally sold under the brand name Regitine. It was developed by Ciba-Geigy and approved by the FDA in 1952 as an injectable agent to control acute hypertension—high blood pressure. When used in higher doses, phentolamine can drastically lower blood pressure. Partly because of this effect, intravenous phentolamine is now used only in rare cases.

Since 1983, urologists have been using a "back-office" mixture of three drugs—phentolamine, papaverine, and prostaglandin—to induce erections when injected directly into the penis. This "trimix" has demonstrated good results. However, it is important to note that clinical studies have shown that phentolamine by itself is ineffective in producing erections, even when injected directly into the penis.

In its SEC filings, Zonagen acknowledged that a formerly available oral formulation of phentolamine had had limited utility in treating erectile dysfunction. Despite this apparently conclusive statement, Zonagen was still alleging that Vasomax was an effective ED treatment because of its "special formulation." However, Vasomax's alleged special formulation does not contain any active ingredient other than phentolamine. Call me dense, but I just didn't get it. Was Zonagen claiming that the same drug that was known not to be effective in aiding erections could now aid erections simply because it had been renamed "Vasomax"?

Zonagen assembled its promoters. Apparently, it isn't hard to find a urologist who relishes the limelight. Dr. Irwin Goldstein, coauthor of the oft-quoted 1994 Massachusetts Male Aging Study, which concluded that more men suffer from impotence than previously thought, was a paid adviser for several nonpornographic erection-inducing companies. These companies and their investment bankers used Dr. Goldstein's report to help them raise millions for product development. What was not widely known was that Dr. Goldstein also held a financial interest in a number of Men's Health Center clinics, clinics that specialize in treating erectile dysfunction.

Dr. Goldstein attested that Vivus Inc.'s (Nasdaq: VVUS) erectile dysfunction drug, MUSE (Medical Urethral System for Erection), really worked. In fact, we analyzed MUSE and researched Vivus, issuing a report on December 10, 1997. In announcing a class action lawsuit against Vivus on May 8, 1998, the firm of Beatie & Osborn quoted language from our report stating that not only was Vivus misrepresenting trial results for MUSE, but also there were concerns about the product sales figures that the company had been reporting.

An Italian research report concluded that MUSE inflamed and

129

enlarged the penis but did not actually cause it to become erect—which I think most women (and men!) would agree is the only worthwhile end point for the test of an impotence drug. Although we can envision a limited use for MUSE, such as for enhancing one's appearance in a locker room or in a Speedo, Vivus was not promoting the drug in this way. Furthermore, just thinking about the proscribed method of applying MUSE is enough to cause an involuntary crossing of a man's legs: It required insertion of a rod into the hole at the tip of the penis.

One of the major traders in the Vivus scam was Jeffrey Vinik, the man who rose to fame by briefly running the Magellan Fund after Peter Lynch retired. According to an SEC filing of September 3, 1997, after leaving Magellan, Vinik and his various entities had rapidly acquired a 2.4 million share position in Vivus. A long-term investment in a quality growth stock? Hardly. A November 4, 1997, SEC Form 13D filing shows Vinik dumping huge blocks on an almost daily basis beginning September 24, 1997.

Dr. Goldstein also said that MacroChem Corp.'s (Nasdaq: MCHM) ED drug really really worked. It didn't. MacroChem was one of the stocks involved in the Michael Schonberg/Dreyfus scandal. Peter Janssen and Bruce Meyers of Janssen-Meyers Associates personally held 1.6 million shares and 1.05 million shares of Macrochem respectively. Schonberg purchased for the Dreyfus funds 1,345,000 shares of MCHM. This recommendation did no credit to Dr. Goldstein's reputation.

Despite these two flops, Dr. Goldstein had no qualms in telling the *Wall Street Journal*'s "Texas Journal" that Vasomax had the potential "to be a billion-dollar drug." No public filings make note of Dr. Goldstein's Zonagen compensation.

Zonagen also enjoyed the support of Dr. Steven Lamm, who previously had hyped the discredited diet drug Phen-Fen. Dr. Lamm wrote a 1998 book called *The Virility Solution*, in which he promoted Vasomax numerous times. In his foreword, Dr. Lamm wrote: "Effective and well tolerated, these amazing pharmacological virility remedies are Viagra, the brand name for sildenafil, and Vasomax (phentolamine)." He also stated: "FDA approval of Vasomax is expected shortly."

Under FDA Regulation 21 CFR 312.7, the Promotion of an Investigational New Drug, a sponsor or investigator, or any person acting on behalf of a sponsor or investigator, "shall not represent in a promotional context that an investigational new drug is safe or effective for the purposes for which it is under investigation or otherwise promote the drug." At the time Dr. Lamm made the above claims, Vasomax was undergoing a Phase III one-year safety study, which had begun enrollment in September 1997.

The Act Itself: Wham, Bam!

As 1997 began, Zonagen's stock was trading down in the $9 range. But Viagra was soon to be unleashed, and the buzz on Pfizer had investors searching for another chance to get in while things were still soft in the hottest drug category since caffeine. The Zonagen promote became tumescent; the stock gradually ascended. It approached its climax in the run-up to November 17, 1997, when Zonagen announced its licensing deal with Schering-Plough for worldwide rights to Vasomax for the treatment of erectile dysfunction. Schering-Plough was red hot itself, basking in the success of Claritin, which, unlike other allergy pills, was not contraindicated by the concurrent use of other drugs.

The Schering-Plough deal called for a $10 million up-front payment and, subject to specific regulatory milestones, an additional $47.5 million, plus escalating royalties. On the day the deal was announced, ZONA shares reached an intraday peak of over $40. The little company based in Woodlands, Texas, had achieved a $446 million market cap. That same day we began circulating a release that summarized our report on Zonagen, which was going to be issued on November 18.

In trying to estimate the impact of our reports before the fact, I ask myself several questions:

- How obvious is the promote? (An obvious promote can be made to look ridiculous much more easily than an abstruse promote.)
- Who's promoting it?
- Who holds the stock, and do they know it's a fraud? (If they don't know it's a fraud, and have bought in on false promises, there's a good chance of a quick and massive sell-off and a substantial price drop.)
- To whom is the stock being sold?
- What are the technicals (e.g., recent price action in the stock and how it has reacted to news and other market developments)?
- How strong is our evidence? Is it easy to understand?

I was surprised at how much impact our Zonagen report had on the first day. I'd been ready for a long-haul battle against Zonagen's combo plate of retail stock promoters and bozobucks institutions. Who could have expected it? Despite the news of this extraordinary deal, ZONA drooped over the course of the day to close below $35. It's as if investors, presented with conflicting opinions, were rating an unknown, short-selling, nonmedical expert's due diligence as superior to the high and mighty Schering-Plough's. Now, what's wrong with this picture?

Disregarding our detailed report and the fact that investors had shown the previous afternoon that Zonagen's Schering-Plough deal wasn't what it seemed to be, on November 19 a *Wall Street Journal* article by Robert Langreth mentioned Schering-Plough and Vasomax in the same breath as Pfizer and Viagra. In the piece, David Saks of Gruntal & Co. decreed there was room for both drugs in the market. I was quoted perfunctorily in the piece as saying there were serious problems

with Zonagen and Vasomax. As usual, the piece stressed my short position in the stock—my financial motivation. Was Gruntal's position or
interest in Zonagen revealed or mentioned? Of course not.

Despite the otherwise inexplicable stock action of the previous
day, the *Journal* piece completely disregarded the controversy over
Zonagen—a conflict that couldn't have been more current or impassioned. A stock drops 6 points (15 percent) on an ultra-positive
announcement, and the *Wall Street Journal* decrees the appropriate
headline to be "Schering-Plough to Sell Impotence Drug." Langreth
completely bought into the Schering/Zonagen hype and decided
that would be his story.

The *Wall Street Journal* is well written and often well informed, but,
just like most other business media, the paper suffers a chronic and de-
bilitating bias toward large institutions, whether they are corporations
or investment houses. This is not only infuriating to skeptics but also
does a critical disservice to the efficiency of the capital markets.

Furthermore, a local *Wall Street Journal* reporter in Texas was be-
having not like an objective journalist but very much like a member
of Team Zonagen. Back on April 9, 1997, Jeff Opdyke wrote a
deliriously positive piece that displayed his ignorance of the truth
about Zonagen and Vasomax. Opdyke even rated Vasomax *superior* to
Viagra! He stated that Viagra's development was six months to a year
behind Zonagen's—which of course was proven wildly wrong.
Opdyke also stated that Vasomax worked faster than Viagra and that
Viagra had undesirable side effects that Vasomax didn't. Could the
"missing side effects" that Opdyke was citing have included one's
mate's sudden interest in going to bed early?

It's shocking to see this sort of shoddy journalism appearing in
such an august publication. But Jeff Opdyke's involvement with Zonagen didn't end here. He left the *Wall Street Journal* on April 30, less than
a month after writing the Zonagen puff piece and went to work as an
analyst for a Dallas-based hedge fund, McGarr Capital Management

Corp. While he was employed there, on November 26, a week after our report questioned the legitimacy of some of Vasomax's claims, Opdyke wrote a report on Zonagen for an Internet site called Multex. His report contained many of the same falsities as his *Wall Street Journal* piece. Opdyke is now back at the *Journal*. Think of Zonagen and Vasomax next time you read a feel-good corporate profile by him.

It's hard to fathom how a *Wall Street Journal* reporter, whether active or on "commercial sabbatical," could read our report and still write a positive story on Zonagen. He didn't even mention any of the serious issues we'd brought up. Our *strong sell* recommendation detailed the homely history of this would-be sexy new drug. Vasomax is a pill form of a 45-year-old generic drug that had been investigated as a possible treatment for erectile dysfunction long before Zonagen got the idea.

The only thing Zonagen *did* have was the Zorgniotti patent. In 1996 Zonagen had acquired Dr. Adrian Zorgniotti's method-of-use patent for phentolamine in exchange for $100,000 cash plus 19,512 shares. (Those shares were worth around $200,000 at the time of the transaction.) The Zorgniotti patent was for the "transmucosal, transdermal, intranasal and rectal" administration of phentolamine as a treatment for ED. Dr. Zorgniotti thought the best way to administer phentolamine was not in pill form at all, but on a piece of paper stuffed between cheek and gums. The patent specifically describes the drawbacks associated with oral administration of a drug in an attempt to effect delivery to a specific site. The Zorgniotti patent was Zonagen's only ED-related patent.

I have never purported to be a medical expert, but I do believe in the absolute truth of research and due diligence, and I have access to some of the world's leading medical researchers. Chief among them was Dr. Judy Stone, whom I've mentioned in the acknowledgments. Judy performed her analyses of medical claims anonymously, as one must in her position. But she was proud to be associated with the public dissection of false medical claims, and she was a vital research ally.

Asensio & Company did extensive research on Zonagen. We did a patent search, which is how we discovered the Zorgniotti patent. We read all of the company's SEC filings including its IPO and secondary prospectuses. Finally, we read Zonagen's own public relations material and the literature produced by the company's Wall Street analysts. Our analysis of Zonagen's clinical trial results led us to believe that the FDA would not approve Vasomax as an oral treatment for organic erectile dysfunction based on these results. And even if Zonagen were allowed to sell phentolamine as a treatment for some form of ED, we believed that doctors would not prescribe such an old, crude drug as Vasomax and that therefore it had no commercial value.

Viagra was a safe drug that was soon to receive FDA approval. It had shown far greater efficacy than that demonstrated by Vasomax's very own highly controversial trials. We believed it was absurd to claim that Vasomax would muscle any market share away from Viagra. Thus we felt that Zonagen possessed no valuable medical asset.

Zonagen had filed a patent application in 1995 to cover the formulation and delivery of oral phentolamine, but the patent was still pending. In any case, we saw no value in a patent on a phentolamine pill for the treatment of impotence since, based on the studies we reviewed, the drug repeatedly had been shown to be ineffective in the treatment of ED.

We studied eight separate clinical trials conducted on phentolamine and Vasomax in four different countries. Neither Zonagen nor any of its investigators ever published complete medical papers for peer review. This failure to make full disclosure of its studies made it difficult for investors and the medical community to assess the validity of Zonagen's trial result claims. Worse, Zonagen disclosed its trial result piecemeal, in a multitude of different documents.

This lack of clarity in published data is a warning in and of itself;

when a magician refuses to open one hand, there can be only one reason. Still, it made our work incredibly difficult. We had to compile little bits and pieces about the Vasomax trials and the results of those trials from numerous sources. We put all of these snippets that were scattered throughout time and among several sources onto a large spreadsheet. That way we were able to re-create information about each of the different trials in different locations. After fitting this puzzle together, we could see why someone would want to cut and shake before baking this cake. But into the oven it went; Zonagen filed these trials with the FDA.

In an SEC filing dated November 14, 1996, Zonagen acknowledged that its Phase II clinical trial results had no statistical significance. One might ask, if that's so, why did the stock continue to rise?

As I said earlier, a promoter never quits. And in this case, persistence paid off. Who would have predicted that Schering-Plough would join Zonagen's parade, kicking millions into company coffers? Who would have guessed Volpe Brown Whelan & Co. would help Zonagen sell $67.5 million worth of stock in a 1997 secondary offering?

While Zonagen didn't have any excuses for its failed Phase II trials, it distracted investors with the miraculous news that, while Phase II didn't go so well, Phase III was a roaring success. Yes, Zonagen was claiming that its Phase III trials (which used the same Vasomax drug used in its Phase II trials) were showing statistically significant positive results. One way Zonagen achieved this was by changing the primary end point from one trial to the next. In its failed Phase II trial, the end point was vaginal penetration. In its Phase III trials, Zonagen did not use penetration as the end point—as if there's this huge market of men out there clamoring for an impotence pill that *almost* works. Furthermore, in its Phase III trials Zonagen altered the type of patients it allowed to enroll and the method of reporting results. Doing this made the data incomparable among the different trials.

Despite claiming success with its Phase III trials, Zonagen did not file a New Drug Application (NDA) with the FDA until July 1998. Instead, the company began a new U.S. trial that was larger than any of its previous trials. Let me repeat that. Zonagen claimed a successful Phase III trial. The traditional move after a truly successful Phase III trial is to move forward with a New Drug Application so that you can get approval to sell the thing and start recouping development costs. Instead, Zonagen backed up and began spending money and time on *another* Phase III trial. We believed that a study of this magnitude, given Zonagen's claims of success with the prior studies, would have been undertaken only if the original Phase I, II, and III trial results had been inadequate to support an NDA filing. Obvious to us. To Schering-Plough, apparently not.

The Climax: Is That All There Is?

Of course, as we have seen repeatedly, with hundreds of millions of dollars at stake, no scam, no matter how meticulously disassembled, ever just throws down its cards and walks away from the table. This little company had some big names behind it. Ross Perot's Petrus Fund, L.P., was an early investor; the head of Perot Ventures remained on the Zonagen board throughout the stock promotion.

On December 16, 1997, with ZONA at $20, David M. Steinberg of Volpe Brown Whelan & Co., which had helped underwrite Zonagen's $67.5 million secondary offering earlier in the year, issued a *buy* recommendation, saying the selling was overdone. His target price: $45.

On January 3, 1998, I received a letter from Charles M. Butler, an attorney representing Dr. Bonnie S. Dunbar and Dr. Balbir S. Bhogal in separate cases against Zonagen. Butler was offering his cooperation. Both of his clients had intimate knowledge of Zonagen and Vasomax.

SOLD SHORT

In the mid–1980s, Dr. Dunbar had generated ideas for some contraceptives that became the basis for the formation of Zonagen. The name Zonagen is taken from the zona pellicula, which is the transparent outer layer of an ovum. Dr. Dunbar's idea—and the company's first promote—was to modify the zona pellicula as a method of birth control. This concept was first targeted at dogs and cats, then at people, using teeming India as its test ground.

Joe Podolski, who became Zonagen's high-profile president, came along a few years later. Dr. Bhogal, personally recruited by Podolski, had been the company's director of immunology from June 1993 through August 1995. Dr. Bhogal was working on the company's second product, an adjuvant called ImmuMax. An adjuvant is an auxiliary ingredient that modifies the performance of a principal component, ideally improving its efficacy like a great cigar topping off a fine meal. In this case, ImmuMax was supposed to enhance the body's natural immune response in the production of antibodies. Dr. Bhogal became aware that ImmuMax was in fact Chitosan, for which two separate patents for medical use already existed, including one owned by a Japanese company for use specifically as an adjuvant. (In any case, Chitosan is simply ground-up shrimp shells, cheaply available in bulk.)

According to Dr. Bhogal's complaint, Zonagen nonetheless went about preparing a patent application for ImmuMax without disclosing to the U.S. Patent Office what it knew of existing patents. The Patent Office rejected the ImmuMax application. Not only did Zonagen fail to disclose this rejection, but the company actually continued promoting ImmuMax and searching for a buyer, including pitching ImmuMax to Schering-Plough. According to Dr. Bhogal, Schering-Plough was advised of this deception in a letter dated July 5, 1995.

We needed to uncover more about Zonagen's claims of pending phentolamine patents. Unable to discover the contents of the company's U.S. patent application—there is no public disclosure of pending U.S. patents—we obtained a copy of what amounts to Zonagen's international patent application. This application, along with Zonagen's own SEC filings, proved what we'd believed to be the case all along: The only medically active ingredient of the secret Vasomax formulation was plain, 45-year-old, generic phentolamine. This application was also how we discovered that Vasomax contained no other ingredient, active or otherwise, that could alter phentolamine's chemistry. (See Figure 7.1.)

FIGURE 7.1 Vasomax Ingredients

Ingredients	Standard Release 40 mg/ Tablet	Rapidly Dissolving 20 mg/ Tablet	Rapidly Dissolving 40 mg/ Tablet	Rapidly Dissolving 60 mg/ Tablet	Rapidly Dissolving Chewable 40 mg/ Tablet
Phentolamine mesylate	40	20	40	60	40
Silicon dioxide (flow)	8	8	8	8	.12
Stearic acid	4	4	4	4	12
Microcrystalline cellulose	120	120	120	120	0
Dicalcium phosphate dibasic (bulking/inert filler)	228	0	0	0	0
Lactose (bulking/inert filler)	0	232	212	192	100
Croscarmellose sodium (disintegrant)	0	16	16	16	0
Sweetrex					348
Aspartame					40
ProSweet					8
Peppermint flavor #860-172					40
Tablet press compression	N/A	N/A	N/A	N/A	N/A
Total tablet weight	400	400	400	400	600

Source: Zonagen international patent filing.

Second, we found evidence that indicated that, contrary to Zonagen's claims, Vasomax was not faster-acting than normal phentolamine. The Zonagen promote was based partly on the claim that its phentolamine pill worked fast and that other pills worked slower. As anyone who's ever used a pill to aid an erection can tell you, speed is of the essence: Nothing "kills the mood" more than sitting around waiting for lift-off.

On March 27, 1998, Viagra received FDA marketing approval. The remaining Zonagen faithful must have felt as if they'd lost a race. But the truth is, they were never in it. And as so often follows a failed promote, the class action suits began raining down on Zonagen. In March and April 1998, shareholders filed a total of eight class action suits against Zonagen. Many of the companies we cover end up on the receiving end of class action suits, and we don't keep track of them all. But eight in two months—this might be a record.

With Vasomax discredited and the class action suits banging into one another, Matt Geller and Daniel Heller of CIBC Oppenheimer, a prestigious financial house, burst out of nowhere to initiate coverage of Zonagen on April 16, 1998, with a mind-boggling *buy*. They set a $40 price target for the stock, which was then trading at $21. They punningly described Vasomax as "a strong competitor that will be able to *penetrate* the market."

This recommendation seems a completely curious and unmotivated move by a major house with no demonstrated financial interest in Zonagen. But a little digging told us more of the story. Daniel Heller, the researcher behind this report, had been employed at Lindsay Rosenwald's Paramount Capital immediately prior to his Oppenheimer job. Paramount held a substantial stake in Zonagen had an officer on its board, and helped it with a 1996 private placement, for which it received warrants.

It wasn't just the little guys who got seduced by this pfakey

By-the-Numbers Stock Promotions

Pfizer wannabe. As of March 31, 1998, T. Rowe Price held 1,069,900 million ZONA shares; Capital Research & Management held 932,000; and Franklin Advisors held 803,000. The Franklin Global Health Care Fund's Zonagen supporter was Kurt von Emster. And these guys hadn't just bought in on the cheap during Zonagen's fledgling days; all had purchased shares in the 1997 secondary offering.

Once again it begs the question: Did they know the truth about Zonagen? If they didn't know, that means that these firms and their analysts were engaging in an incredibly incompetent version of due diligence. Did they bother to read my reports? The facts were right there; all they had to do was click on NEWS. If they knew and didn't care, then, worse in my view, they were thinking they could play a dangerous little game with the share price.

It is our belief that the eight class actions suits impelled Zonagen to sue (unsuccessfully) what it deemed to be the source of its misery: Asensio & Company. How many times have we seen officials of outright blatant scams blame their troubles on short sellers? No legitimate company with a real business to attend to would bother wasting valuable corporate resources, including management time, suing a short seller. Only stock promotions waste shareholders' money filing lawsuits to try to quiet their critics. We've established a clear record that any company that tries to muffle us with lawsuits will experience the exact opposite. We have been vindicated in every case. When investors see public companies expend vast resources to silence their critics, they might want to tread carefully.

I have some advice for any company that finds itself under attack from short sellers: Continue to develop, market, and sell your product if it's so wonderful. Prove them wrong in the marketplace. If you can do this, your stock will thrive. The shorts can't stop it.

SOLD SHORT

On May 10, 1999, Zonagen announced it had decided to forgo an FDA Advisory Panel review of the Vasomax NDA until the results of additional clinical studies could be submitted to the FDA. This action caused Zonagen to automatically receive a nonapproval letter from the FDA for its Vasomax New Drug Application. Zonagen tried to spin this as a long-term positive, but nonapproval is nonapproval, and the market knows this. The stock, scuffling along at around $20, lost half its price and many of its believers that day, on extraordinary volume of almost 5 million shares. And this was the lesser of two blows the FDA delivered in 1999.

On August 10 the FDA announced that clinical trials of phentolamine-based drugs would be put on hold until certain issues surrounding a two-year rat study had been resolved. From there all but the truly deluded bailed out, and the stock began a drift downward to $5. I'm sure there is some sort of joke I could insert here about the deflated hopes, the drooping stock, maybe work in the test rats somehow, but that's not the sort of thing I do. I'm an investor, not Robin Frickin' Williams.

By the time of this second FDA thunderbolt, Schering-Plough had plowed at least $20 million into Zonagen. And the partnership persists. Since May 1998, Schering-Plough has been trying to sell Vasomax in Mexico under the brand name Z-Max. It has yielded Z-Minimum revenues. Zonagen and Schering-Plough, despite the class action lawsuits, the FDA nonapproval and clinical halt, and the dizzying drop in stock price, are still claiming to be working on a new toxicity study and analyzing results from the latest clinical trials. They plan to resubmit the NDA. And by the time this happens, perhaps there *will* be a market for the drug—because maybe there will be people living on the moon then, and the lesser gravity will turn even flaccid Vasomaxers into rigid Viagrans.

Drug Dealing Made Easy

Any company can produce any chemical or biological component it wants in any quantity it wants and call it a drug. However, if that company wants to sell that drug to treat a disease and to claim that humans can in complete safety take prescribed dosages of that drug to effectively treat that disease, it has to go through an approval process with the U.S. Food and Drug Administration. This process occurs in a sequence of three phases. After each phase, trial results are submitted to the FDA, which decides whether trials may continue.

Phase I

Phase I trials are nothing more than toxicity tests, measuring the drug's safety. Because this phase requires little more than not hurting or killing subjects, Phase I trials are especially prone to promotion. For example, in 1999 SafeScience Inc. (Nasdaq: SAFS) promoted great Phase I results for its cancer cure. Its product was derived from fruit pectin. Pectin may be a popular emulsifier for foods and drugs, and it probably won't hurt or kill you, but as a treatment for cancer it's dubious to say the least.

Phase II

Phase II is a dosing trial. While testing for efficacy—does the drug work?—clinicians are also trying to find the right dosage and/or schedule for administering the product (e.g., once a day, twice a day). Phase II will give the drug company some idea about whether to spend the money to go on to the next phase or not.

Phase III

Results from Phases I and II, while included in the FDA submission, are not sufficient for marketing approval. Phase III is the pivotal trial. Phase III trials must be double blind, which means that neither the patients nor the clinicians know which patients are receiving the drug and which are receiving a placebo. Phase III trials must meet certain protocols agreed on with the FDA. These protocols can include the number of trial sites, doctors, and patients involved in testing; the method of determining which patients are appropriate for the trials; and, crucially, what is the end point of the trial—the result that is deemed successful treatment.

Publishing Results

There are no regulations regarding the publishing of trial results. However, fraudulent stock promotions usually lack openness and complete disclosure—in peer reviews, medical journals, and even press releases.

Promotional Regulations

Under FDA guidelines, drug companies may not promote the safety or efficacy of drugs that have not been fully approved for general marketing. Often a fraudulent company will try to bypass this regulation, either blatantly or through third-party endorsements, using "advisory groups" and other faux "outsiders" to promote its drug.

New Drug Application and Approval

After a company completes Phase III trials, it may submit a New Drug Application. The FDA then decides whether the safety and efficacy statistics generated in the clinical trials actually demonstrate that the drug works safely and effectively. If so, the drug will be approved for marketing. However, just because the FDA approves the drug doesn't mean that doctors will prescribe it for their patients.

Timeliness

Although no exact schedule is given, a tacit time frame exists for the testing and approval process for various classes of drugs. Medical frauds may claim to be on a "fast track" for drug approval, but often that is the last thing they want. It's easier to sell the sizzle of a steak than an actual rancid piece of Spam. When a company continues to go through the motions with underenrolled Phase III trials many years after receiving Phase III approval, it's a safe bet that it is far more interested in filing to register stock shares for insiders than in filing an NDA.

For an interesting website of health frauds and quackery, check out www.quackwatch.com. Quackwatch is a participant member of the Fraud Defense Network, an Internet-based alliance of insurance companies, government agencies, and other interested parties working to prevent, detect, and investigate fraudulent activity.

Turbodyne: The Missing Banker, the Phony U.N. Guy, and the Engine Thingy That Was Going to Save the World

Turbodyne Technologies, Inc. (OTC:TRBD), suffered by far the single largest one-day plunge of all our initial short-sell advisories—on unprecedented volume of over 11 million shares—and was delisted just 169 days after our report, but that's not what makes it so memorable. No, it's the convoluted story behind this stock's rise and fall that makes it one of the most weirdly compelling schemes I have ever encountered. Turbodyne is also one of the four companies that have had the nerve to sue me. And it maintained its lawsuit long after both the EASDAQ and the NASD charged the company with issuing misleading press releases, long after a six-month suspension from trading was imposed by regulators in the United States and Europe.

The company was claiming to possess an add-on that lowered a diesel engine's emissions and made it more fuel efficient. But even if you did no analysis of this company's technology, the genesis of Turbodyne certified it as a no-doubt, "put it in the freezer 'cause it's ice," slam-dunk, $700 million short when we found it. It began on Vancouver's Howe Street, where penny stocks abound and charismatic scammers are celebrated as much as reviled.

Turbodyne began as a shell company called Clear View Ventures, whose shares traded on the Vancouver Stock Exchange (VSE) in January 1993 at 4 Canadian cents. The man who controlled Clear View Ventures was Harry Moll. Moll was a legend among legends, involved in more Canadian stock promotion schemes than you can shake a hockey stick at. My favorite Harry Moll scam was Cross Pacific Pearls. According to the *Vancouver Sun*, Moll said this company was breeding clams capable of producing pearls "larger than a fivepin bowling ball."

The VSE eventually banned Moll. His current whereabouts are officially unknown, but he is thought to be living not especially frugally in the Cayman Islands. Among other deals, Moll was involved in Dynamic Associates (OTC Bulletin Board: DYAS).

On March 15, 1994, Clear View underwent a reverse takeover by California-based Turbodyne Systems, in which Turbodyne gained a listing on the VSE by letting itself be taken over by Clear View. Edward Halimi of Turbodyne became the new CEO of Clear View, which changed its name to . . . Turbodyne. According to the *Vancouver Sun*, Moll passed control of Turbodyne to his longtime associate Logan Anderson, who in turn passed control to Leon Nowek. Nowek had been associated with Moll in Northfork Ventures Ltd., which ran into regulatory trouble in 1992 after its founder, Dr. Anthony Nobles, was found to have falsified his academic credentials.

A fellow named Nick Masee, who for 37 years at the Bank of Montreal had been a private banker for many of Howe Street's best-known promoters—including Harry Moll—resigned his job and became a director of the new Turbodyne. According to the *Sun*, Masee was known to have a taste for the good life. He con-

By-the-Numbers Stock Promotions

sorted with Moll and his associates in a world of yachts and fancy restaurants. Masee reportedly invested in his clients' deals, although he was said to have no "street smarts." As described by the *Sun*, Masee looked more like a flashy promoter than a plodding banker: perpetual tan, bronze-colored hair, gold jewelry, and an exotic-looking Asian wife.

According to published interviews with acquaintances, Masee had become frustrated earning $80,000 a year while watching his clients scarfing millions with their stock schemes. He wanted a piece of the action. Masee joined the Turbodyne board in March 1994, soon after the reverse takeover. According to the *Vancouver Sun*, the Vancouver Stock Exchange required Masee to sign an undertaking that he would have no further dealings with Moll, who had been banned from the VSE by then.

On August 10, 1994, just a few months after changing careers, Masee and his wife, Lisa, were supposed to meet an unidentified prospective financier at Trader Vic's restaurant in Vancouver. The couple disappeared that night and were never seen again. There were no signs of foul play but also no evidence that the couple had chosen voluntarily to disappear. Their beloved black cat, Spider, was found at their house days later, half starved, and they had not taken their passports.

According to the *Sun*, despite being a banker, friend, and confidant to many of Howe Street's most notorious scam artists, Masee was considered clean. There was an unsubstantiated rumor that he may have guaranteed Moll's gambling debts, and that those debts had been assigned to a group of nasty bikers. Masee also had been subpoenaed as a witness in an embezzlement trial involving a client. The bottom line: Because he was a Howe Street cynosure, almost *all* of Nick Masee's chums could be considered suspects. An irony pointed out by the *Sun* is that, while Turbodyne's share price was only 10 cents when he disappeared, in just a few years his holdings and options would have made him the millionaire he aspired to become.

Turbodyne, looking for a quick charge, engaged Pecunia Gmbh to sell shares privately in Germany. Whether Turbodyne had seen the advantage of placing its stock overseas, especially in a non-English-speaking country that might not be able to properly investigate a company's background, is not known. Teutonic Turbodyne investors probably wouldn't recognize the name Harry Moll or remember a strange story about a couple mysteriously disappearing. In any case, Turbodyne was a hit among the Germans. Later, after we translated our reports into German, the German press would become enchanted with the Asensio-Turbodyne saga.

By March 1995 Turbodyne's stock, pumping mightily but not nearly at the point it would reach a few years later, had risen to $1.18. *Canada Stockwatch*, a sporadically useful publication that epitomizes the simultaneous revulsion and fascination Howe Street has for its stock promoters, printed several positive pieces about the company at the time. But when Turbodyne's Edward Halimi, queried by *Stockwatch* about a sudden price plunge, lamely punted that it was due to "more sellers than buyers," the publication tore into Turbodyne as an "also-ran promotion" of "Harry Moll and his followers."

At this point Turbodyne lacked sales. Now, it's usually easier to promote a company's future promise than to try to explain why a moribund product already on the market is suddenly going to enjoy explosive sales growth. But Turbodyne apparently felt that if it acquired a manufacturing business in the automotive field, it would add fuel to its story and substance to its earth-saving product claims.

In October 1995 it announced the acquisition of California-based Pacific Baja Light Metal Holdings for $12 million cash and $18 million in stock. Pacific Baja, a "real" company with actual sales and earnings ($14.7 million/$2.1 million as of the previous year), had ostensibly been a supplier to Turbodyne. Not only did the deal afford Turbodyne sales, but also, just like Diana Corporation's money-losing Atlanta Provision meat distribution holding, maybe it could help obscure lack of earnings from the front and center promote. (Pacific Baja and its subsidiaries commenced Chapter 11 bankruptcy proceedings in the United States Bankruptcy Court for the Central District of California on September 30, 1999.)

In April 1996 Turbodyne was forced to make a strange announcement that one Melanie St. James had been acting as a secret market maker for the stock since June 1995. The company disclosed that St. James is a relative of Edward Halimi, then the company's president. (Other reports specify that she is Halimi's stepdaughter.) No further details were disclosed, but insider trading reports show that Halimi transferred 800,000 shares to St. James in June 1995 at no cost to her. The company also awarded David St. James, who lived at the same address as Melanie, an employee option to buy 150,000 shares at $1 each. Evidence of wrongdoing? Not per se. Suspicious? Hell, yes.

In June of that year the company overstepped itself in a release, announcing that Granatelli Performance Technologies had agreed to act as worldwide distributor for the auto and motorcycle gasoline-engine aftermarket. Granatelli would be required to purchase at least 15,000 Turbopac units in 1996 for USD$9.4 million and 50,000 units at USD$31.3 million in subsequent years. Although it was never implied directly, many investors may have believed that this automotive company was associated with Indy race car driver Andy Granatelli.

A later prospectus, however, revealed that Granatelli Performance Technologies had purchased not 15,000 units but only 125 units, for USD$78,000, and that the company was in fact merely a shell formed specifically for the purpose of marketing Turbodyne products, with no significant assets or sales history. Plus, Granatelli was forced to change its name to Grand Technologies, reportedly because Andy Granatelli, who had no connection to the scheme whatsoever, had threatened legal action. In other words, the company had announced and promoted a marketing "deal" with a business even funnier than its own. (On January 21, 2000, Turbodyne announced it had paid a judgment to Grand Technologies in response to liens that Grand was holding against Turbodyne and Edward Halimi.)

Nonetheless, the promotion rolled on, and in March 1997 Turbodyne began trading on the Nasdaq, at around $8 a share. On April 11 Turbodyne announced in a press release that it had been awarded designation by the United Nations Flag Technology Program: "The special acknowledgement by the Global Technology Group has been given only to technologies that assist developing countries through the creation of employment, improving health conditions or enhancing the environment. The Turbodyne system meets all three criteria." The letter of designation was issued by Joseph D. Ben-Dak, described in the release as "chief of the U.N. Global Technology Group." Ben-Dak praised Turbodyne in the release.

This Flag Technology designation was invoked repeatedly in future releases. And there's a useful lesson here. Often a stock promotion will claim credibility via some impressive-sounding imprimatur. And what could be more impressive than the United Nations? But you must ask yourself: "Have I ever heard of Joseph D. Ben-Dak? Have I ever heard of the Flag Technology Program? Do I know of any legitimate companies that have been so designated? What does the U.N. have to do with any leading-edge product or commercial activity? What does the U.N. know about *any* technology?"

This U.N. anointment brings to mind some other scams that announced real deals with known entities that vastly overstated potential revenues, such as Zonagen with Schering-Plough, Solv-Ex with Shell Oil, and Diana Corporation with Concentric.

On July 30, 1997, Turbodyne joined the European EASDAQ exchange, becoming one of the few companies to trade on both the Nasdaq and the EASDAQ. (In 18 months it would be one of even fewer companies to have had trading forcibly *halted* on both exchanges.) On August 14 Turbodyne delisted itself from the Vancouver Exchange to trade exclusively in North America on the Nasdaq.

In October 1997 Turbodyne promoters figured out a way to get into the *New York Times*: They were able to get a small article regarding their pledge, as thanks for the U.N. designation, to donate half a percent of their gross sales to the United Nations. Hmm. And to whom were they going to send this check? Boutros Boutros-Ghali? Ted Turner? Superman? Regardless of my mockery, it was a masterful publicity ploy.

The so-called analysts were falling into place, as well. On February 2, 1998, Christina S. Kohlhaas of CSK Securities Research in Novato, California, issued a *strong buy*. Her lengthy report looked like it was straight from the Turbodyne PR department, with no negatives or cautions whatsoever regarding a company that had yet to ring up a sale from its new invention. "An impressive management team . . . to bring it all together," she burbled. The impressive management team hadn't yet brought it all together, however; the price held steady at $3 a share.

On March 3 Turbodyne shareholders voted to become U.S. domiciled, in Delaware, rather than in Canada. This change caused the removal of the Scarlet "F"—designating a foreign stock—from the stock's symbol; it went from TRBDF to TRBD. By getting the "F" out of there, Turbodyne raised the comfort level of chauvinistic U.S. investors.

On April 27, 1998, Fox News presented a feature on Turbodyne in connection with Earth Day. Two days later the company announced a purchase order from Italy for 40 car units. On May 13 CA IB, the investment bank of the Bank Austria group, issued a *buy/buy*, with a headline touting "increasing torque for earnings growth." Shares had risen from February's $3 to over $11.

On May 26 came a big, vague announcement: "A major European vehicle and engine manufacturer has selected Turbodyne's Turbopac models 1500 and 2200 for incorporation on three classes of engines being manufactured for the 1999 model year." Turbodyne claimed it was "contractually restricted" from divulging the name of this manufacturer.

On June 16 a Turbodyne announcement claimed that Paris Transit was going to test the Turbopac. It went on to claim: "The custom kits reduce emissions by more than 50% while saving fuel and other operational costs." On July 2 Turbodyne began waving around a purchase order for $30,675,000 from the TransBusiness Group of Moscow. The Russians supposedly were ordering 10,500 TurboPacs for Moscow Transit Buses, with the first shipment due October 1. In the week preceding the announcement, the stock ran up from $7 to $9 a share.

I picture Harry Moll on the deck of his beach house in the Caymans, dropping his phone in wonderment when he learns how far Turbodyne has been able to run with his little 10-cent shell company. Not only has the company amassed a stunning market cap built on press releases, but it's also postured itself as the environmental savior of the world. As Edward Halimi stated, "Turbodyne's technology is now considered as the only technology available which can reduce the global warming effect of diesel vehicles."

Despite the company's "highly speculative status," a number of respectable institutions were making a market in Turbodyne, including Salomon Smith Barney (which moved almost 3 million shares in April 1998) and our old friends at Neuberger Berman. Neuberger Berman was a frequent and voluminous trader in Turbodyne, becoming a significant market maker just prior to the run-up. It shifted over a million shares a month during mid-1998.

In the first seven months of 1998, Turbodyne issued 33 press releases. A July 20 release stated that Turbodyne was engaged in preliminary discussions with "several major industrial concerns regarding the possible establishment of a strategic alliance with, and the possible acquisition of a minority interest in Turbodyne." The engine of this little company with the big ambitions was roaring.

By-the-Numbers Stock Promotions

On August 3 it overrevved at $16.63 per share. Was Turbodyne ready to blow a gasket? A penny shell that acquired a car-part patent for $200,000 in stock now had an insane market cap of $700 million.

You'll recall that Diana was another San Fernando Valley–based promotion whose bogus technology was obtained for $200,000. Diana, which received a slew of media attention and was championed by major investment houses, attained a peak market cap of only $600 million. I believe Diana received more attention because, with only 5 million shares outstanding, it was able to blow people's socks off with a price rise from $5 to $120. But Turbodyne, with over 40 million fully diluted shares out, priced its shares cheaper. Doing this made the stock more attractive to people who were willing to take a flutter. Psychologically, it's more satisfying to purchase stock in big round numbers; at $120, 100 shares of Diana cost a hefty $12,000. For whatever reason, this Vancouver filly outpaced the New York Stock Exchange's entry in the 1990s Promoters Cup race by $100 million.

Unfortunately, Turbodyne's peak performance coincided with my undergoing a major surgical procedure. On July 28, 1998, I spent 10 hours horizontal on an operating table. It was one of the few times since becoming an active short trader that I wasn't in touch with my office during trading hours, closely checking stocks in which I am involved or have an investment interest. Relative to our capital base, Asensio & Company generally has large, undiversified positions that require constant vigilance. That's the way I like to trade. I always stayed in touch with the markets. After having waited so long for the Turbodyne Express, however, it took off without me.

I was in the hospital for three days. And in those three days, Turbodyne stock traded up to new highs. I had been following the stock for months, waiting for the opportunity. I could tell from the price and volume action that new buyers were entering the stock. I laughed at my predicament and realized that the time had come, so I decided to issue a report on Turbodyne. I began preparing the report from my hospital bed.

I couldn't speak; my head was bandaged. I couldn't even suck liquids through a straw. I was eating by injecting soup stock with a syringe through a rubber hose running into my mouth behind my wired jaw. I communicated with my office via e-mail. But I was in great spirits, enjoying the kindness of my mother and my ex-wife, who'd both come to New York to be with me. It was the first time since 1993, when we started the public brokerage, that I had taken any time off. But Turbodyne called: "Come get me. Come get me." I got bored with chicken soup through a rubber hose. I had to get me a taste of that sweet, sweet Turbo sugar.

On August 4 we initiated coverage. Our 400-word, no-frills report hit the overblown Turbodyne stock hard. We unveiled our research on Turbodyne and detailed that over the previous five years, Turbodyne had claimed deals with 12 different companies in over 14 different countries, yet no manufacturer had ever incorporated a single Turbodyne product in a new engine. During this same sales-free period, Turbodyne had sold over 25.6 million shares at an average price of approximately $2.18 per share to the public. None of these shares was sold under a U.S. registration statement and underwriting. The vast majority of Turbodyne's 44.2 million fully diluted shares had been sold through below-market private sales to insiders who then resold the shares to the public.

We had never seen a stock crack like Turbodyne did that day. I was home so I missed the thrill of the dancing numbers. From its previous day's high of $16.63 it dipped as low as $5.63, a drop of 66 percent. Bloomberg covered our report and the stock action in Turbodyne as one of the top global stories that day. But I didn't have a quote machine at home, and I couldn't speak. I woke up late, checked the price, and almost choked on my watery split-pea soup.

By-the-Numbers Stock Promotions

My Turbo hunger was sated, but it was almost a letdown to see the company capitulate without a fight.

On August 17 a frazzled Edward Halimi returned to company headquarters in Woodland Hills, California, claiming to have spent the previous 10 days in "negotiations" in London and Moscow. (Hmm. London and Moscow. Perhaps he was planning to buy a bridge? Some of those cute li'l Russian nesting dolls?) Traveling with him had been Ben-Dak "of the U.N. Development Program." With the stunning drop in the stock price, the earlier promotional excesses would have to be increased exponentially—now the numbers would have to be *huge*. In a press release, Halimi described Turbodyne's Russian market as "representing more than $1 billion in potential sales to the company." He also claimed that the company was "poised to access" Mexico's "potential market of $1.2 billion." Regarding the "libelous and loathsome tactics" of the short sellers, Halimi stated, apparently in reference to the Bloomberg coverage, "The good news is [they] have brought our important breakthrough technology to the attention of the world press." This is like Nixon thanking the *Washington Post* for establishing his place in history with its delightful Watergate coverage.

A late August research foray produced a nugget of solid gold for us, but we really had to work for it. The United Nations' anointing of Turbodyne had been gnawing at me. I'm not a big U.N. fan, but I felt something more than bureaucratic hoopla was involved. Either U.N. officials were unaware of this low-level bureaucrat, Joseph Ben-Dak, and his imprudent granting of U.N. endorsements, or, much worse, they *were* aware. If they were aware, this would be a much bigger story. And if they weren't aware, we decided to make them aware and solicit comment.

I can't imagine any more difficult research assignment than trying to thread one's way through the fractured structure of the United Nations hierarchy. Who the hell knows *how* to reach the proper person there? And the problem was compounded many times over by the fact that it was August, when most of the world is on vacation. We began with the inspector general of the U.N. and the Office of Human Resources. No one there was helpful in any way. Thereafter we decided never to let anybody go without either releasing a statement or giving us the name of someone more directly involved.

It was like unpeeling the layers of an onion: All steps were small, incremental. We gradually bored our way in toward the proper authority. Finally we reached the United Nations Development Program (UNDP) and from there the internal Human Resources department. We sent them copies of the Turbodyne press releases exploiting the "U.N. Flagship Technology" designation. Several days later we received an amazing fax from François Loriot, the chief of the legal section of the UNDP's Office of Human Resources. Here is what he told us.

Ben-Dak had left the United Nations Development Program on April 1, 1997, 10 days before Turbodyne's original announcement of its designation from the U.N. Flag Technology Program—that's 10 days before the first of Turbodyne's many descriptions of Ben-Dak as an "official of the UNDP." The Global Technology Group that Ben-Dak managed had been terminated. Turbodyne's press releases concerning its "U.N. Flag Technology" endorsement or status were not authorized by the UNDP and in no way represented the UNDP's position with regard to Turbodyne's technologies or related financing.

Further work revealed that Ben-Dak was involved with affixing a false U.N. seal to other stock promotions, as well. On March 18, 1997—just two weeks before Ben-Dak left his U.N. post for greener pastures—GK Intelligent (GKI) Systems, Inc., announced that it had received official notification from the UNDP that it had been designated as a Flag Technology.

According to GKI's Form 10-SB-A, filed October 2, 1997, Ben-Dak had served as vice chairman of its board of directors since September 1996, six months before the designation—and five and a half months before he left his U.N. post. It also stated that Ben–Dak had recently undertaken a "full-time project" for the company. In this form, Ben–Dak was also listed as owning 6.4 percent, or 1 million shares, of GKI. This did not include an additional 500,000 unvested warrants.

During the first half of 1998, GKI's stock rose from less than 50 cents per share to a high of $19.75. On August 13, 1998, GKI announced that its chairman and several other key employees, including a board member, its chief financial officer, chief information officer, and corporate counsel, had resigned en masse and without comment. The company is now gone, its doors literally locked, but it still trades a few shares every day (OTC: GKIS) at around 30 cents.

That same month Turbodyne issued press releases regarding tests at Southwest Research Institute and Goldenwest Emissions Laboratories. Take that, short sellers—in your face! But we learned something of interest: The tests at Southwest Research were conducted by one Magdi K. Khair. In July 1997 Khair had sold a patent to Turbodyne for an undisclosed amount. And Goldenwest turned out to be a college laboratory class.

Turbodyne applied to cease being a reporting issuer in British Columbia, where it had traded on the Vancouver Stock Exchange, on January 12, 1999. Trading in Turbodyne was halted by the Belgium-based EASDAQ just eight days later, on January 20. The stock closed that day at $5.34. The EASDAQ announced that it planned to initiate disciplinary procedures against the company for, among other things, allegedly issuing a number of press releases that contained false or misleading information.

The Nasdaq, ever wary of alienating even the foulest of paying constituents, failed to halt the trading of Turbodyne until February 26. And despite a preponderance of evidence regarding the company's bogus promotional efforts, trading was resumed on the EASDAQ on March 8, 1999, with the price by then in the $1 range.

Nasdaq, perhaps reluctantly, finally delisted Turbodyne as of

SOLD SHORT

April 1, 1999. The Nasdaq Listings Qualification Panel alleged that Turbodyne "engaged in a pattern of issuing misleading and incomplete news releases, which often were unsupported by an adequate basis in fact."

In mid–1999 Turbodyne underwent a sweeping management change. On July 2 Peter Hofbrauer replaced Edward Halimi, Turbodyne's longtime leader, as CEO. On October 8 Hofbrauer became chairman, and Gerhard Dels was named president and CEO. Notably, the new guys came to me to settle our ongoing legal dispute. It's sad that, just to reach this point, I had to pay $1 million in legal costs defending my right to free speech. Still, Hofbrauer and Dels seemed legitimately interested in building some sort of business.

Unfortunately for them, the new regime inherited the sins of the old. On August 1, 2000, a Turbodyne press release stated that there was enough working capital to remain a going concern only until the end of the month. And that was the *good* news. The company also announced it had conducted an investigation into prior management's 1999 issuance of approximately 8.7 million shares of common stock for an aggregate purchase price of approximately $9.5 million. Tubrodyne concluded that it had not effectively registered those shares under the Securities Act of 1933 and had not disclosed this failure in its SEC filings. It stated that the issuance of the shares, to eight institutional investors and three individuals, each of whom was located outside the United States, had been erroneously reported in SEC filings as being the result of a repricing and subsequent exercise of options.

The next day, with the stock trading below 50 cents, the EASDAQ suspended trading in Turbodyne shares. On August 17 the suspension was reaffirmed through at least October 3, 2000. And so ends the saga of the missing banker, the phony U.N. guy, and the engine thingy that was going to save the world.

Anatomy of a Stock Promotion

A stock promotion is like a disease. And just as a disease can be transmitted in many different ways, there are many different kinds of stock promotions. But, like a disease, there are typical symptoms that let you know the patient is unwell. Here are some of those symptoms.

- The underwriters of the initial public offering have a tainted reputation.
- Promoters of the company and others receiving private, below-market shares and warrants have been involved in other stock promotions, often in unrelated businesses.
- The product is often in a sexy, hot field with hard-to-quantify, hard-to-understand performance specifications.
- If made available for independent scrutiny, the product could easily be proven to be of lesser value than claimed. But any tests or trials regarding the product are delayed beyond reasonable expectation, and results are never disclosed completely and precisely.
- The company creates new stock shares on an ongoing basis. Insiders buy these shares directly from the company at below-market prices. Often the increase in shares outstanding coincides with press releases containing claims that are false or misleading. The company then applies to the SEC to register those shares for its recipients so they might freely sell the shares without further disclosure.
- No analyst is "covering" the company. Or the market maker, IPO underwriter (often one and the same) and compensated others are the only "analysts" covering the company. These analysts rate the company's stock a *strong buy*. No matter how damaging the news about a company, these analysts will simply say the stock has "overcorrected" and is "undervalued," or will blame short sellers for unfairly driving down the stock price.
- The market in the stock is tightly controlled. Borrowing shares to short is difficult.
- The company changes auditors, or its auditor is unknown. (Even if the company's auditor is one of the Big Six, however, this is by no means a guarantee of a squeaky-clean audit—far from it.)

SOLD SHORT

Ergobilt: Brother Smart and Brother Dumb, the Dynamic Duo, and the Dopey Promote That Got Even Dopier

Wall Street may be a public institution, but it has the narrowminded values of a private club. Anyone can join in, as long as he or she fits into the Street's prevailing *modus cogitatus*. The McMillan brothers, Mark and Gerald, were able to convert a humble little mom-and-pop chair-making business into a vast stock scam thanks to Wall Street's misperception of Gerald, who possessed an advanced university degree, as the sophisticated brother. In fact, it was cunning and street-smart Mark who turned a bankrupt company into a vehicle he could use to gain access to the public coffers. And it was Gerald, Ph.D., who started the acquisition of a shell corporation with absolutely no assets or technology and then oversaw one of the most bumbling, transparent promotions ever, and helplessly watched his high-flying hot-air balloon burst.

If you step back and look at what the McMillans were selling, you wonder how they ever got anywhere. It's as if they couldn't even come up with an idea for a corner shop, let alone a publicly traded company. But for some reason two serious investment firms, Cruttenden Roth and Principal Financial Securities, whom I call the Dynamic Duo, got behind this company and stayed with it, fighting loyally till the end, even after we reported in excruciating and gory detail that the king was naked.

For starters, Dr. Gerald's corporation claimed to own an obsolete technology that it didn't actually own. For several months, however, the McMillan brothers had investors convinced that a 12-year-old product was the greatest thing since, well . . . since the same product had been pitched years earlier by its previous promoters, before *those* guys went down in flames.

Besides Brother Dumb & Brother Smart not bothering to come up with much of a product to sell, the ErgoBilt (OTC: ERGB) story

160

includes a company official who tried to change his name to disguise his past but couldn't be bothered to change his name very much. And it involves Rooney Pace, one of the more notorious sleaze brokerages of the 1980s.

There are only two possible explanations for such a dumb promote. Maybe Dr. Gerald & Co. didn't know about the earlier promote. Or maybe they knew and thought that *this* time, with Gerald's superior intellect behind it and the chances of anyone remembering or finding out being pretty low, they could get away with the deal. What could they possibly have been thinking with this maladroit farce? (Of course, when they got caught they denied the whole thing.) But how could the underwriters and analysts continue trying to defend it—and try, try they did—after we exposed the scam?

The best way to explain this lunacy is to go back to the beginning. The story you are about to read was revealed to the public only years after the fact, when we first began our investigations into this shaggy-dog story of a stock promotion.

In 1979 two Los Angeles court stenographers, Jerrold Lefler, 24, and William Cuff, 45, began a small firm that performed computerized typesetting. Lefler invented the steno theory that was central to the company's method. The company purportedly performed a job for a client, Jeffries Banknote, faster than the client thought possible. In 1983 Jeffries's parent, the Charles P. Young printing company, advanced Lefler and Cuff $4.5 million to expand and form a new company called Digitext.

Digitext, based in Thousand Oaks, north of L.A., went public in February 1986. The 1.4 million shares in its offering enjoyed a solid first-day rise, from $4.25 to $6.25, and soon nested between $7 and $8. The Digitext machine supposedly facilitated high-speed stenography through the use of special computer software that simplified the typist's keystrokes. The computer-aided transcription system, combining a computer with a steno machine, was quite similar to a system that was already widely available in 1986 courtrooms. The not-so-revolutionary Digitext-ST, consisting of a keyboard and software, cost $14,500. Remember, by 1986 we were already well into the personal computer age; the first Apple Macintosh (128k) was rolled out in 1984 and cost only $2,500.

A few months after the IPO the company was deeply unprofitable, and its stock dropped to the $4 to $5 range. Lefler and Cuff were at odds. Both held 410,000 shares, stakes worth well over $1.5 million each, even after the price drop. Cuff left the company but not the overall picture. He teamed up with two Digitext board members, including Martin Bell, the president of Charles Young, their parent company, to foment a shareholder rebellion against management. Martin Bell worked for Morty Davis at the notorious D. H. Blair brokerage. D. H. Blair ceased retail operations in 1998 and has been fined millions for securities violations. Bell, acting on behalf of shareholders, claimed company officials were squandering money on luxury perks and unauthorized payments.

Years later I met Bell. When the Digitext scam resurfaced in its Smart Brother/Dumb Brother incarnation, he called and we had a good little laugh. Overall, ErgoBilt was a funny story made even funnier by the seriousness and stupidity of the Dynamic Duo: Cruttenden Roth and Principal Financial. There's nothing funnier than an unsmiling broker caught with his pants down on the corner of Broadway and Wall Street.

A particular target of Bell's was Lawrence West Melquiond, who had been the president of Digitext since June 1985 and its CEO since May 1986. Bell accused Melquiond of excessive first-class flying and other abuses. In what passed for a defense, Melquiond responded that no one had ever complained before.

In February 1987, with the company roiled by dissent, Patrick Rooney joined the board. Rooney, who had been chairman of the Rooney Pace brokerage firm from 1978 to 1985, had suddenly found himself with some time on his hands—the previous month his company had been shut and filed for bankruptcy. The firm was permanently barred from membership in the New York Stock Exchange because of alleged securities violations. As a board member, Patrick Rooney received an option to buy 500,000 Digitext shares (10.1 percent of the company) for $2 a share.

Things began to look up for Digitext when 1980s computer giant Wang signed as the exclusive marketer of the Digitext-ST and announced that it planned to buy $800,000 worth of the machines for resale. But things turned sour again in October 1987. Digitext announced that production of the machines for Wang would be delayed for several months because test models showed flaws in some of the keyboard's main parts. Melquiond was booted back to the ignominy of coach-class travel; he resigned as president and CEO on October 13. The stock dropped that day from $5 to $3.75, far from a $9 high in July.

In 1988 Patrick Rooney was convicted in New York's District Court on one count of filing a false income tax return in 1983 and one count of conspiracy relating to that crime. He wasn't the only one suffering; by June 1988 Digitext's stock price had fallen to $1.87. Rooney wasn't through with Digitext, however. In January 1989 he acquired 573,000 shares, or 11.6 percent of the company.

More Rooney Pacers took an inexplicable interest in the moribund Digitext that year. In September, with its stock trading around 50 cents, Tom DePetrillo, the former head of Rooney Pace's Providence, Rhode Island, office, bought a 14.6 percent stake in Digitext and was appointed to its board. Besides his lamentable Rooney Pace connection, DePetrillo had been at Josephthal Lyon & Ross when the NASD accused that firm of securities violations. DePetrillo himself had been suspended more than once prior to that. He was involved in penny stock deals with Harold Schein, who was appointed to the Digitext board at the same time as DePetrillo.

SOLD SHORT

Now, what's all this got to do with ErgoBilt? That's the same question the Dynamic Duo would be asking themselves eight years later.

Shortly after DePetrillo and Schein became directors, Digitext stopped filing all required documents with the SEC and its stock ceased trading. Altogether, Digitext had raised over $17 million in two public offerings.

On August 8, 1994, long after it stopped reporting to its public shareholders, Digitext assigned its patents to a California corporation named Computer Translation Systems & Support, Inc. (CTSS). Melquiond and Lefler used CTSS to raise fresh funds from investors. Of course, public Digitext shareholders had just seen the only asset of the company snatched away.

On March 14, 1995, Schein filed a lawsuit claiming that Digitext had defaulted on a $56,324 debt. The suit asserted that DePetrillo had authorized the granting of Digitext assets as collateral for the alleged loan, and therefore he was to get the first $56,324 to be derived from the Digitext patent. Digitext failed to file any answer or objection to Schein's lawsuit, which allowed Schein to obtain the Digitext patents without a trial. But wait a minute: Remember CTSS? Weren't the patents assigned to *that* company seven months earlier?

We obtained and reviewed Schein's Complaint, Security and Assignment Agreement, Conditional Assignment of Trademarks and Letters Patent, Promissory Note, and the Default Judgment. Now remember, we're just short sellers, not underwriters conducting due diligence before selling stock to the trusting public. We also reviewed certain correspondence between Schein and Digitext concerning the amount due on the debt. Based on this review, we believed that Schein was entitled to receive from the Digitext patents only the amount he was owed. He did *not* win outright ownership of the patents. (Not that they had value anyway.)

Let's leave the floundering Digitext shell, its business a shambles, its board infested with Rooney Pace refugees and other promoters, its patents twice spirited away, and move back a few years and a thousand miles east to College Station, Texas. Here the second half of the incipient ErgoBilt empire was gestating.

In 1985 Dr. Jerome Congleton earned a patent on a chair design he called "neutral posture," referring to the way an astronaut in zero gravity experiences no stress on the spine. Congleton formed a company called BodyBilt Seating, Inc., to produce and market the chair, employing his wife, daughter, and son Drew. By 1988 the company had fallen deeply in debt.

In June 1988 Congleton hooked up with Mark McMillan, a local entrepreneur and fellow parishioner at the local Methodist church in College Station. McMillan paid $11,000 for the company's assets at auction and allowed the Congletons to continue the business. McMillan and a partner pumped an additional $250,000 into BodyBilt, but the firm continued to lose money.

According to an account in the February 14, 1994, issue of *Forbes*, one night McMillan told the Congletons he'd had enough and asked for his money back. Immediately upon leaving McMillan that night, the Congletons reportedly raced back to strip the Body-Bilt office of its assets. Young Drew Congleton finked on his family, however, informing McMillan of their pillaging. McMillan, apparently impressed by Drew's honesty, trustworthiness, and complete lack of family loyalty, offered him 25 percent of the company to help him run it. And together they managed to turn BodyBilt around. By 1993 it became profitable, on sales of $5 million.

Meanwhile, the other Congletons formed a new chair company, Neutral Posture Ergonomics. It, too, became profitable, earning $1 million in 1993 on sales of $7 million. And when both firms started earning money, Congleton and BodyBilt began to engage in a family feud—protracted mutual patent-infringement lawsuits, to be specific. Neutral Posture would capitalize on ErgoBilt's disgrace to go public by positioning itself as the Chair Guys Who *Weren't* Involved in That Stock Promotion Thing.

In 1996 Mark McMillan's brother, Gerald, formed a shell company called ErgoBilt, Inc. Gerald's ErgoBilt business existed simply to provide services to Mark's BodyBilt—it appeared that Mark was throwing his egghead brother some crumbs. But Gerald's apparent intent was to use ErgoBilt to make a reverse acquisition, or "back-door" public offering, of Mark's BodyBilt. As of December 31, ErgoBilt had cash of $32,150, a negative net worth of $267,251, revenues of $372,808, and a loss of $313,594 for that year. ErgoBilt's revenues came from service fees paid by BodyBilt.

Gerald, who held a Ph.D. and B.S. in Economics from Texas A&M and taught economics at the University of Dallas Graduate School of Management, began wooing investment bankers. His pitch may have been that his hick brother—who may have been less educated than Gerald, but was by this time the chairman of the chairs—had this nice little company but was unable to take it to "the next level." He, Dr. Gerald, a distinguished professor at the elite University of Dallas, could take it to "the next level."

The Dynamic Duo bit hook, line, and sinker, and then began gnawing on the pole. Normally, a company with such dismal financials and insignificant sales in a boring business is not an ideal IPO candidate. But Cruttenden Roth and Principal Financial Securities swallowed Gerald's story—well, we don't know that for sure, but we do know they agreed to sell the story to the public. They underwrote an offering for approximately $11.9 million through the public sale of 1.7 million ErgoBilt shares at $7 per share on February 3, 1997.

Now, I had to ask myself: What's with the Dynamic Duo's appetite for Dr. Gerald's Brother Smart/Brother Dumb pitch? Could the Duo's thinking have gone like this? "Gerald smart. Ergo, he make good company. Ergo, we should underwrite. Ergo . . . bilt. ErgoBilt! We like."

By-the-Numbers Stock Promotions

And what was in it for not-so-dumb brother Mark? Let's just say that after the IPO, he didn't need no fancy chair to be sittin' pretty. Mark McMillan and his two other BodyBilt shareholder buddies received $7.2 million in cash—more than 65 percent of the cash the company netted from the IPO. And, just in case they were the kind of people who don't even get out of bed for such piddling sums, they were also granted almost 1.5 million ErgoBilt shares, around 25 percent of the company.

ErgoBilt's "shell" shareholders, whose company had less than nothing immediately before the offering, were given 2.8 million shares, equal to 46.5 percent of ErgoBilt, for an average price per share of, erm . . . $0.00. This extraordinary dilution—a result of giving a no-cost interest of over 70 percent to the company's promoters—raised its public shareholders' cost of acquiring BodyBilt to preposterous levels. Not to mention all that cash that was taken out.

Let's recap. After the offering there were 5.7 million outstanding shares of ErgoBilt. The public, which had kicked in $11.9 million, owned only 28.6 percent of the company, which retained only $2.7 million of that money. Insiders shoveled $9.2 million and over 70 percent of the company off the table and into their own pockets. As ridiculous and unattractive as that sounds, it was clearly disclosed in the Dynamic Duo's IPO prospectus.

ErgoBilt made its second move the following month, on March 26, 1997, when it entered into a licensing agreement with CTSS, the licensee of the Digitext patents—or, as it was described at the time, its "state of the art proprietary computer and keyboard system," then being marketed as the IMPACTwriter. ErgoBilt claimed that an operator could enter data up to 4.5 times faster with the Digitext/IMPACTwriter than with a traditional steno keyboard. Company shares traded that day at $6.

With performance like this, sales must be gr-r-r-r-reat after 10 years of development, right? A fantastic deal for ErgoBilt shareholders? Maybe even 4.5 times as great as any other deal? Nope. Not in this book. No such luck for the Dynamic Duo.

The keyboard claims were apocryphal, but the promotion certainly went into action 4.5 times faster than a traditional scheme. By June 1997 ErgoBilt's Dynamic Duo had somehow attracted institutional holders with their ergonomic mumbo-jumbo. Gardner Lewis Asset Management held 175,000 shares, Wellington Management 172,500 shares, and Putnam Investments 138,000 shares.

On July 30, 1997, Cruttenden Roth, ErgoBilt's IPO underwriter, issued a *strong buy* report. This exceedingly poor advice was reiterated on September 18, this time with an increased earnings-per-share estimate. Even more ghastly, Cruttenden Roth continued to recommend the stock on September 24, September 30, October 6, and October 31. These were all issued *after* Asensio & Company had discovered and revealed—with all source documents specified, just so there was no doubt—that CTSS was a redo of the Digitext scam.

My point is not: How could they fail to heed our word?! My point is: How could they not at least examine for themselves the specific documents and facts we'd cited in our reports?

Principal Financial Securities, the other IPO underwriter, chimed in on September 18 with a reiterated *buy* on ErgoBilt and a $22 to $25 price target. (It was trading at $13 that day.) Principal Financial also published after our September 24 initial report, on October 1.

ErgoBilt went beyond its ludicrous licensing deal to acquire the "assets" of CTSS outright on August 28, 1997. A principal of CTSS, Jerry Lefler (the original inventor of the Digitext), became the executive vice president of technology of ErgoBilt's newly formed Ergo-Fon'iks subsidiary. The ErgoFon'iks president was another CTSS principal, someone named "Larry West." (Hmm . . . sounds vaguely familiar. Wasn't there a guy named Lawrence West Melquiond out there in the murky past? Coincidence?) Gerald McMillan was the chairman of ErgoBilt, and Mark McMillan the president and CEO of BodyBilt, ErgoBilt's only operating subsidiary. According to an ErgoBilt press release, the CTSS patents (read: Digitext) were now being marketed under the name "Fon'iksWriter." (For a company devoted to simplifying text entry, it certainly devised a product name that's a pain in the ass to type.)

By September 1997, thanks to the summer promotion, the share price had risen to $13. Cruttenden Roth brokers started working the phones. One of the people they tried to pitch on ErgoBilt was . . . me. Oops. Some hapless guy wanted me to listen in on the ErgoBilt conference call. I demurred, but he told me about an "impressive" presentation for brokers where Larry West would speak and Jerry Lefler would transcribe. When West finished his presentation, the computer had the whole presentation on screen for brokers to see. I listened and noticed that when the question-and-answer period started, they stopped transcribing.

This made me think two things. First, I've seen live sportscasts and other events where they have onscreen transcription almost immediately, so what's the big deal? I mean, if this were, say, the 1960s, then the Fon'iksWriter would be quite an impressive product indeed. And the fact that its promoters stopped transcribing the *unscripted* Q&A . . . Could it *be* more shifty? It made me wonder if the whole thing hadn't been a scam. We began to research the company.

On September 23 a release from Dallas-based ErgoBilt made the seemingly impressive claim that Fuller & Parker, a Dallas-based deposition and litigation-support services agency, endorsed the Fon'iksWriter. (As we have seen so often, scamsters seek co-conspirators to convey the illusion of legitimacy. The less sophisticated ones simply enlist their golfing buddies. A far-flung "customer" is no guarantee of authenticity by any means, but some unknown customer in the same town is extra-suspicious.)

On September 24, with ErgoBilt trading at $13.88, we released our first report. Our work had shown that CTSS did not in fact possess any patents or trademarks. We knew of no legitimate purpose for ErgoBilt's alleged acquisition of CTSS. What was there to buy?

ErgoBilt had failed to disclose publicly that "Larry West" was in fact Lawrence West Melquiond, former first-class-flying president, CEO, and director of Digitext, and that Lefler, too, had been a key Digitext promoter. Nor had ErgoBilt disclosed that the Digitext/Fon'iksWriter had been unsuccessfully on the market for over 11 years under at least three other names, including the Intellitex, AccuWriter, and ImpactWriter.

In our reports we dissected the reasons why the Digitext shorthand machine and software were widely known in the transcription industry to be an old, inferior, failed product. Both its input and translation capabilities were materially inferior to those of its competitors. Fon'iksWriter operators must think of the way a word is spelled and broken down before they can key the word into the machine. This causes errors and slows operators significantly. Competing machines allow operators to input sounds. Skilled operators on modern machines can have bursts of up to 700 words per minute, more than three times ErgoBilt's slower but still exaggerated claims. In addition, the Digitext/Fon'iksWriter theory is extremely rigid and does not allow operators to improvise. Competing machines and software allow operators to modify their input methods. Finally, ErgoBilt's software is prone to mistranslation errors. It was easy to see why the thing didn't sell.

A second Asensio & Company release that same day debunked ErgoBilt's "endorsement" by Fuller & Parker's president, Reesa Parker. We discovered that Fuller & Parker, a small Dallas freelance court reporter agency, had had a long relationship with ErgoBilt's promoters. Ms. Parker, who is herself a shorthand reporter, did not even know the Fon'iksWriter writing theory and therefore could not operate ErgoBilt's machine. In fact, none of Fuller & Parker's court reporters owned a Fon'iksWriter, and none knew how to use the machine. In other words, it was an endorsement as hollow as, say, William Shatner pitching hair mousse.

On September 24 I received one of those e-mails that periodically remind me there are real people out there who are gratified by our exposing fraudulent stock promotions. A former senior manager of BodyBilt Seating wrote: "I can offer much corroboration to your report as well as more details that will support it. As a senior officer I was entitled to a large number of stock options, but willingly gave them up in order to leave the company, as I felt that while they were not worthless, they were not worth much. You have made many accurate findings in your report, but there is much more that has nothing to do with CTSS or ErgoFon'iks. While I am not in the habit of trashing former employers, there are many strange things about this company that should be explored."

While this was interesting, it was not surprising. It would be inappropriate for me to describe what the former senior manager said about those "strange things," because they were not documented. And I did not need his information, because I already had seen enough "strangeness" about ErgoBilt.

The following day, ErgoBilt issued a pro forma press release claiming that the Fon'iksWriter was a great advance over the Digitext-ST, that I am a short seller—how did it figure that one out?—and that it had retained legal counsel to advise the company on its options, blah blah blah. Always the same—I can recite these lines in my sleep. My only regret at these times is that a bunch of cheesy lawyers make a lot of money encouraging these sleazy companies to try to perpetuate their scams by abusing the courts.

This already leaky promotional vessel was now taking on water from all sides. On September 30, 1997, we published again, this time examining the Congleton vs. BodyBilt patent dispute. ErgoBilt had failed to disclose that on August 22, 1997, U.S. District Judge Lynn N. Hughes had dismissed BodyBilt's lawsuit against Jerome Congleton. ErgoBilt also failed to disclose that BodyBilt had acknowledged it no longer held a license on the complete patent.

On the other hand, Congleton's infringement suit against Body-Bilt was still pending. A ruling against ErgoBilt could have resulted in an injunction preventing BodyBilt from selling any of its chairs, plus socking the company with a large monetary judgment. BodyBilt was the only part of ErgoBilt that was generating any sales at all, and its Congleton-designed chairs represented substantially all of those sales. ErgoBilt had failed to include any mention of past or pending patent disputes in the risk section of its prospectus, an egregious omission that even the most prevaricating promotions rarely commit.

ErgoBilt had been bombed and strafed; there was nothing left. Nevertheless, the news didn't stop the indefatigable promoters cum analysts at Principal Financial from reiterating both their *buy* and their revised price target of $22 to $25 on October 1, 1997. Laughably, the shill at Principal Financial was attempting some sort of perversion on the concept of due diligence, claiming to have "revisited" company management and to have conducted an "in-depth background review of the Fon'iksWriter." In retrospect, it looks like the only diligence he could possibly have performed was to double-check that Stoo'Pid spelling of Fon'iksWriter.

Somehow the ErgoBilt share price held above $10 into October. It then began a long, slow descent over several months, finally crashing below the $1 barrier in July 1998. After that, it was time to type T-H-E E-N-D. Today the stock trades for pennies on days that it trades at all—which is not to say that the McMillan boys haven't become multi-McMillionaires.

Finally, a word about ErgoBilt's underwriters. By all appearances Cruttenden Roth and Principal Financial Securities were unaware of the fraud when they underwrote the ErgoBilt IPO. When we drew their attention to what they had helped hatch, they chose to persevere with the promotion. Okay, I've never seen an underwriter go back and repudiate one of its hatchlings, but the Dynamic Duo were in a class by themselves. On October 31, 1997, more than a month after this scam was publicly depantsed, Cruttenden Roth again reiterated its *strong buy* and raised its 1997 earnings-per-share estimate, now up to $0.63. It's not clear where and how any sales were going to be produced. The Cruttenden Roth report stated: "The negative rumors and innuendos circulating about the company and its products are either unfounded or based on partial information." Say what you will, the McMillans *really* got their money's worth from these guys.

An ironic sidelight to all this is that Cruttenden Roth's yeoman promotional effort was what focused us on ErgoBilt in the first place. A scam this blatant and dopey might have caught our attention anyway, but you never know. To top it off, we did some of our short selling of ErgoBilt through Cruttenden Roth itself. It was happy to have our business. I can only imagine the company's reaction when it learned that one of its valued customers was the guy who was reporting on the ErgoBilt Follies.

Crystallex: Fool's Gold

In early 1997 a Canadian corporation called Crystallex International (AMEX: KRY) was telling investors that it owned the rights to Venezuela's Las Cristinas Numbers 4 and 6—one of the world's richest gold mines. Ooh, shiny—investors wanted in. There were a few problems, however: Someone else already owned the mine. Their partners were the Venezuelan government. And Crystallex had absolutely no right to the mine. None. In fact, it even was precluded from making a claim on the mine. The Crystallex promoters may not have had a leg to stand on, but thanks to the AMEX they did have a floor to trade on.

Now, you'd think after a century and a half of legendary swindles, the words "gold mine" would at least raise the antennae of any remotely prudent 1990s investor—especially when the company's name ends with an "X." But whereas the classic "We get the mine, you get the shaft" gold scams, from city slickers preying on feckless '49ers on up to the notorious Bre-X, relied on "salted" *lodes*, the Crystallex scam relied on a salted *claim*.

The Crystallex fraud was augmented by the fact that most small American and Canadian investors would be unable to apply serious diligence; after all, documents relevant to the assessment of this company were inaccessible in this country and required considerably more than a Taco Bell understanding of the Spanish language. So, without anyone to counterbalance its totally false public statements, Crystallex promoters not only proclaimed ownership rights over those gold mining concessions but also stated that the Supreme Court of Venezuela was considering enforcing those rights. And when the company began to assert with confidence that a favorable decision was imminent, the price of KRY shot up over 250 percent in just seven weeks.

But in fact there was no ongoing legal proceeding or pending decision in any court that could have possibly resulted in Crystallex having an interest in Las Cristinas. And our research showed that Crystallex had a fully diluted market value of over $300 million on iffy sales of $2.2 million in the prior nine-month period, administrative expenses of $3.3 million, and an operating loss of $950,000. Labeling this stock "grossly overvalued" would be grossly understating the case.

From 1996 through early 1998, Crystallex issued 10 million shares of stock, none in a legitimate public underwriting, all sold at a profit by insiders benefiting from the company's false Las Cristinas declarations. At least three Crystallex insiders sold stock in February 1998, shortly after several promotional stories were published on the Internet. The stock they sold was purchased at less than $2.25 per share and then sold at an average of over $7 per share. This is when we stepped in. But let's back up a bit first.

By-the-Numbers Stock Promotions

In 1986 a Venezuelan company, Inversora Mael, C.A., apparently purchased mining rights for Las Cristinas 4 and 6. Three years later, with nary a nugget having been dislodged from the site, the Venezuelan Ministry of Energy and Mines (MEM) extinguished this concession and denied its renewal. We would later discover that the 1986 Las Cristinas "purchase" by Inversora Mael was in fact an attempt to execute and register a fraudulent transfer of title from its actual owner, who was deceased. Registration was properly denied, the fraudulent transfer was never effected, and the Republic of Venezuela sued Inversora Mael to remove any possible doubt of ownership of the mine's title.

In 1991 the MEM granted the Las Cristinas rights jointly to the government-owned Corporacion Venezolana de Guayana (CVG) and to Placer Dome Inc. (NYSE: PDG), a $3 billion Canadian mining concern. Placer Dome held 70 percent of the rights, CVG 30 percent. On August 14, 1991, Inversora Mael, under threat of criminal prosecution, was forced to abandon its efforts at official recognition of its Las Cristinas claim.

But hold on. In 1993 gold fever struck at kilometer 88 of Las Cristinas 4 and 6. Suddenly this mine was worth a ton. On May 16, 1996, Inversora Mael petitioned the Venezuelan Supreme Court to disregard its forced 1991 abandonment and bless its fake ownership. Judgment of this petition was still pending on March 3, 1997, when Crystallex claimed to have acquired Inversora Mael, reportedly for $30 million cash plus up to 206,667 KRY shares.

Let's recap: Inversora Mael had its illegally obtained rights taken away in 1989, and in 1991 it was forced to officially abandon its claim under threat of criminal prosecution. Yet in 1997 Crystallex issued a press release stating without qualification that it owned the rights to Las Cristinas 4 and 6. Crystallex also claimed to have installed measures to protect shareholders in the laughably improbable event of a takeover attempt—in effect, the company was attempting to hide a poison pill inside a box of poison.

But investors conned into buying KRY—and adding $100 million to its market cap—weren't the biggest losers. From February to June 1997 the spurious uncertainty generated by Crystallex helped cause Placer Dome, which held legitimate rights to the mine, to lose $1.5 billion in market cap.

In most other scams I've encountered, some incremental twist on the truth causes a stock to be grossly overvalued. Here, however, Crystallex was simply *inventing* information. On April 17 Crystallex claimed that the Supreme Court of Venezuela had issued a final and binding ruling ordering a transfer of rights to Inversora Mael. Oddly, though, on April 25 the company stepped back and said it had commenced an action to seek a Supreme Court ruling. On June 4 a company spokesman actually attributed recent market activity to the company's "ownership rights of Cristinas 4 and 6." It was as if the language and distance barriers between U.S. and Canadian investors and events in Venezuela were emboldening the promoters to new heights of audacity.

On June 24, 1997, Crystallex joined the AMEX—welcome to the snake pit. The stock also continued to trade on the Toronto Stock Exchange. Its opening day listing price was $5.13.

By July 11 the Crystallex promotion was in full bloom. An analyst named Kenneth S. Friedman, in his newsletter's "Interim Bulletin," promoted the stock thusly: "The Venezuelan Supreme Court has issued several rulings which give Crystallex the rights to Cristinas 4 and 6." No doubt he received this information directly from the source—from his Crystallex source, that is.

A few days later, on July 16, KRY trading was halted after the company received a negative Supreme Court judgment. Crystallex somehow spun this as a victory—not that I've ever seen a fraud throw up its hands and admit defeat—but the market wasn't so sanguine. The stock dropped from $8 to close at $3.80. Was this the end?

It never is. On July 31 John D. Attalientl of Barrow Street Research in New York City issued a *strong buy* on KRY. Attalientl would reiterate his *strong buy* on February 26, 1998. As I've said before, you always have to take analyst recommendations with a huge grain of salt, but when it comes to analysts you've never heard of working for firms you never heard of wildly hyping obscure penny stocks . . . we're talking Bonneville Salt Flats.

An August 14, 1997, article in Canada's *Financial Post* quoted Crystallex CEO Marc Oppenheimer as suggesting that KRY and Placer Dome might become partners in Las Cristinas. Placer Dome's president, John Willson, incensed by the very thought, responded *no way*: "They are, in our opinion, claim jumpers." They weren't even that. Maybe he didn't understand. Or maybe he was too outraged to dignify KRY with a more detailed, thoughtful, conclusive statement. Willson's comments, while seemingly tough and no-nonsense, typified the ineffective Placer Dome response to Crystallex's attempted trespass. He was giving Crystallex too much credit, implying that through some devious, unsavory means it might somehow have stolen the Placer Dome claim.

Institutions bought into the Crystallex fantasy. As of September 10, 1997, the Altamira Equity Fund and Royal Precious Metal Fund each held 1 million shares, and a Fidelity fund held 450,000. Scudder Gold became a holder in early 1998. Crystallex's Oppenheimer took advantage of the pumped-up price to dump 108,000 shares that month.

Let's take a look at Marc Oppenheimer, dynamic CEO of Crystallex. He had been CFO for Serena Resources Ltd., which had changed its name from IBL Equities in January 1996 and was suspended from trading March 3, 1998, due to unpaid fees in the amount of $652.15 owed to the Vancouver Stock Exchange. He was the CFO of Concord Camera Corp. of Avenel, New Jersey, as of May

9, 1991. Concord's chairman, Jack Benun, had been accused of embezzlement by the previous CFO, Micheal Rea. Benun fired Rea, and Rea sued—this is all public knowledge. Rea's suit alleged that he had been fired because he refused to let the embezzlement go unreported. Rea agreed to an out-of-court settlement. In his search for a presumably more pliant CFO, Benun found Oppenheimer.

On September 15, 1997, Oswaldo Ruiz, described as the former general director of mines and geology for Venezuela's Ministry of Energy and Mines, was named a vice president of Crystallex and president and board member of Crystallex de Venezuela. His February 9, 1998, resignation would be buried at the bottom of a bogus press release spreading more false rumors about Las Cristinas. Ruiz was unwilling to stick around at this cushy sinecure for even five months.

I was in Miami and saw a money manager promoting the stock on CNBC. At first I thought it might be a special-event arbitrage play—if the company had a chance of winning the court case and obtaining rights to the mines. But when I learned that the man touting the stock on TV had only around $2 million in assets under his management, I became suspicious of his appearing on CNBC and decided to investigate. We began studying Crystallex in October 1997. I retained an attorney and political adviser in Venezuela to dig up the facts.

An obstacle in the propaganda battle was Placer Dome's less-than-aggressive response to Crystallex's bogus challenge. The company didn't seem to understand what it was up against. I've seen this time and again. A real company is roped into another's fraudulent activity, yet it fails to understand what is happening. It doesn't understand the character (or lack thereof) of the opposition. You can't stake your hopes on your company's product or business model being superior, because that's not what these frauds are about. The scamsters will continue to release false statements and to withhold unpleasant truths until someone exposes their game. Placer Dome reacted as if Crystallex were simply some legitimate rival.

By-the-Numbers Stock Promotions

Throughout 1997 and 1998, a website called VHeadline/ VENews, "edited" by one Roy S. Carson and purporting to be "Venezuela's Electronic News," served as a chatty mouthpiece for delirious Crystallex distortions. One piece claimed that Placer Dome had offered $23 a share for Crystallex and had been turned down, because another mining company had offered far more. A January 29, 1998, posting shamelessly stated that Placer Dome was planning to abandon its claim to Las Cristinas.

In fact, amid a fog of uncertainty caused by its inability to dissipate the Crystallex smoke, Placer Dome on January 20, 1998, did stop construction on the Las Cristinas mines. Imagine what a major coup this was: A plain and simple scam is able to stop construction by one of the world's largest gold exploration companies on one of the world's most promising gold mines.

Another uniquely despicable aspect of the Crystallex campaign was its continual "reporting" of rumors. On January 30, 1998, and again on February 9, the company attributed share action to "rumors" of impending judgments in favor of its ownership claims. On the February date trading was actually halted on the Toronto Stock Exchange for three hours for pending news—and the "news," of course, turned out to be those gosh-darned rumors.

You didn't need a crystal ball to see where this overinflated stock was heading. On February 10, 1998, we began shorting KRY. We sold shares from $6.63 to $8.13.

On March 4 we exposed both the fabricated claim to Las Cristinas and the Crystallex statement that "the Supreme Court of Venezuela is currently considering its application seeking to enforce its ownership rights over" those gold concessions. Crystallex shares declined from $7.25 on March 3 to $4.81 at the close on March 5, a 34 percent drop. Still, the company was grossly overvalued.

That afternoon Crystallex shot back with a press release denying my claims and excitedly revealing, as if it were some big secret, "we have since learned that Asensio is a notorious short seller." The release, like all standard responses to my initial reports, pointedly explained that short sellers profit from stock prices going down. (It failed to note, however, that stock *promoters* profit from stock prices going *up*. And in this case they would sell all they could when they could.)

Crystallex also announced it had retained the legal firm of Cleary, Gottlieb, Steen & Hamilton to pursue "all appropriate legal responses." Cleary, Gottlieb is the home base of Ed Mishkin, whom you may recall as the attorney Solv-Ex put in charge of the Asensio hit squad. Mishkin was left egg-faced after the Solv-Ex offering was found in court to be fraudulent. Crystallex, abandoning its noble re-portage of rumors for the time being, also stated, "We do note for the record that our motions to enforce ownership rights over the Las Cristinas 4 and 6 gold mining concessions in Venezuela are before the Political Administrative Chamber of the Venezuelan Supreme Court." Actually, this was neither fact nor rumor; it was an outright lie.

Dorothy Atkinson, an analyst with Whalen, Beliveau & Associates of Vancouver who had placed a $25 price target on the stock in February, reiterated her *buy* on KRY. She stated, "Crystallex is not a fraud, there is a court case ongoing, and that is why the senior banking companies aren't making loans to Placer." In a March 4, 1998, report she asserted, "Concessions Cristinas 4 and 6 acquired by Crystallex constitute ownership rights that are recognized and protected under Venezuelan mining law and have been confirmed by the Supreme Court of Venezuela and leading Venezuelan law firms." I wonder how good Ms. Atkinson's Spanish is, because no official document ever existed that remotely stated such a thing.

Ms. Atkinson said a lot of things about Crystallex. But what she didn't say was that her employer, Whalen, Beliveau, did a $21 million institutional financing for Crystallex in June 1996, receiving an 8 percent commission plus a warrant to purchase 10 percent of the warrants sold. Whalen, Beliveau was the top seller of KRY from December 1997 through March 1998, moving over $4.5 million worth of the stock.

On March 5, 1998, we revealed that, contrary to their claim of a year earlier, Crystallex had loaned $13.7 million to a private company to acquire all shares of Inversora Mael on behalf of Crystallex. As you'll recall, Inversora Mael was the false claimant to Las Cristinas. This loan was noninterest bearing and had no stated terms of repayment. Guess who owned this private company getting all that free money: certain directors of Crystallex.

The Crystallex promoters sank even deeper into despair on March 18, when Venezuelan congressman Rafael Rodriguez Acosta of the Congressional Committee on Mining held a news conference at the Fontainebleu Hotel in Miami Beach during a conference on Latin American mining investment. He discussed the congressional investigation of Crystallex's false Las Cristinas claims. In a simple, straightforward speech, Acosta stated that Crystallex had no rights to the mines and would never win even the right to pursue any rights. Furthermore, Acosta's subcommittee had investigated Crystallex and found it guilty of bribery and fraud. Crystallex had failed to disclose any of these material events.

The promote was rapidly deteriorating. In addition to making false claims of ownership to Las Cristinas, Crystallex failed to disclose that the Venezuelan minister of energy and mines had "absolutely voided" several *other* gold-mining concessions it claimed to own. In its latest annual report filed with the U.S. Securities and Exchange Commission and the Ontario Securities Commission, Crystallex had claimed that it had "good title to" the voided concessions, which presumably represented a significant portion of the company's already minute mining assets. When we publicly disclosed the gaping discrepancy between its PR claims and its SEC and OSC filings, Crystallex had the audacity to take out newspaper ads disparaging Asensio & Company and refuting our information—information that could not have been more indisputable.

March 18 was truly a double-barreled blast at Crystallex. That day, despite a halt in trading, the stock (which had slowly crept back up in the preceding days) nose-dived from $4.63 to $3.25, an almost 30 percent drop.

The next day Crystallex promoter Roy S. Carson published a despicably untrue report in his VHeadline/VENews claiming that Rafael Rodriguez Acosta was "to be hauled before an internal disciplinary committee" by Bernardo Alvarez, the president of the Committee of Energy and Mines. I phoned Alvarez in Venezuela. I learned not only that this report was completely false, but also that Alvarez had been fired the preceding week after serving for only a brief period.

A few days later all the key figures in the Venezuelan government backed Acosta. The coup de gras was a definitive decision by the Supreme Court of Venezuela denying once and forever Crystallex's pleas to be allowed to make a claim. By June 12, 1998, Crystallex stock had fallen to 75 cents.

It's hard to believe that Crystallex could have strung along investors with ever more convoluted statements of certainty that a court would award it the rights to Las Cristinas. But what's even harder to believe is that regulators at the AMEX, who do so enjoy our short-selling efforts, to this day allow Crystallex to continue trading on their prestigious exchange floor.

CHAPTER EIGHT

GROSS MISMANAGEMENT

You've heard of a shotgun marriage, right? That's where a couple with about as much in common as Aung San Suu Ky and Donald Trump are forced together through mutual necessity. Well, this is the story of a shotgun ménage à quattre. Through a set of circumstances unlikely in the extreme, a telecom megagiant and one of America's most prominent governors found themselves in bed with a group of Florida penny stock promoters and a small-town lawyer who had managed to receive a political appointment. These strange bedfellows then skipped the honeymoon and went straight on to the cover-up and deceit part of the marriage.

Our story begins a decade earlier, however, with an unremarkable penny stock promote. Unlike most such transient trifles, this one just went on and on and on. It grew bigger and bigger every year, like some mutant omnivore with terminal indigestion, until its repeated doses of accounting trickery could not keep it from exploding and splattering the innocent with the gore of red ink.

For over a decade investors had been hoodwinked by a series of little scams that the penny promote produced. Then somehow in 1998 this paltry promote, at best a money-losing ditch digger, managed to convince a lot of people that it was in fact a sleek tele-com with mouthwatering prospects. Finally the promote hit the big time, and the spotlight was dazzling. Unfortunately, bumbling bureaucrats, led by that small-town lawyer, were unable to muster even the minutest bit of pressure that would have ended this of-fense on the markets once and for all. What follows is a story best described as "inaction packed."

On November 23, 1996, the New Jersey commissioner of trans-portation, Frank Wilson, stepped down from his post. He had been accused by Lockheed Martin IMS, a bidder on a major state con-tract, of discussing his personal job prospects with prospective con-tractors. In the ensuing shakeup, a small-town New Jersey lawyer named Ed Gross was named the executive director of the New Jer-sey Turnpike Authority (NJTA). Gross was a local political operative with ties to Governor Christine Todd Whitman.

Gross joined the NJTA at an eventful moment. The contract that was being bid—and that Frank Wilson allegedly tried to use to grub a new job—involved a consortium of five agencies, of which the Turnpike Authority was by far the largest and most important. The undertaking was an expensive and ambitious project called EZ Pass. The EZ Pass system allows drivers to prepay tolls and, thanks to a small radio device affixed to the windshield of a vehicle, cruise through toll booths with the toll automatically deducted from the prepaid account. The project requires the installation of sensors in the EZ Pass lane, software to manage the system, and, trickiest of all, a reliable, automated method of detecting and fining violators. Lockheed Martin, which had already successfully installed an EZ Pass system in New York State, was seeking the New Jersey consor-tium contract.

On March 25, 1997, the consortium awarded the $488 million EZ Pass contract to MFS Network Technologies, Inc., known as NT. At the time, NT was a subsidiary of MCI/WorldCom (Nasdaq:

Gross Mismanagement

WCOM). Yes, *that* MCI/WorldCom. Lockheed Martin was left out in the cold.

As the future of New Jersey transportation was taking shape, Ed Gross managed to steal the local media focus away from the hotly anticipated EZ Pass project and cast it on himself—and not in a flattering light. It was a side issue that served as an hors d'oeuvre to the mess of a stew that Gross would soon be serving. An October 28, 1997, headline in the *Bergen County* (NJ) *Record*: "Two Women Sue Turnpike Authority; Managers Claim Sexual Discrimination." The women were the turnpike's chief information officer, Lynn Fleeger, and Ann Christine Monica, its assistant director of law.

Both Gross and a turnpike spokesperson, John Sheridan, immediately dismissed the claims. On October 29, however—the very next day—NJTA comptroller Catherine Schladebeck stepped forward, also accusing Gross of sexual bias and harassment.

In a potentially more damaging assertion, Schladebeck also alleged the toll agency's projected EZ Pass revenues had been overstated by $40 million. Schladebeck quoted Gross, upon seeing projections that the state would lose money on EZ Pass, saying "I know you thought I was stupid, but I'm not so dumb after all. I got all the other agencies to pay for our equipment." Gross responded that the $40 million difference was a result of moving the cost of maintaining fiber optic cable from an outside vendor to NT.

Ed Gross withstood whatever repercussions, if any, resulted from these accusations and was still in the saddle on March 11, 1998, when the EZ Pass contract with NT was finalized and the job officially commenced. The Monica/Fleeger suit was settled in August 1999, with the New Jersey Turnpike Authority paying the women's attorney and court costs. The Schladebeck suit was settled in June 2000 with similar terms.

Even before taking on this formidable assignment, NT was in serious trouble with other ongoing projects. Its $8 million Atlantic

City Expressway project was slated to be finished June 1998, 18 months behind schedule. Its $30 million California project was almost two years behind schedule. Well, New Jersey would have none of that in their $488 million deal. The consortium set penalties for noncompletion: $5,000 per day, plus $500 per day for each of the 700 tollbooth lanes that were not completed in time. This meant a potential maximum penalty of $355,000 per day, seven days a week, for every day the project was overdue. No problem for NT and MCI/WorldCom.

The Secaucus-based Violation Processing Center (VPC), one of the more difficult aspects of the project, was due to be operational by November 11, 1998.

On April 27, 1998, just 47 days after commencing the EZ Pass project, MCI announced it had sold NT to a former blind-pool penny stock company based in South Florida called Able Telcom [sic] Holdings Corp. (Nasdaq: ABTE). At the time, Able had a very, very, questionable market cap of around $100 million—just one-fifth the value of the EZ Pass contract alone! MCI's market cap was over $150 billion. You would think this drastic weakening in the quality of ownership should have been a cause of concern for consortium officials. And if that wasn't cause for concern, how about the fact that Able Telcom was not only *not* a telecom, but it couldn't even spell the word.

Even a disinterested observer might muse over how a very, very questionable $100 million nonentity like Able could possibly win the bidding for a company like NT. After all, NT had to fulfill a $488 million New Jersey contract, and others as well. A consortium manager responsible for the largest public works project in state history might go beyond idle curiosity and wonder if this new parent company, with no background in advanced transportation technology, was capable of overseeing the EZ Pass project. The contract had been awarded to a division of the mighty MCI/WorldCom, not to a shaky unknown. Could Able even finance the NT acquisition, let

Gross Mismanagement

alone the EZ Pass project? Furthermore, consortium managers should have demanded assurances that the company contracted to do the job would be the one that actually performed the job—would NT's key managers remain in place after the merger, or would they jump ship?

Ed Gross most certainly must have been advised about the transfer of NT before it closed. The day he learned of the deal, Gross should have asked himself one key question: *If NT had been owned by Able rather than MCI during the bidding process, would NT have been allowed to bid—much less been awarded—the EZ Pass contract?*

Had the answer somehow been "yes" or even "possibly" or even "remotely possibly"—and it really couldn't have been, but let's play out the argument—then Gross should have examined Able's finances. Had he done this, he would have discovered that Able was in dreadful financial condition, a condition made fatal by the NT purchase. He would have learned that NT had not been an independently funded subsidiary of MCI. He would have learned that NT had been thoroughly dependent on MCI's deep pockets to survive. Able's pockets, on the other hand, were so bare, they couldn't even feed themselves, let alone the "new kid."

And then Gross could have moved to protect the state and its taxpayers.

How do I know that Ed Gross had the right to protect the EZ Pass project? Because there was a contract. And this contract was chock full of provisions that were being flagrantly violated. The state could have examined Able's finances. The state could have prevented MCI transferring NT to Able. MCI had no right to dump the EZ Pass contract. And Gross and his colleagues could have acted to protect the state. Unfortunately, no one objected until after we had sold Able short and exposed the whole thing. Ed Gross was caught off guard. By that time the EZ Pass contract was in shambles and the cover-up had already started.

SOLD SHORT

The answer to "Was Able able?" was categorically *no*. This response fulfilled a key provision of Article III, the "termination/default" part of the contract. Section 3.02b describes "reasonable grounds for uncertainty with respect to Contractor's ability to perform the work." It specifies that the contractor must provide assurances that the contract can be fulfilled, or else the contract will be deemed in default. Could Able have possibly provided credible assurances? No. Gross should have considered calling in MCI's performance bond and canceling NT's contract. He did none of the above.

Gross was asleep at the wheel on the turnpike. And by the time he woke up, he had driven into a ditch and become stuck in the mud. As the months went by, as the cash vanished and the EZ Pass project went nowhere, it became apparent that Gross had done nothing to safeguard the contract or the taxpayers of New Jersey. As Asensio & Company began its research into Able Telcom and the EZ Pass project, several salient facts emerged, and several even more damaging developments took place.

We learned that NT had been shopped around for more than a year, but no one in the industry—hey, no one in the whole world—had wanted it. NT, historically and hugely unprofitable, was locked into over $1 billion worth of money-losing contracts backed by MCI/WorldCom performance bonds. MCI was desperate for someone else to assume the responsibility of managing those loser contracts and their massive liabilities.

Actually there had been one other interested party. A Canadian penny stock called Sirit Technologies had hooked up with NT's president and CEO, Kevin Moersch, and other NT managers in an effort to execute a management buyout. They tried for over a year to arrange financing but failed. In fact, Sirit claims it approached Able, thinking for some misguided reason that Able could provide financing for the purchase, and that's how Able got the great idea to purchase NT for itself. I guess that Sirit, a Canadian penny stock, saw

Able, a U.S. penny promote, as a gateway to a richer market. After NT was "sold" to Able, Sirit launched a lawsuit against Able for stealing this great company from under its nose. And incredibly, in July 2000, Sirit won its suit and was awarded a judgment for millions of dollars in "damages." Can you imagine the luck? Not only does Sirit manage to escape being dragged down by this money-sucker, it also becomes the only party in this quagmire to emerge with a profit—and a sizable one at that.

Anyway, with no other viable bidders for NT and a desperate desire to rid itself of this albatross, MCI was forced to finance Able's purchase of NT itself.

So what was Able Telcom? Originally formed as a blind pool in the late 1980s, Able literally was a penny stock. Its founders ran into trouble with the SEC and the U.S. Army; its underwriters were barred from the securities business just months after the Able public offering. The company had declared profits in 1993 and 1994, boosting its stock price, allowing insiders to cash out options and bringing a little equity into the company. But in 1995 and 1996 the company wrote down these same profits. The reality was, far from being a "telcom," Able was in fact a ditch digger for the telecom industry and had never recorded a legitimate profit in its entire history. It had survived for 10 years thanks only to questionable extraordinary accounting entries, which drew the active attention of the SEC. And now it had taken on a debt so huge and a project so unprofitable it couldn't possibly remain a going concern.

Soon after Able's takeover of NT, 12 senior managers departed NT, including the president and CEO, Kevin Moersch, who left on May 5, just a week after the Able buyout. Moersch told Herb Greenberg of TheStreet.com that he decided not to join the Able family when Able's chairman, Gideon Taylor, chummily suggested to him that all construction managers skim money from projects. "I have no confidence in the new people," Moersch said. Taylor allegedly said, "I looked at your deals and I know there's a whole lot more money in there than you guys have shown. . . . I'm certain that you are running your business the way most of us do, in that you step in to almost any job and draw a little extra money out." This time ol' Gideon hadn't stepped in to any old job. EZ Pass was the biggest deal of its type in history. Just how much "little extra money" Able drew out from Jersey and MCI will never be known.

On August 19, 1998, Able announced new hires for NT. The following day we issued a report regarding the severe deterioration in the quality of NT management. Besides Moersch and others, we learned that NT had also lost Bill Thompson, president and COO of MFS Transportation Systems; Robert Thurman, senior vice president of estimating and engineering; Rick Bonds, vice president of legal and regulatory affairs; and Bob Eide, senior vice president of network sales. The new hires announced by Able displayed little of the knowledge, training, or experience of their predecessors. And let's keep in mind that NT under its previous, experienced management, had already been behind on several projects. The situation was shaping up as a morass that made the New Jersey Meadowlands look like the gardens at Versailles.

"Section 1.25—Personnel" of the EZ Pass contract, Part H, spells out the "key personnel" clause common to all such contracts. Among other stipulations, it states: "In the event the Contractor wishes to substitute personnel for any key personnel . . . the Contractor must notify the Authority in writing and request written approval for the substitution. . . ." In a sense, Gross hired Frank Sinatra for a concert and Tiny Tim showed up. And then Gross approved the switch, apparently deeming Mr. Tim an equally competent performer. Our reports caught Ed Gross tiptoeing through the tulips.

Able's stock had run up to $20 in response to bogus management and analyst claims that the NT purchase had added great value to the company. When these claims were shown to be false, the stock plummeted to as low as $1 a share. This company had for 10 years applied the Pac Man theory to stock promotion: It hungrily devoured a series of small companies that showed sales, thus pumping up its stock price. But this time Pac Man had violated the first principle of fine dining: Never eat anything larger than your head.

Before we began issuing our reports on Able, a charitable soul might have suggested that perhaps Gross was unaware that MCI had sold NT to a group of penny stock promoters. But then, this is the man responsible for overseeing the entire EZ Pass project on the New Jersey Turnpike. Gross himself, upon awarding NT the contract, had described the project as "the single most important development on toll roads since they began in the 1940s." And Governor Whitman had stressed the significance of this project, terming the EZ Pass agreement "the largest, most innovative transportation procurement in the world." You'd think Gross should have been aware and must have been notified.

Once he knew what was happening, instead of acting on behalf of New Jersey taxpayers, Gross tried to conceal the problem. On August 26, 1998, Gross told Pat Gilbert, a staff reporter for New Jersey's *Bergen Record*, that KPMG Peat Marwick, the turnpike's auditor, had been retained in July 1998 to review Able's acquisition of NT. Gilbert then sought comment from Peat Marwick.

Peat Marwick spokesperson Suzanne Hayat denied Gross's statement, saying the company was never hired to examine Able. "They think because we're doing the auditing work for the Turnpike that this is an extension of the work we're doing," she stated. "That's not how it works. Any other projects, they hire separately for."

Now, let's think this through. Gross told a reporter that Peat Marwick had performed an examination of Able. The reporter subsequently discovered that Peat Marwick had never been *asked* to perform this analysis, let alone actually having performed it. At this point, Gross *still* could have stepped back and asked Peat Marwick to perform the analysis. But it never happened. Peat Marwick *never* performed an analysis of Able. There is something seriously amiss about this.

Gross should have acted when MCI transferred ownership of NT to Able. Able could never have qualified to be a bidder for the EZ Pass job or to get a bond for the job. A simple check would have revealed that. Even accepting that this didn't happen, how could Gross possibly have thought he had commissioned an analysis and declared this to a reporter? And, then, when that reporter discovered that in fact he hadn't directed Peat Marwick to do the work, as Gross thought he had, how could Gross not have commissioned an analysis at that time?

It gets worse. The Atlantic City Expressway EZ Pass project, due to be completed June 1998, 18 months behind schedule, was . . . delayed. It was finally activated on November 11, but there was a slight problem: The EZ Pass system didn't work. New Jersey transportation officials never disclosed this. On February 5, 1999, the *New York Times* reported that cars were cruising through the EZ Pass lanes on the Atlantic City Expressway without paying and without being caught. Even in this article, which came months after the NT debacle had been exposed and EZ Pass had become a $500 million money pit, Gross refused to utter a critical word on NT. "What is more important than losing a month or two is that we have a quality system," he told the paper. "We are committed to the highest standards of performance." Jayne O'Connor, a spokesperson for the governor, said of Gross and other NJ transportation officials: "They have showed that they are not afraid to take action when they need to."

November 11, 1998, was an apparent "good news, bad news" day for NT: It was the day the Atlantic City project was finally "completed," but it was also the deadline for the Violations Processing Center. The VPC was nowhere near completion—it was, in fact, a shambles. (And since the Atlantic City EZ Pass system didn't work properly, actually it was a "bad news, worse news" day.) Gross allowed NT to push the VPC deadline back to December 23 without penalty—that's what "taking action" must mean in New Jersey.

Gross finally sent Able a letter of default on December 29, 1998, announcing that the state would begin assessing a $5,000-per-day fine as of December 23 until the Violations Processing Center was operational. In the letter, Gross also demanded delivery of an operational VPC by January 15, 1999.

Able failed to notify investors of its VPC failure and the notice of default. Given the company's past omissions and misrepresentations, perhaps this is not surprising. But it's hard to excuse the fact that neither did Ed Gross publicly disclose the notice of default. This is a case of a public servant concealing material information from the very public that was funding the project. Fortunately, a copy of the notice was faxed anonymously to us. After verifying its authenticity, we issued a report dated on January 8, 1999, on NT's failure to meet the VPC deadline.

You know what? Disseminating information unwillingly and indirectly via Asensio & Company's research and reporting does not constitute full, candid disclosure. If not for our report, any investor trying to research Able—not to mention any New Jersey taxpayer trying to learn what was up with EZ Pass—would have had no access to this incredibly salient information.

Fortunately, not everyone at Able and NT was in cover-up mode. Also on January 8, I received an e-mail from a former NT employee who had read my reports and had specific information about the extent of the EZ Pass boondoggle. She described the role of each departing NT employee, telling how crucial each of them had been to the EZ Pass project. She also told me that software vendors were not being paid. The repeated missing of deadlines, the 1998 departure of top NT execs—these told me the sad condition of NT's EZ Pass project. But now I knew who exactly was doing the work and how poorly that work was being done.

The former employee informed me that work on the VPC was now being done by outside consultants. Previously, NT employees had done the job. She told me that one of the key software developers had a full-time job with Texaco. NT was on its third or fourth replacement for vendors that had cut the firm off for nonpayment or late payment. Many NT consultants had left because their bills, though undisputed, hadn't been paid for over 120 days. The former employee also said that the new managers did not have staff support.

She wrote, "What has been spent is more than the job is worth." There was no question; this was most definitely an insider. "Why do I tell you this?" she wrote. "I really don't care what you do, and I don't own any Able stock, short or long. But I have never been so disgusted by the actions (or lack of actions) by corporate managers before, and I would hate for anyone to lose any more money buying into this mess without knowing the truth."

At long last, when we disclosed the notice of default, the story attracted some media attention. On January 16, 1999, another VPC deadline passed, and the noncompletion fine was raised to $25,000 per day. But really, if Able couldn't pay a $5,000-per-day fine, what made anybody believe it could or would pay a $25,000-per-day fine? Going through the motions of imposing a fine to impress the public that "Ed Gross means business!" wasn't going to get EZ Pass installed. The only way to accomplish that would be to fire NT and hire another firm.

On January 20, 1999, we wrote to James Weinstein, the New Jersey commissioner of transportation, citing Able's dreadful financial condition as a possible explanation for its contract default. We also expressed our belief that Ed Gross had not only allowed Able to gain control of the EZ Pass project but also had allowed it to persist in harming the project by covering up Able's default and failing to take decisive corrective action.

On that date we also published the news that Joseph Andre Schmidt, the Able executive who was the EZ Pass program manager, had resigned. Over the previous two and a half years Schmidt had first been involved in the negotiations for the EZ Pass contract and then managed the project for NT. Once again Able Telcom—and Ed Gross—had failed to disclose this significant negative development. Only some short seller's report on the Internet made this information public.

Our research uncovered details of specific obstacles NT was having with the VPC. The system had failures in its integration and components. Among the failures were the inability to: take readable pictures of the license plates of violating vehicles; digitally read the images and automatically retrieve the vehicle's registration information; and issue a summons matching the vehicle and the time, place, and type of toll violation. Basically, the whole shebang.

The little pictures were fuzzy but the big picture could not have been clearer. Able was in default of its debts. The debt holders were not foreclosing because Able had no assets that could be sold to cover any meaningful part of the loans outstanding. In fact, Able's businesses may have had negative cash flow even before incurring the large NT losses. NT's contractual obligation to continue to pay the California and Colorado expenses had been part of the reason for MCI/WorldCom's inability to find any legitimate bidders for NT.

We thought that the December 29 VPC deadline failure and the lame attempt at a cover-up had finally exposed Ed Gross. At this point, if it hadn't been obvious before, Gross certainly had the contractual right—not to mention the obligation—to call MCI's performance bond on the project or otherwise act to sever New Jersey's ties to Able. We thought that Gross would not be allowed to continue disguising his inexplicable leniency behind a facade of tough love. When Able had the gall to publicly ridicule the notice of default from the state as "not uncommon," we thought it would be the last straw.

Ed Gross's failure to disclose the default on the VPC had blown up in his face. On January 21, 1999, the five members of the EZ Pass Consortium and their staffs met with representatives from Able and NT to hammer out an "absolutely, positively, last chance, and we mean it this time" agreement and schedule for the successful completion of the Violations Processing Center.

There must have been at least 20 people in that conference room. Because of our involvement in disclosing the VPC default notice, we became a de facto clearinghouse for reports from the meeting. We were receiving calls not only from members of the media but also from well-placed, politically astute New Jersey contractors who had been lined up as subcontractors on the Lockheed Martin bid and were drooling at the prospect of NT and their subcontractors being dumped. They would be glad to step in and claim all those juicy jobs and do the work that needed to be done. Those subcontractors had contacts at several of the agencies in that meeting. And they contacted me in hopes of exchanging information. Many of them, astute businessmen, knew how dismally the project was progressing and had themselves shorted Able Telcom. I liked that. Also, disgruntled former NT employees with contacts still at NT or in the consortium would tell me what they were hearing from the meeting. It was as if I were right there at that big table.

Suddenly Ed Gross was pulled out of the meeting—he'd been summoned by the governor. My phones lit up like a Christmas tree. This was it, we all thought: Either Ed Gross was going to dump NT, or the governor was going to get rid of Gross and install someone who *would* dump NT.

Gross Mismanagement

Fat chance.

The governor's chief of staff, Michael Torpe, and I had had extensive conversations on the Ed Gross/NT situation. It so happened that I was on the phone with Torpe when Gross arrived to meet with the governor. Of course, we don't know what happened behind closed doors. However, we know that instead of Gross or NT being dumped, nothing was done—nine months after we exposed the whole enchilada. The state could have stopped writing checks to NT. But then Able Telcom would have gone bankrupt, and the whole scandal would have been exposed.

I want to be clear that I am not bashing the policies of the Governor's Office. Governor Whitman was a prominent member of the Republican party and has since, of course, gone mega. I am a social liberal. Not a Republican. Not a Democrat. I believe that Republican governments tend to be good administrators. They generally don't overpromise or overhire, they are careful with tax dollars, they don't create bureaucracies. This was simply one case where one governor was apparently *not* implementing appropriate administrative procedures.

You might think it unconscionable and indefensible that once the Able/NT problem rose to Governor Whitman's desk she didn't attend to it with seriousness and alacrity. The project was a huge, important one with an enormous sum of money at stake. But somebody in Governor Whitman's office, perhaps the governor herself, allowed the boondoggle to persist. It's unfortunate, but it's what happened.

By the time this problem hit Governor Whitman's office NT was in default of its contract and the state's payments to Able had exceeded the work delivered. The governor could have:

1. Immediately stopped the payments to Able and determined how much money Able had been paid to date.

2. Had her lawyers check the contract with NT and discover her rights.
3. Called for an audit of all subcontractors to see what work they had done, how much they'd been paid, and how much they were owed.
4. Audited the work done and determined how much it should have cost the state.
5. Calculated how much money was missing.
6. Threatened to call in the performance bond.
7. Negotiated a settlement with NT/Able.
8. Declared the contractor in default and put out the job for re-bid.

As best we can determine, here is the point-by-point scorecard of action that was taken:

1. None.
2. None.
3. None.
4. None.
5. None.
6. None.
7. None.
8. None.

On January 22, 1999, the *Newark Star-Ledger* reported that, prompted by a letter from Asensio & Company, the Governor's Office had told the New Jersey State Attorney General's Office to examine our claims of mismanagement and Able's insolvency. When the media picked up on the story and questioned Gross, he ingenuously replied, "We don't have a contract with Able. Our contract is with MFSNT. Who owns them does not drive our process."

This statement is inexplicable and ignorant. NT never existed as an independent unit. NT was no less dependent on MCI for sustenance than a lamprey sucking nutrients off a whale. But when the giant mammal shook loose the parasite, NT suddenly found itself frantically sucking at the wizened husk of a failing stock promote— and slowly starving to death. In fact, the new host had turned the tables on the parasite; Able was using NT as a vehicle for siphoning funds from New Jersey state taxpayers. Furthermore, Able was also using the state's demonstrated leniency to pump up its stock price; evidently, no matter how badly the company screwed up, the state would never pull the plug.

Although New Jersey was making payments to Able, those payments were not flowing down to the company's subcontractors. The issue of unpaid subcontractors would rear its ugly head on March 2, 1999, when Able announced it had fired the software designer for the EZ Pass project, American Traffic Systems (ATS), on grounds of incompetence. We contacted James Tuten, the president of ATS. He told us that Able simply had refused to pay for his company's services. In fact, it was ATS, which was suing Able, that pulled out of the project. "They weren't legitimate," said Tuten. "They weren't fair, they weren't ethical, and they weren't professional."

Section 3.02 of the EZ Pass contract, subsection a) vii, describes one "event of default" as "the Contractor has failed to make prompt payments of amounts that it is contractually obligated to pay to Subcontractors or Suppliers for Materials or labor for which it has received payment." Yet another airtight cause for the state to pull the plug; yet another missed opportunity.

As the VPC default was heating up a cold January, Able also defaulted on bank, senior subordinated, and preferred financial obligations, and was being sued by its own stockholders for withholding material information and disseminating false information. If Able's debt holders were forced to call their loans, the company would have had to declare bankruptcy. The preferred shareholders knew that and so were unable to force payment. It was a classic stalemate.

Just as Able was about to go under for the last time, a mysterious savior appeared. On January 26, 1999, Able announced that a newly formed entity called Interfiducia Partners LLC had bought the Able debt and promised not to convert the preferred shares. Interfiducia may have looked like a white knight, but it was really just an old guy riding a donkey. We discovered that it was a recently formed corporate shell with no assets and no business. This alleged deal was never consummated.

You may ask: Didn't the annual audit disclose the company's insolvency? One of the reasons the bankruptcy wasn't exposed and the wheels hadn't fallen off the promote was that Able's audited 10-K statement for the year ending October 31, 1998, was completely inadequate, as the SEC found when it required a sweeping restatement of their financial statements.

Arthur Andersen performed the 1998 year-end audit for Able. It was hired on October 9, 1998, right before the fiscal year ended, after Able had bought NT. It became Able's seventh auditor in 10 years. Andersen also happens to be the auditor for MCI/WorldCom, which was one of the world's largest audit clients. According to a February 17, 1999, piece on the Dow Jones News service, MCI had originally backed the NT construction performance bonds. Able was supposed to replace the MCI bonds with new ones but failed to do so. So MCI was liable for hundreds of millions if Able failed to deliver in New Jersey.

But that's not all. MCI was also liable for NT performance bonds in New York State and Colorado. Able reported in a 1999 SEC filing that $499 million in NT contracts were backed by bonds. Former NT employees told writer Craig Karmin of the Dow Jones Newswire that all of those bonds were from MCI. MCI had a huge, huge stake in keeping NT/Able afloat.

Gross Mismanagement

Able delayed release of its 1998 SEC 10-K filing for so long that the letter "E" was appended to the company's trading symbol—now ABTEE—an indication of a late filing, and a warning sign to investors. Finally, on February 24, 1999, the 10-K was filed. In it, Arthur Andersen allowed a highly dubious $40.5 million intangible asset, which saved the day.

On February 26 we published a report titled "Able's Accounting Fraud Fully Exposed." We stated our opinion that Arthur Andersen's conduct and material omissions were flagrantly fraudulent. How could we characterize the work of this accounting giant so harshly without ever receiving so much as a threatening letter from the company in response? How could it just absorb the whole thing? Could it have been because they knew that we were totally right? Andersen had done no more or no less than what we researched and disclosed. Its lack of response speaks for itself. And if it didn't speak for itself, a December 1, 1999, Able announcement that the SEC was investigating its accounting spoke quite loudly and articulately.

And in February 2000, Able announced that its 10-K for 1999 would be delayed, just as it had been a year earlier. Time for the mathemagicians at MCI/WorldCom and Arthur Andersen to conjure more accounting wizardry on the tattered Able books? Or would the glaring beams of the ongoing SEC investigation make it a little risky to pull off this not-too-slick feat of ledger-demain?

This time it was impossible to conceal the truth. Arthur Andersen was forced to issue a statement that questioned Able's ability to continue as a going concern. Even Vik Grover of Kaufman Bros., the loyalest lapdog analyst you ever did see, turned on Able, biting its hand with a comical after-the-fact downgrade.

As ABTE sunk into oblivion, it seemed doomed to be designated every spring as ABTEE—the Scarlet E of a late filer. Or perhaps the company will decide that it will be easier for investors to find it if it just makes the extra E a permanent appendage. Meanwhile NT has changed its spots by renaming itself Adesta Transportation. Christine Todd Whitman has joined the Bush II Cabinet as head of the Environmental Protection Agency. And finally, with MCI's help, in August 2000 the remains of Able were merged with a Toronto-based company, Bracknell Corporation (Toronto Stock Exchange: BRK).

As for EZ Pass, which we dubbed "Sleazy Pass," New Jersey state officials claim that it's up and running, at least on the Turnpike. How much did all the machinations cost the New Jersey taxpayer? No one will ever know.

CHAPTER NINE

ABUSING
THE PROCESS

Avanti: Copycats

You might think that some of the bad guys in this book should be behind bars. Well, this is a case where there was once a chance that could have happened. According to the cops, the key executives of Avant! Corp. ("Avanti," Nasdaq: AVNT) were caught red-handed with stolen software. This was not just some commonplace civil dispute between two squadrons of corporate lawyers. For several years the only reason that six members of Avanti's board of directors were clad in pinstripes instead of prison stripes was that they were out on bail.

My major professional gripes are the biased rules against short selling and the abuses against freedom of speech that are detailed in this book. I believe we can put up with a few scams as a cost of freedom from excessive government regulation. I would never want to be the judge of anyone's conduct, let alone decide who owns what software code and whether the taking of it should be a crime. But we do make judgments about what's good and bad for business. And having a chance to lose your product because a state prosecutor has charged you with theft ain't good for business.

SOLD SHORT

This irrefutable jeopardy to Avanti's stock had been almost completely ignored by the market—a market that is usually so adept at analyzing risk and pricing stocks accordingly. A powerful cadre of major institutions stood behind Avanti long after its brazen executives were arrested for stealing software. The stock capitulated once, then climbed back, and then again, and then back once again. Avanti now trades way down from where it was when we initiated coverage—closer to the true market value of a company that could suddenly find itself bereft of leadership and liable for crushing punitive damages.

Avanti's official company name is for some misguided reason "Avant!" It is pronounced "Avanti," however, and I am not about to subject my readers to the frustration of having to wade through gratuitous punctuation. When's the last time anyone printed Yahoo!'s exclamation mark? Apparently someone thought it would be clever to invoke the Italian word *avanti*, meaning "forward," but at the same time try also to tie in the French phrase for "daring and trendy," that is, *avant garde*. The result is a corporate name that is silly and meaningless. This having-it-both-ways greed, which instead backfires, is an appropriately potent symbol for the company and its management.

Many who do not understand what I do label me cynical, when in fact I am the opposite. I have faith in the self-regulated, free market system. Yes, I am skeptical of corporate statements, having seen so many misrepresentations. But I believe that, in the end, corporate misbehavior is punished by the markets.

You know what "cynical" is? Cynical is promoting and purchasing shares of Avanti knowing the company has been criminally charged with having been constructed on a foundation of stolen software. Cynical is a self-described 21-year-old hotshot analyst at Fidelity Management named Tony Huang who pseudosagaciously chirps, "Software product cycles move faster than the wheels of justice." Cynical is Fidelity Management wagering great sums of money in support of this sentiment.

In other words, everybody was aware of the grave charges, but several large shareholders believed that by the time any punitive action might be taken, Avanti would be so well established, profitable, diversified, and beloved that the impact on its runaway train would be like a gnat hitting its windshield. I disagreed.

This cynicism is compounded by Avanti's entrenched position in Silicon Valley. In a few short years, in the fast-forward manner of Valley growth, Avanti has swallowed up so many other companies that its business is no longer solely based on the allegedly stolen software that made it all happen in the first place. So now it's harder to view Avanti as merely a company selling someone else's product. Plus, software cycles *do* advance rapidly; by the time Avanti was first enjoined from selling certain plundered software, the company smirked and chortled that it was no longer selling that product anyway.

Situations and personnel change so fast in Silicon Valley that it seems there is little virtue in corporate loyalty or integrity. The industry response to the hard evidence presented against Avanti was a collective yawn. They were willing to accept that the theft occurred; they just didn't see the heinousness of the crime.

The software was stolen from Cadence Design Systems, Inc. (NYSE: CDN), which at the time pretty much dominated the market in an esoteric software niche. Cadence created Electronic Design Automation (EDA) software to design integrated circuits. Avanti not only stole Cadence's software but also muscled in on its market allegedly using Cadence's own technology.

In February 1991 four top Cadence employees departed to start Arcsys Inc., which later became Avanti. Avanti grew quickly after Gerald Hsu, general manager of Cadence's largest division, left Cadence in March 1994 to take over as Avanti's CEO. Total revenue rose steadily from $51 million in 1994 to $81 million in 1995, $124 million in 1996, $164 million in 1997, $227 million in 1998, to $347 million in 1999, as many former Cadence customers switched over to Avanti products. EDA software requires intensive development over many years and sells under contracts worth millions of dollars.

The hyperaggressive Hsu is a professed admirer of Sun Tzu's *The Art of War* and is said to quote from it often. According to Cadence's former CEO, Joseph B. Costello, Hsu developed a campaign at Arcsys called "JFK Cadence," or "Just fucking kill Cadence." When pressed, Hsu offered with a wink a denial, stating that this actually meant "joint floor-planning kernel." Hmm . . . Which sounds more like a phrase coined by a man weaned on *The Art of War*? Costello was reportedly furious when Hsu defected, but after all, when they say "All's fair in love and war" in Silicon Valley, they're not talking about love.

Cadence and Arcsys signed a peace pact on June 6, 1994: Hsu could join Arcsys, but he could not hire any Cadence employees for six months. More significantly, Cadence exonerated Avanti of all claims regarding trade-secret theft committed prior to the pact. This limited release proved a keystone of Avanti's later defense. Apparently Hsu didn't respect the six-month poaching embargo. According to Costello, in August 1994 Hsu began recruiting Mitsuru (Mitch) Igusa, one of Cadence's most talented engineers. On September 15, one day before Igusa left the company, Cadence network administrators observed him sending a 5.3 megabyte file to himself at a private e-mail account.

Although Igusa never actually went to work for Avanti, Costello smelled a rat. He complained to Santa Clara County authorities, and on November 10 police searched Igusa's residence. Source code to key Cadence place-and-route programs was found on the hard drive of Igusa's Sun workstation. Specifically, authorities found a key enhancement to the place-and-route software, a so-called area-based program that lets the computer help do the work in chip design. The software had been stripped of Cadence copyright notices.

The Cadence "soft-lifting" continued. According to court documents, in January 1995, on his next to last day at Cadence before joining Avanti, engineer Chih-Liang "Eric" Cheng copied a program he had written over the previous two years onto a file. He named this file "byebye.tar" and stored it on a backup tape. (A ".tar" file is a compressed file that can contain numerous other files.) Called VSIZE, this program helps designers figure how big a chip must be to handle a given number of circuits. Avanti had planned to market the product in 1996.

Arcsys/Avanti's flagship place-and-route software was called Arc-Cell. It was a direct competitor of Cadence's Symbad. Arcsys developed ArcCell in no more than two years, while Symbad had taken Cadence six years to develop. In June 1995 Arcsys, cashing in on the value of its stolen software, went public.

On August 29, 1995, Cadence engineer Jeff Markham was on a routine visit to Cirrus Logic Inc., a customer across the bay in Fremont. He happened to boot up a chip-design program by Arcsys and compared it to Cell3, an older Cadence program. He spotted a tiny flaw he had unintentionally written into the Cadence program years before—a misaligned edge of a rarely used screen that made it appear fuzzy. Markham notified Cadence executives, who hired a software analyst, John Navas. Navas found thousands of features in the Arcsys software that matched Cell3, including identical misspellings and grammatical errors.

Meanwhile, Mitch Igusa set up shop as a consultant a block away from Avanti. Just down the hall from Igusa, Avanti's chief of engineering, Stephen Wuu, and Shiao-li Huang, Avanti CEO Gerald Hsu's administrative assistant, had for unknown reasons rented an office, too. Howdy, neighbors! They and other former Cadence executives claimed to have set up something called the Saurus Fund, supposedly to endow start-ups. Igusa received at least $15,000 from this fund, which was never registered as an official venture capital fund, never incorporated, and appears to have been invented after the fact solely to explain payments to Igusa.

The affidavit in support of an April 1997 arrest warrant for seven Avanti principals strongly suggests that Huang's private Bank of America checking account was used to make payments to Igusa. Huang deposited a series of large checks from the indicted Avanti principals, then either withdrew several thousands of dollars in cash at a time or wrote checks (at least three for $5,000 each in July and August 1995) to Igusa.

Igusa was arrested in August 1995 and charged with misappropriating trade secrets. Huang's suspicious checks and cash withdrawals continued even after Igusa's arrest. On October 20 private investigators hired by Cadence photographed Igusa receiving an envelope from Avanti's vice president of technology, Y. Z. Liao, in Avanti's parking lot.

On November 27, 1995, Arcsys stock began a week of giddy highs and stupefying lows. It bought Integrated Silicon Systems Inc. for $264 million in stock and named the newly merged company "Avanti." The stock hit $51 a share. Then, on December 5, more than a year after the raid on Mitch Igusa's home, police and FBI agents searched Avanti's offices and found what was later alleged to be stolen Cadence software.

An electronic log taken as evidence suggested that Stephen Wuu, Avanti's chief of engineering, spent his final weeks in 1991 as a Cadence research and development manager copying its basic place-and-route program, Symbad. Wuu denied the accusation, claiming the 47,000 lines of code mentioned in his log were his original work, which he had completed in 19 days. A normal day's work for a programmer is 100 lines. Wuu was alleging a daily output of almost 25 times that. Even jaded Silicon Valley denizens had to chuckle at the Herculean outrageousness of his boast. It's as if they weren't even trying to cover their tracks, deeming themselves invincible.

After the raid, Avanti stock took a tumble. But in the first of several Avanti PR coups, the *Wall Street Journal* reported that the SEC was probing at least four current and former Cadence employees for short selling AVNT after gaining confidential, advance information about the recent raid. Avanti claimed that Cadence CEO Joe Costello was one of those who illegally traded in its stock. Costello replied that he had dumped a large short position at a loss several months before the raid precisely to avoid the appearance of impropriety. Imagine what a bitter pill for Costello: losing money shorting a company he believed to have stolen the very basis of its business from his own company.

Whether it was Cadence employees or not, *somebody* had aggressively shorted AVNT soon before the raid—and unfortunately it wasn't me. The short interest in the stock ballooned from 350,000 in August 1995, when Jeff Markham discovered hard evidence of outright theft, to 1.4 million in November. The average daily trading volume in November was 60,000 shares. On December 4—the day *before* the raid—volume hit 376,000. On December 5, the day of the raid, the stock dropped from $41 to $35, and the following day it slipped all the way to $23. It would fall as low as $12 before reviving.

Nevertheless, the company was still registering sales and acquiring other firms. Any indictments against the Avanti principals seemed part of a remote and hazy future. And large investment funds continued to buy. The stock price slowly began to rise once again. It hit $24 in March 1996, $28 in July, and $32 by the time January 1997 rolled around.

On March 19, 1997, U.S. District Court Judge Ronald M. Whyte issued a preliminary injunction, prohibiting Avanti's further use of trade secrets and copyrighted source code and overturning

the immunity Avanti was claiming from Gerald Hsu's 1994 employment agreement.

Still, current sales figures were not being impacted, and Avanti's
stock price held. Institutions continued to hold AVNT, subjecting
the savings of countless small investors to the very real and tangible
possibility of a total loss if Avanti's executive team should be tried
and convicted. Amerindo held a giant 5.8 million block of AVNT
shares. Van Wagoner Capital Management held 1.6 million shares;
Warburg, Pincus had 461,000 shares; and Wellington Management
had 351,710 shares. All would significantly increase their holdings
in 1997.

On April 11, 1997, seven former Cadence employees, six of
whom were Avanti directors, were officially charged by the Santa
Clara County district attorney with illegally helping Avanti obtain
Cadence trade secrets. They were arrested, booked, and released on
bail. Defendants included Avanti's CEO, Gerald Hsu; its VP of technology, Y. Z. Liao; its VP of engineering, Stephen Tzyh-Lih Wuu; and
an Avanti director, Eric Cho.

This time the market did react to what could only be the worst
of possible news. The image of a corporation's key officers being fin-
gerprinted was too much for even the most cynical trader. On the
first trading day after the arrests, the stock closed at $24.50 on vol-
ume of 604,000 shares. The next day, however, it nearly halved,
down to $12.50 on a volume of 6.5 million shares. It would ulti-
mately fall as low as $9.75 after the arrests. And once again, as the
image of Gerald Hsu and his henchmen sullenly breaking rocks or
clanging tin cups across the bars of their cells receded in investors'
minds, AVNT shares bounded up.

By May 1997 AVNT was back at $20.75. For very good reasons,
analysts were cool to the stock. Jennifer Smith of Robertson
Stephens issued an ignominious *market perform* on AVNT. Even
Alkesh Shah of Morgan Stanley was *neutral*. Neutral. Avanti had paid

Abusing the Process

Morgan Stanley $500,000 plus expenses in 1996 to render a finan-
cial opinion of the company.

The institutions, though, were more enthusiastic than ever. On
June 30, 1997, Amerindo upped its holdings to 6.1 million shares;
Van Wagoner to 2.3 million shares; Warburg, Pincus to 954,000
shares; and Wellington to 676,000 shares. In addition, Robertson
Stephens had jumped aboard with 649,000 shares, Hartford Investment with 547,000 shares, and eight others had acquired over
100,000 each. Finally, Fidelity Management, which would later
prove the most, shall we say, "perplexing" holder of Avanti, held
983,000 shares, though that figure would rise to 2.8 million by
October 9.

Meanwhile Avanti was trying to have Santa Clara County
Deputy District Attorney Julius L. Finkelstein dismissed from the
case on the grounds that his office had availed itself of Cadence-
funded software experts.

This is where we finally stepped in. On August 1, 1997, we published a report regarding Avanti's characterization of this recusal motion against the DA. The report was not an outright stock-buster, it
was simply an attempt to initiate a public dialogue.

On August 15 Cadence attorneys made the oral argument that
ArcCell was a definite copy of Symbad. Avanti backed off its absurd
plea of complete and utter innocence and instead argued that whatever Cadence code was stolen was of minimal importance. Cadence
responded that this "minimal amount" represented 100,000 lines of
code, or over two engineer-years of work. In addition, Avanti's
overall product was made possible only by the employment of the
stolen code. Any newly written code, no matter how brilliant or
miraculous, would be unusable if a judge enjoined the use of the
stolen code.

On August 21 we reported that Avanti was misleading investors
by claiming technical superiority and increasing market share over

the very Cadence products it had stolen. In reality, despite the IC-design-tool market's extraordinary growth and Avanti's small histori-cal sales base, Cadence was still growing faster than Avanti.

Avanti's apparent strategy was to use its inflated stock to grow beyond a mere alleged software pirate. It was using the value of its stock to buy other businesses. And the institutions buying into Avanti and bidding up its price made this plan all the more effective. As the company expanded, the prospect of a total loss in the Ca-dence litigation became less of a knockout punch. On the surface it seemed a brilliant if wholly unfair scheme.

On September 23, 1997, a federal judge issued an injunction preventing Avanti's customers from using its ArcCell place-and-route product, making the risk of design-flow interruptions more immediate and tangible to those customers. Despite this dreadful news, the next day 4 million shares traded and the stock rallied, as if the inability to market a key product was a positive. The explanation for this defiance of market logic might be that near the end of Sep-tember, all of Avanti's top five institutional holders, which had al-ready controlled over 51 percent of its outstanding shares, bought more stock. But sometimes when you think you've cornered a mar-ket, you've actually painted yourself into that corner.

I have never seen such trading as on September 23 and 24, 1997. On the twenty-third, when the judge's gavel had fallen, the stock dropped from a daily high of $33.62 to a low of $18 in the after-market. But the next morning, a huge order imbalance on the buy side—4.4 million shares, more than 10 times Avanti's normal vol-ume—pushed it back up to $30.

By September 30 the level of support for Avanti from just a few institutions was mind-boggling. Van Wagoner held 2,456,000 shares; Warburg, Pincus, 881,120; AIM Advisors, 2,211,000; John Hancock Advisers, 630,000. The holding of Fidelity Management & Research Co. (FMR) as of October 9, 1997, was 2,772,500 shares, or 10.73

percent of the company. This wasn't a patch on Amerindo, which by November 21 would accumulate 6,422,603 shares—almost 25 percent of this deeply troubled company.

Avanti issued a press release claiming great results in the quarter. On October 15 we reported our view in a report titled "Avanti's Dismal Third-Quarter Results." We discussed the manner in which Avanti promoters were misleading investors regarding the quality of those earnings and future prospects. We found the company's criminal problems to be suppressing earnings; we discovered customers who were concerned about future support, upgrades, even their ability to continue using already installed Avanti products. The promoters were claiming that Avanti possessed an earnings reserve and that its reported earnings were understated. We determined that no such earnings reserve existed and that Avanti had no backlog of shipped and fully accepted yet unbilled product. The ridiculous claims by the longs, of course, would have been illegal anyway.

Analysts took a dim view of what was happening at Avanti—in their understated way, of course. Alkesh Shah of Morgan Stanley reiterated his *neutral*. Doug van Dorsten of Hambrecht & Quist issued a *hold* due to litigation but noted that the strategy of ongoing acquisitions seemed to mitigate the importance of Avanti's Aquarius software—which might soon be enjoined—to the company's bottom line.

Wessels, Arnold & Henderson declared a *current buy—aggressive growth* rating for Avanti on October 21 and reiterated this rating several times. Wessels had worked on Avanti's public offering and received a $2 million fee for advising on a merger.

On October 21, 1997, Joe Costello resigned as the head of Cadence, becoming vice chairman of Knowledge Universe, a "buzzy" new company that treats education as a business. (Knowledge Universe's chairman and cofounder is Michael Milken.) Costello was much respected for his leadership at Cadence if not widely beloved in the industry. Belying Avanti's untrue claims of superiority and growth, Cadence was still far in front of its market. However, rumors began to fly that Costello had been the only true hard-liner at Cadence and that the new CEO, Jack Harding, would settle with Avanti. Some even said that Costello had been pushed aside so that a settlement could be arranged. We spoke to Harding, however, and he said, "No way." And it turned out that indeed no settlement had been in the works; the legal process continued.

On December 19, 1997, Avanti issued a press release with its own deceptive spin. Avanti, discounting any chance of an injunction against its Aquarius software, crowed that the injunction against ArcCell was meaningless because it had stopped selling or licensing ArcCell products or code in mid-1996 and that current users were permitted to continue using it. Gerald Hsu bragged later that all ArcCell customers had already switched to Aquarius.

We contacted Amerindo to inquire about its use of New York City pension funds to buy Avanti. We received a threatening letter from its counsel and then a personal reply from Alberto Vilar, chief investment officer of Amerindo. Vilar accused us of "intentionally and wrongfully interfering with our economic advantage, defaming us and willfully and intentionally attempting to manipulate the price of Avant! stock." He concluding by saying "Your activities are mean, shameful and loathsome. They are motivated by appalling avarice and greed and they will not be permitted to go unanswered." Boy, was he mad. "Me so rich. You so poor. Me squash you." Either these people were ignorant or in complete denial of Avanti's tenuous position, or they were simply attempting to intimidate me with bluster or threats of lawsuits.

I was disturbed about public pension funds being invested so irresponsibly, especially funds from the city where I live. Twice I wrote to the deputy comptroller of New York City, John Lukomnic; he never responded.

We went public with an accusation of institutional involvement in the manipulation of Avanti stock. Several newspapers played the story prominently, including an amazing piece on the front page of the *Boston Herald* business section on January 7, 1998, headlined "Investor Fires on Fidelity Buy." The piece made the usual insinuating noises about how short sellers profit from a share decline, but it was still oddly amusing to see coverage of puny little Asensio & Company questioning an investment by the great Fidelity in its own hometown newspaper. It was particularly astonishing to see a cynical punk like young Tony Huang, the "analyst" who reportedly first recommended Avanti to Fidelity, actually fingered in print for his deed.

An even more damaging piece appeared in *Pensions & Investments*. It laid out the story, including the ridiculous number of shares held by Fidelity, Van Wagoner, and Amerindo, and the fact that all three had continued to purchase AVNT even *after* the April 1997 indictments. It also detailed the fact that Amerindo had invested millions in New York City pension funds in Avanti.

A pair of class action lawsuits on behalf of Avanti shareholders, filed in 1995 and 1997, were consolidated in 1998. The combined suit accused Avanti principals of making a series of false and misleading public statements and omitting material information. Specifically, it cites the misrepresentation and minimalization of the following three thefts:

1. Avanti founder Stephen Wuu copied a place-and-route program called Symbad before leaving Cadence and used it to bring ArcCell to market in 1993.
2. Cadence engineer Mitch Igusa sold stolen Cadence source code for advanced area-based place-and-route software to Avanti executives.
3. Eric Cheng copied a Cadence program called VSIZE onto a file named "byebye" and took it to Avanti to be used to develop Avanti's DSO products.

SOLD SHORT

As part of its ongoing effort to delay action on its case, Avanti had been fighting for years to have the Santa Clara County deputy district attorney taken off the case. Prosecutor Finkelstein had to survive two challenges in the forms of recusal motions by the criminal defendants. Avanti, with its bottomless legal funds, had in the past been able to force the prosecutor to submit to cross-examination by the defendants, an astonishing and distressing situation. A California law has been enacted to allow judges to rule on motions for recusal without allowing evidentiary hearings, thus protecting prosecutors from this type of rich man's legal contrivance.

On December 16, 1998, a grand jury issued an indictment on the pending charges plus an additional securities fraud charge. The new charge specifically stated that Avanti marketed computer programs containing software code that it neither owned nor was licensed to use. Each of the defendants (all current or former Avanti executives, including Gerald Hsu) was individually subject to $27 million worth of damages. And the case was moved up from municipal to superior court.

In an effort to buff its image, the company set up the Avanti Foundation. Frequent radio advertisements extol the foundation's efforts to buy computers for the elderly and to help them get online. Avanti officers, after speaking to an elementary school class in a low-income section of East San Jose, made a highly publicized offer to pay for the college education of each student in the class.

On September 9, 1999, a federal judge barred all copyright claims arising prior to the 1994 release signed by Cadence but allowed all postrelease claims to proceed. Avanti characterized the ruling as a victory, because the claims still pending were for two products that it no longer sold: ArcCell and Aquarius. Avanti claimed its current program, Apollo, would be protected. In fact, there were damaging aspects, and the criminal trial—the true determinant of Avanti's future—was still looming. Nonetheless, the stock soared from $14 to $23 in one day—and then, over the following month, it slid back to $14.

The powers that be in Silicon Valley, where employees flow freely from tech firm to tech firm, seem to have no interest in opening this legal can of worms. Trade-secret cases are notoriously tricky, even the seemingly open-and-shut variety like this one. It may be a distasteful policy, but it is effective. Entrepreneurs would apparently rather risk a certain level of theft than see their profits dissipated by a flock of buzzard lawyers.

Fiends in High Places: Network Solutions

This is a simple story. They won. We lost.

But there were extenuating circumstances. If we hadn't been distracted by the lawsuits, things could have turned out a little bit differently. Still, we had never encountered a foe with more political power or a stock with greater market clout than this. There aren't many others out there like Network Solutions. Thank goodness.

Network Solutions (Nasdaq: NSOL) achieved its fortune on the basis of a government affirmative action contract that was snatched up by a huge, money-laden defense contractor. The contractor then leveraged this prize many times over by working the political system, applying a political headlock at the highest levels of the federal government.

Until 1999, Network Solutions had for over five years been the sole registrar of Internet domain names—Web addresses ending in ".com" and so forth. If you wanted a .com address on the World Wide Web, you had to come to this company. It was able to charge an excessive, monopolistic price for this service. Despite dozens of other companies that wanted to enter this business and provide more service for less money, Network Solutions managed to stave off the onset of competition. And even when limited competition was let in, Network Solutions, in reality nothing more than a bought-and-paid-for database and a government contractor, was able to apply massive influence to arrange a sweet long-term deal for itself.

How did the firm do it? How did a private company stick it not only to the U.S. government, but also to everybody in the world who wants to register an Internet address?

Network Solutions has extended its reign thanks to a supremely well-connected parent company capable of diddling masterfully with the federal political system. Without a bevy of Washington lawyers and lobbyists and a brothelful of complicit politicians, Network Solutions would never have been able to gouge the public for as long as it has, let alone *continue* to maintain its otherwise inexplicable power.

After we ceased coverage, Network Solutions extended its rampage, its political front persons crashing through all checks and balances, its stock screaming skyward, culminating in a historic buyout for a tasty sum. When asked about Network Solutions and its resounding success, I can respond only with the facts.

Until it was awarded the registry monopoly, Network Solutions had been subsisting on government jobs, building and maintaining large computer networks. Its founder, Emmit McHenry, was an African American who had formerly been a vice president of an insurance company. Network Solutions often got subcontracts from large firms like AT&T under affirmative action programs.

In 1992, a few years before the Internet began its explosive growth, the National Science Foundation (NSF) awarded the domain-registry contract to Network Solutions. NSOL would facilitate all registration of the most popular domain-name extensions: ".com," ".net," ".org," and ".edu," including maintenance of the domain-name database. The company received a flat annual fee for this service. For the first two years, this was a money-losing proposition. In March 1995 McHenry and his partners sold Network Solutions for $48 million to Science Applications International Corp. (SAIC), a huge, privately owned, astonishingly well-connected defense contractor based in San Diego.

SAIC has about $4 billion in annual revenues, roughly 80 percent of which are derived from federal contracts. SAIC board members include Retired Admiral Bobby Ray Inman, who was offered the job of defense secretary by Bill Clinton, and two retired generals, from the army and the air force. Past board members have included former Defense Secretary William Perry; Melvin Laird, Nixon's defense secretary; Donald Hicks, former head of research and development for the Pentagon; and former CIA directors Robert Gates and John Deutsch. The firm and its executives contribute over $100,000 to political campaigns in each election cycle.

I was advised by several of my closest associates not to enter this fray. They were concerned that NSOL was perceived as an Internet stock, and when we approached it in early 1999, everybody knew what a short seller's nightmare that group was, defying all reasonable methods of valuation. But mainly the fear was of the SAIC political juggernaut. Never before had so many people I trusted warned me off a stock.

SAIC had a vision for Network Solutions and its money-losing domain-registration contract. It recruited another plugged-in individual to run Network Solutions: Gabriel Battista, the former head of U.S. operations for UK-based Cable & Wireless PLC. Within four months of the March 1995 acquisition, SAIC managed to use its political muscle to convert NSOL's registration income from an annual stipend to a pay-per-name fee. Network Solutions charged $100 upfront for a two-year registration, of which $30 went to something the NSF created called the "Internet Intellectual Infrastructure Fund." NSOL and the NSF were criticized for running a monopoly of the domain registration system. As a result, the $30 "infrastructure" charge was eliminated, but NSOL got to retain its $70-per-name fee.

As the Internet took off, so did Network Solutions' business. NSOL not only collected $35 per year for most every Internet address, it also controlled the master list of registered domain names. SAIC truly had a gold mine on its hands. And the NSF found itself engaged in an ongoing affirmative action contract that had been reassigned to a coven of superrich white men. By September 1997 Network Solutions had become so attractive that SAIC decided to float a small amount of stock. The stock began in the $6 range, drifting down to $3 by the end of the year. (All prices in this chapter have been adjusted for a March 1999 2 for 1 split.) It wasn't until a secondary offering in 1999, however, that SAIC insiders would *really* start registering large amounts of cash—$729 million, to be more precise—into their bank accounts.

This bonanza had not gone completely unnoticed. When a government contractor starts coining money faster than the U.S. Treasury, you can bet that a mixture of fairness seekers and greed heads will try to stick their noses into the trough. The greedy ones tried to hop aboard the NSOL gravy train; the altruistic ones tried to open up the registration process.

In late 1997 a politically diverse group called CORE, the Internet Council of Registrars, tried to create seven new top-level domain names (TLDs) in order to introduce competition with NSOL. (A TLD is ".com" or ".net," for example. Examples of new TLDs might be ".biz," ".sex," or ".fun.") However, the NSF, which had authority in this matter, felt that adding new TLD names would be destabilizing and premature. (Not to mention the questionable demand for lame top-level domain names like ".biz," ".sex," or ".fun.") Several new TLDs were finally approved in November 2000.

At the end of January 1998, the U.S. government issued a "Green Paper" that set forth its preliminary intentions to create competition in the domain registration business. Meanwhile,

Abusing the Process

CORE, which represented small and large U.S. Internet companies as well as companies from Europe and the Pacific Basin, continued on its own path of introducing competition. In February 1998 CORE was in the process of testing its own Shared Registry System when someone broke into a server facility in San Francisco and stole two 200-pound servers belonging to CORE. The thief or thieves also stole the software used to run the registry system.

CORE decided not to pursue the establishment of new TLD names. Instead, it chose to wait and try to work with the U.S. plan to reform the domain-name registry system.

Ira Magaziner, who ran the Clinton administration's ill-fated healthcare initiative, was the government's point man on domain names. He helped produce a "White Paper" that eventually led to the creation of a group called ICANN, the Internet Corporation for Assigned Names and Numbers. ICANN had a mission to open competition for the ".com," ".net," and ".org" extensions. The group was started in 1998 through the spearheading efforts of Jon Postel, one of the Internet's original founders. Postel had personally administered the addressing system during the Internet's pioneer years.

ICANN is answerable to the U.S. Commerce Department. Becky Burr, a senior Commerce Department adviser, was supposedly the government official responsible for seeing to the transfer of control of ".com" registrations from the U.S. government to ICANN. Then, theoretically, or perhaps just for PR purposes, ICANN's duty was to put the brakes on NSOL's runaway train. Postel set up the ICANN board, which included Esther Dyson, a well-known webhead who is considered on the cutting edge of new technologies, a veritable *Wired* magazine poster girl. Unfortunately, soon after setting up ICANN, the highly respected Postel suddenly died. Amid a small outcry that seems to have been orchestrated by NSOL about the closed-door nature of board nominations, Dyson became the ICANN chairperson. By November 1998 ICANN was officially formed.

It should be apparent that the creation of ICANN was anathema to the continued profits of Network Solutions. SAIC wasn't just sitting back and waiting for its monopoly to end. An October 8, 1998, piece in the *Wall Street Journal* detailed Network Solutions' intense lobbying effort. Al Gore's former technology adviser and Harold Ickes, the former White House deputy chief of staff, joined NSOL. Network Solutions also hired Dutko & Associates, an influential D.C. lobbying firm. Dutko was the largest fund raiser for the Democratic National Committee in 1997. Perhaps most important of all, Network Solutions, based in Herndon, Virginia, had a very good friend indeed in Virginia Republican congressman Tom Bliley, a bowtie-wearing, coiffed-white-haired smoothie who happened to be chairman of the House Commerce Committee. As in "Department of Commerce." As in "the people overseeing ICANN."

The battle lines were drawn as early as October 1998. SAIC/Network Solutions had its deep, deep cash reserves and its intimidating battery of lobbyists, paid-for congresspeople, and ultra-well-connected board members. The government, whoever that is, was supposed to have the will of the people, the principle of fair and open markets, and ICANN. Ullp!

On November 16, 1998, with competition talk heating up, came a surprise announcement. Gabriel Battista abruptly resigned as CEO of Network Solutions. No new CEO would be named until May 24, 1999, when James Rutt, chief technology officer of the Thomson Corporation, stepped in. In the interim the company was headless, but investors were heedless; the stock price *doubled* before the year was out. It doubled *again*, to $60, in the first week of January 1999.

Of course, Battista's bowing out might have *benefited* Network Solutions—and SAIC. SAIC controlled NSOL's stock. Three of NSOL's most senior managers were current or former SAIC employees, and six of NSOL's eight directors were current SAIC employees. Now they wouldn't have to go through an outsider to implement SAIC's policies.

SAIC was preparing a massive secondary offering of NSOL stock. Prior to releasing the "red-herring" prospectus for this offering, the company received notification of official Department of Commerce recognition of ICANN. Well after this notification was received, the company solicited buyers with this preliminary prospectus—a prospectus that omitted critical language regarding the planned delegation of DOC's authority over the Internet .com business to ICANN.

The final prospectus for this offering, dated February 8, 1999, states, "We have agreed with the Department of Commerce to transition to a shared, or competitive, registration system. . . . This transition will occur in a phased approach with limited competition scheduled to begin by March 31, 1999." The implication was that Network Solutions would be "allowing" others to get into the business. In fact, it supposedly was being stripped of its monopoly contract and supposedly would have no greater standing than any other company in the new registration system. Although it seemed likely to be permitted to be one of the approved registrars, NSOL didn't have any guarantee of even that status.

It's like Network Solutions was renting a house and got evicted, but figured that since it still had a set of keys, it could come in and use the bathroom anytime it wanted. It was willing to share the bathroom with the new residents, though, as long as it got to go in first. Isn't that nice?

Let me repeat: NSOL was a simple government contractor, nothing more. Period. Network Solutions had no business other than a government contract that was scheduled to be terminated.

"We may not be able to sustain the revenue growth we have experienced in recent periods," warned the prospectus. "If we do not successfully maintain our current position as a leading provider of domain name registration services or develop or market additional services, our business could be harmed." While true, this was a huge understatement.

Once competition enters, the domain-name business becomes all about price. Anybody can perform a registration at a cost not much higher than whatever the company that is willing and able to offer the lowest price decides it should be. But nowhere in the prospectus is a brutally curtailed registration fee even mentioned as a possibility.

In the secondary offering of February 8, 1999, SAIC sold 4.5 million shares at $170 each, raising $650 million and reducing SAIC's stake in NSOL from 72 percent to 45 percent. SAIC had seen well over a 1,000 percent cash return on its $56.4 million investment of just four years earlier—*and* it still retained 45 percent of NSOL. This remaining equity stake was worth another $1.3 billion on the day of the secondary offering, and it would grow substantially.

The stock closed the day of the offering at $74—13 percent below the offering price. For those who held on longer than a month, however, riches were pending.

That same day James Pettit of Hambrecht & Quist, a colead manager of the secondary offering, stated in a company press release: "Many steps still remain, and it will take a while before we ultimately see competition. Under these guidelines Network Solutions would retain its position as the registry in .com, .net, and .org top-level domains and would function as a registrar as competition begins to evolve in 1999 at the registrar level." Hambrecht & Quist issued non-stop *strong buys* through 1998 and 1999. In December 1998 the company's Pettit and Matthew Davies had predicted, "We continue to believe true competition is at least 12++ months away."

Hambrecht & Quist wasn't the only friendly investment house behind NSOL. On February 11, 1999, PaineWebber issued a *buy* on the stock. PaineWebber made a market in NSOL and has acted as an investment banker for the company. When Battista resigned with no successor in sight, PaineWebber reiterated its *buy* and actually *raised* its price target. Now, normally the resignation of a CEO is considered a negative development. And when there's no replacement in sight, it's a cause for serious concern. But not in SAIC-land. Amazingly, J.P. Morgan Securities Inc. also raised its price target and reiterated a *buy* when Battista resigned. Morgan would later act as a manager in the secondary offering. Only Prudential, an NSOL market maker that eventually would issue one of the most fancifully optimistic reports ever seen, rated NSOL an unimpressed *accumulate* at the time that Battista resigned.

On February 25, 1999, BancBoston Robertson Stephens held its Tech '99 Conference. Robertson Stephens was a market maker in NSOL and was an underwriter of the secondary offering. Its analyst Keith Benjamin asserted that, apropos ICANN, "there's no competition coming." Nonetheless, NSOL had dropped 19.9 percent from February 1 to March 5. But this was no pump and dump. The institutional ownership of NSOL in March 1999 was over 20 percent. The stock was about to become a day trader's darling, zooming up from $70 to $150 in just 20 days.

ICANN announced that as a first phase of opening up the registry, it would soon begin a test bed for a shared registry system. It put out a call for applicants. Perhaps preparing for a worst-case outcome, on March 2, 1999, Network Solutions announced that it was receiving 90 percent of its business through channel relationships. This may have been meant to imply that even with competition, its 150 partners, many of the Internet's biggest names, such as Yahoo and Netscape, would continue funneling registry business exclusively to NSOL.

Network Solutions realized that no matter how hard it fought, it would no longer be the sole registrar of domain names. It could be the leader, as AT&T was when long distance was deregulated, but the registration part of its monopoly was kaput. So the company focused instead on the value of the existing registry—the database of all Internet addresses, including the name and contact information for the owner of each address. Not only would new registrars need interactive access to the database to perform registrations, but also, since each registration has only a two-year term, the list also could serve as a prospect list for new clients. If NSOL did not make the registry available to any and all prospective registrars, fair and open competition would be impossible.

NSOL was a U.S. government contractor. One might think the government should own the registry. But that's not how Network Solutions saw it. It claimed ownership of the registry and asserted that maintaining the registry and making it available to competitors would cost $16 per name. Even if you concede the company the right to control the registry that American taxpayers funded, the $16 fee, as we would learn later, was wildly excessive.

ICANN held a meeting in Singapore in early March to decide major issues in opening up the registration to competition. On March 4 Prudential's Paul Merenbloom and Aydin Tuncer reported on that meeting: "With the first days of the Singapore-based meeting of the ICANN complete, we believe NSOL shareholders should be jumping for joy right about now. . . . Looks like a long road to deregulation. NSOL shareholders should continue to benefit. Reiterate *strong buy*." The stock ran up 30 points, to $110, on this and similar reports.

In reality, the analysts completely misrepresented the events in Singapore. The resolutions were as negative to Network Solutions as we could have possibly imagined. Naturally, we chalked this distortion up to just another case of dumb analysts swallowing corporate spin. Little did we know we were "through the looking glass" with this one.

We knew what happened in Singapore because we stayed up all night monitoring the meeting live over the Internet. The meeting was well organized and fast moving. ICANN successfully scheduled such events as the test bed start date and the registering of candidates for the test bed.

Abusing the Process

Anyone who watched the meeting could see that ICANN was clearly committed to removing the U.S. government's control over domain-name registration and fixing agreements among ICANN, the registry, and the registrars. Anyone who understood the language of Amendment 11, which had been adopted October 7, 1998, could see what was supposed to be coming. Amendment 11 is an extension of the cooperative agreement between the Department of Commerce and NSOL. It calls for NSOL to recognize ICANN, allows NSOL to continue operation of the Domain Names Registry during the transition to a competitive environment, and provides for the development, deployment, and licensing by ICAAN of a mechanism that allows multiple registrars to accept registrations.

Of course, in the end that's not what happened. But at least we gave it the ol' college try. Before things turned Network Solutions' way, things were going to get a whole lot hairier—and the stock price a whole lot trimmer—than its cheerleaders had predicted.

ICANN was prepared, willing, and able to take over supervision of the Domain Names Registry. In a way, this stock was a short seller's dream. There was so much hot air being pumped into the stock price, it was ripe for a noisy deflation.

Over the weekend of March 20 and 21, Network Solutions, perhaps drunk on its stratospheric $150 share price and $3 billion market cap, perpetrated such an outrage that only its political clout could keep it from facing severe penalties. NSOL "rerouted"—let's call it what it was; it was, in effect, a website-napping—Internet traffic from the U.S. government–owned InterNIC directory to the NSOL home page. InterNIC is a generic, non-NSOL–owned registering site. Network Solutions had maintained this site as part of its government contract. On this day NSOL turned a quasi-public utility into a promotion and a forced link to Network Solutions.

It's stunning how brazen the company could be while under such intense scrutiny, at a time when ICANN supposedly held

Network Solutions' future in its hands. The next day, although the news of NSOL's offense had not yet appeared in traditional media, Internet sites and chat rooms were abuzz. Meanwhile, the public outcry had become so severe that even the NSOL-compliant U.S. Commerce Department had to act. Becky Burr, the Commerce official charged with overseeing the transition, stated, "We're very concerned. This was undertaken without consultation with the United States Government."

This may not seem like very strong language, but it was enough to hit NSOL, and hit it hard. In the last half hour of trading on Monday, March 22, 1999, NSOL cratered. It swiftly crashed from over $150 to $120—down an average of a buck a minute for 30 minutes.

Two weeks later Network Solutions would partially establish a far less functional InterNIC website. As usual, however, the company was let off with a warning. The unauthorized use of U.S. government property by a government contractor is a serious offense. At this point I should have seen that the U.S. Commerce Department was paying way too much deference to this company's clout.

I had been looking forward to Wednesday, March 24, and not because that would be the day of the NSOL stock split. I was ready to publish my first report on Network Solutions, and I knew that Bob McGough of the *Wall Street Journal's* "Heard on the Street" column was interested in a story on the company. Hoo-boy, imagine all the things we knew about Network Solutions, its misrepresentations to investors, its bully tactics, all published in the "daily business bible."

I hoisted the *Journal* off the floor outside the door of my office. The headline hit me with a thud: "Potential Competition Isn't Hurting Shares of Network Solutions, the Web Site Registrar." Despite the preponderance of negative information I saw, McGough's eyeballs led him to a positive story. At the time, given the facts, this slant was ludicrous. In retrospect, and for all the wrong reasons, the *Journal* had got it right.

Abusing the Process

The next day, March 25, the stock was trading down to $110. This was the day we initiated coverage. We reported on the facts that convinced us that NSOL's management had led investors to believe that the expiration of its contract would be postponed or that it could not be terminated totally and easily. Investors had also been led to believe that even if the contract was terminated, NSOL's business value would continue to grow. In reality, the termination of NSOL's contract should have eliminated all barriers to entry in the domain-name business. As a result, we believed that NSOL's $2.2 billion market cap, which placed it in the top 10 among Internet stocks, was grossly overvalued.

Based on research with potential competitors, we estimated the total annual cost to operate the registry comfortably was less than $3 per name. We believed that the registry function ultimately would be transferred to an ICANN-accredited cooperative. In any case, we did not believe that the temporary, test bed registry price would remotely approach what analysts were estimating NSOL wanted to charge annually for running the registry: $16 per name.

Our reports continued. We believed that the U.S. government and the Internet community were not going to let NSOL set an exorbitant price for the registry function. The cooperative or some other, less-greedy company would get the contract. As a result, we believed that NSOL would quickly become one of hundreds of registration services operating in a small-dollar-value, low-margin, no-value-added business. NSOL was trading at a large premium to legitimate Internet stocks, which unlike NSOL had promising, not diminishing, futures. Even assuming a strong Internet equity market, we believed that NSOL would trade below $40 per share after the test bed was concluded and well below $20 per share after the contract was terminated. We were right about the fundamentals, but we hadn't factored in the power of SAIC to manage the system and effect an outcome that made no sense to anyone except Network Solutions.

SOLD SHORT

Unlike some of our other shorts, which managed to wobble on their feet for a few more rounds before succumbing to the facts, NSOL did the opposite. The stock tanked. Clearly the company had not fully informed investors about the risks they were facing, and NSOL was blindsided. But NSOL had the stamina for a long battle, and in the end it got off the mat and returned to hoist the gold belt.

April 7, 1999, saw the release of one of the most highly misleading and cynical analyst reports I've ever seen. Prudential, raising its price target from $125 to $188, titled its report "Forget the Shorts and Check the Facts—ICANN Needs NSOL's Blessing to Proceed & Technology Delays Lie Ahead For Potential Competitors; STRONG BUY." It's hard to believe anybody could think the U.S. government would need the blessing of one of its contractors. Worse, the report was apparently telling investors that NSOL could block potential competitors with technology delays. Among other deceptions, the report stated, "NSOL's agreement with the Department of Commerce stipulates that both ICANN and each of the registrars must have separate agreements with NSOL prior to the initiation of competitive access to the NSOL controlled registry. No such agreements currently exist." No such agreements existed because no such agreements were necessary.

On April 8 we published a response titled "NSOL Analyst Issues False Report." Regarding Prudential's assertion that separate agreements would be needed for each registrar, we pointed out that Amendment 11 of NSOL's agreement with the Department of Commerce specifically states that ICANN, not NSOL, will exercise Domain Name System regulation responsibility and that ICANN, not NSOL, will subject registrars to consistent requirements. Amendment 11 further states that even if NSOL were allowed to continue to operate a provisional Shared Registration System (SRS), it must give all licensed Accredited Registrars equivalent access.

In the event that NSOL failed to provide a shared registration system or made unacceptable demands on ICANN's accredited registrars, the U.S. government could simply and readily terminate the company's contract. It could then solicit competitive bids or allow ICANN to develop a cooperative registry. In fact, through our due diligence we discovered that the U.S. Department of Commerce had already requested and reviewed cost information from database management companies interested in providing a Shared Registration System. Some of these companies claimed that they could provide these services at $2, versus the $16 fee NSOL was attempting to obtain. But NSOL said that some of these companies have never run a registry so their estimates were not based on reality. We also broached the topic of the inappropriate use of SAIC's political influence, declaring that this undue pressure, along with NSOL's baseless, excessive demands, might backfire and lead to an early termination of its entire domain-name contract.

In an April 19, 1999, *Business Week* article titled "By Any Other Name, A Monopoly.Com," Debra Sparks picked up on my April 8 report. She reported on NSOL's utterly false claim that it cost the company $16 per name to maintain the registry's database. A company called Emergent, a division of computer-services company Keane Inc., estimated it could do the same job for $2. Not only was Network Solutions asserting primacy in a business it controlled solely on the basis of an expired government contract, but it was also attempting to impose an 800 percent markup.

On April 21 ICANN announced the five companies that had been selected to participate in the initial test bed phase of the Shared Registry System for the ".com," ".net," and ".org" domains. (Network Solutions refused to apply to become an ICANN-accredited registrar.) These included AOL, CORE (the Internet Council of Registrars, the earlier would-be ICANN), France Telecom/Oleane, Melbourne IT, and register.com. The test bed was to begin on April 26 and last through June 24. (This date was later extended to July

16.) ICANN also announced that 29 other applicants—including small and big names, such as AT&T—had met its criteria and were expected to join the competition after the test bed phase.

That same day BancBoston Robertson Stephens, asserting that the ICANN announcement was already built into NSOL's stock price, reiterated its *buy*. "We are slightly surprised by AOL," stated Robertson Stephens, "because NSOL is now marketing through Netscape. We suspect ICANN encouraged AOL to join, to create a perception of competition. We don't expect AOL to become an aggressive competitor." Says who? How could a Robertson Stephens analyst speculate on AOL's future competitive interests? To be fair, however, this speculation now seems plausible. Virginia-based AOL, with all its technology and marketing might, has as of this writing *not* become a player in domain-name registration. Another particularly cynical if all too correct June 25 Robertson Stephens report would mention NSOL's "friends in Washington," referring to a letter that Virginia congressman Tom Bliley sent to the Department of Commerce.

The coverage of NSOL didn't shy away from extolling the company's political might. The analysts also played up recent earnings, which were of course bounteous. They did not disclose, however, that these lavish numbers reflected a monopoly that no longer existed. Once the government contract was terminated, there was no reason to expect any earnings at all from sales. If only an analyst had said, "You'd think they'd be doomed when they lose the monopoly. But ICANN hasn't got a prayer. NSOL has so much cash, the Commerce Committee is in their back pocket, and their parent company has loads of political juice. So they'll probably be able to delay competition as long as possible and even then extract an inflated fee from the new registrars." *That* I would have respected. *That* would have been honest. And of course, *that's what happened.*

With the April 21 ICANN announcement of the test bed participants, competition suddenly became all too real. The hypesters, in one last pyrotechnic burst of truth-spinning, carried the day: The stock opened at $60 and closed at $92. But in the end, no spinmeister could possibly distort *this* reality. NSOL's stock finally succumbed, free-falling in a few days back down to $60, where it sat for the next two months.

The market was trading on speculation over whether NSOL would be the permanent registry or only temporary, and how much it could charge for the service. The Department of Commerce was soliciting other Internet companies for guidance on how much it would cost to administer the Shared Registry Service; we were doing pretty much the same work. We confirmed that perfectly capable companies were willing to charge $2 per name for the service. Despite all his legwork, despite the $2 offers, William M. Daley, the secretary of commerce, awarded the contract to what might have been the highest bidder. He allowed Network Solutions to collect $9 per name, a scandalous markup. Daley's late father, Chicago's venerable, patronage-doling mayor Richard J. Daley, would have been proud.

On April 28, 1999, we wrote to Secretary Daley regarding NSOL's $9-per-year fee for registry services, a fee that violated both the White Paper directives and the regulations contained in Amendment 11's cost-plus pricing restrictions. Equally important and disturbing was that the Department of Commerce had obligated the ICANN test bed participants to pay NSOL for two years of registry services up front. The stated and primary objective of all parties involved, except NSOL, was to terminate NSOL's entire domain-name contract as soon as possible. In fact, according to Amendment 11, it should have been canceled no later than September 30, 2000. Therefore, the ICANN test bed participants were required to pay NSOL for two years of registry services with no guarantee that NSOL would escrow their funds and be obligated to repay the prorated unearned balance when its temporary position as the registry was terminated.

On May 5 Network Solutions shares fell as much as 14 percent as the company said the Justice Department wanted more information for a two-year-old antitrust investigation. The probe focused on the company's control over the database of customer names and Internet addresses. That day the *Washington Post* reported that Justice Department investigators had trained their sights on that issue. "We're looking at the possibility of anti-competitive practices in the Internet addresses registration industry," Justice Department spokeswoman Jennifer Rose said.

Despite this threat of government intervention, Network Solutions was funding a monumental disinformation campaign to turn the media and public against ICANN. To fund its ongoing activities, ICANN was requesting a $1 fee to be tacked onto registration costs. Through its high-placed champion, Representative Tom Bliley, NSOL made this request look like grand larceny, an abomination— even though NSOL had been overcharging for registration, and by a lot more than a dollar, for *four and a half years!* Even Jeri Clausing of the *New York Times*, who had been covering the story on an ongoing basis, swallowed this spin. She wrote a piece on June 7 titled "Critics See Internet Board Overstepping Its Authority." If ICANN was "overstepping," then NSOL had stomped without permission across more borders than Genghis Khan.

Even more disappointing was Ralph Nader, someone I generally respect. On June 11, 1999, Nader came out against ICANN, perceiving a lack of checks and balances. Imagine that! NSOL had been running amok with no regulation or competition, and he's complaining about ICANN. It's hard to understand how a commonsense guy like this could possibly abet NSOL in its efforts to weaken and discredit ICANN and delay competition. Even if ICANN was totally out of control—and it wasn't—let it first rein in NSOL, open competition, and create the market, and *then* have the Department of Commerce deal with ICANN. On June 16 Esther Dyson tried to "turn" Nader; she asked for his help in breaking up the NSOL monopoly. It never happened.

On June 22 House Commerce Committee chairman Tom Bliley wrote to Secretary of Commerce Daley, blasting ICANN for the $1 fee. The old campaigner labeled it a "tax" that would threaten the growth of the Internet. He also questioned ICANN's right to terminate Network Solutions if it failed to enter into a registrar accreditation agreement with ICANN by June 25.

It would be foolish to assert that this sort of lobbying didn't have a positive effect on the stock. Around this time, the stock rose to a new plateau. Opening the month at $50 and looking like a future $20 stock, it instead enjoyed a steady incline to $80.

The NSOL media counteroffensive against ICANN continued. On June 24 Herb Greenberg of TheStreet.com—normally a refreshing font of antiestablishmentism—told a dubious-sounding story of an alleged short seller who researched NSOL and decided that not only was it not a short, it was in fact a stock to buy. Greenberg ended the column: "In the words of [*I Love Lucy*'s] Ricky Ricardo: How 'boud dat." Strange, but I don't recall that being a particular catchphrase of either the Ricky Ricardo character or Desi Arnaz, the *Cuban-born* actor and musician who portrayed him. Am I being too sensitive?

Network Solutions even went so far as to fund an anti-ICANN campaign on Internet message boards. An October 14, 1999, *New York Times* article revealed that Jay Fenello, the former president of Iperdome, an Atlanta-based domain-name registration company, had posted against ICANN on 10 online message boards, including NSOL's. He admitted to being a hired consultant for Network Solutions.

On July 9, 1999, we issued a report titled "NSOL's Political

Campaign Fails to Alter Termination Process." We discussed the funding activities of Network Solutions, with which it was gathering political support in an attempt to delay the termination of its DNS government contract. We believed (okay, we pretty much *knew*) this activity might have resulted in the highly publicized letters critical of ICANN from Citizens Against Government Waste, Americans for Tax Reform, and Ralph Nader of the Consumer Project on Technology. We viewed this flurry of opposition to ICANN, particularly that of longtime NSOL defender Tom Bliley, as a clear indication that Network Solutions was acutely aware that its delaying tactics had been exhausted. Finally, we felt that NSOL's political campaign would not alter the process and might even backfire.

We were wrong.

A functioning Shared Registry System, which could have been readily accomplished with or without NSOL's participation, was one of the final steps needed to complete the planned termination of NSOL's DNS government contract. Commerce Secretary Daley, in response to our letter of April 28, confirmed that the Department of Commerce did not agree that NSOL's fee to administer the SRS temporarily complied with Amendment 11's cost-plus-reasonable-return pricing limitations. Furthermore, the secretary stated in a letter to Asensio & Company dated June 17, 1999, that the department granted the interim price for Phase I only. This interim price was established to allow Phase I to commence and to further "the introduction of competition," which was the euphemism NSOL coined for the planned termination of its DNS government contract.

As the year progressed, we began to realize that Network Solutions, specifically its parent, SAIC, had far more political might than we had reckoned. And juice counts far more in D.C. than it does on Wall Street. Even though the stock had drifted back down to the $50s and $60s, it was beginning to look as if the Department of

Abusing the Process

Commerce and the White House had been White Paper tigers, forced to go through the motions. They had never been willing, zealous foes of the NSOL monopoly.

On September 27, 1999, Secretary Daley stated that the Commerce Department's negotiations with Network Solutions had been "contentious" and "could have idled the Internet." What?! Can you imagine any other branch of the U.S. government caving in to such an outrageous threat? Yet the U.S. government appeased a mere arrogant contractor ostensibly to keep things running smoothly in the short term. And in doing so, it delayed the development of an open and competitive ".com" registration system.

I never saw it coming. For once my flair for observing the obvious failed me.

Daley also announced an agreement between ICANN and Network Solutions. NSOL will continue to manage the registration database until 2003. Under the new deal, Network Solutions received $9 per year for each registration until January 2000. Since then it has received $6 per registration. NSOL rose $5.88 on this announcement, to $72.81. The next day the stock gapped up into the $80s. The beginning of a long, uninterrupted bull run can be traced directly to this event—this caving in to the lobbying forces, this thwarting of the public's best interests.

In March 2000 Network Solutions received a stunning $500-plus–per–share, $21 billion buyout offer from VeriSign Inc. (Nasdaq: VRSN), based on VeriSign's stock price that day. It was by far the largest Internet merger at the time. The offer coincided, however, with a major pullback in tech stocks. VeriSign tanked, and NSOL shares careened between $500 and $200 for months, never actually reaching the ballyhooed buyout price.

The day of the VeriSign announcement, Tom Bliley announced he would be resigning from Congress. Meanwhile, William Daley resigned from the Department of Commerce to spearhead Al Gore's presidential campaign, later entering the history books as Gore's front man during the Florida vote-counting hoo-ha.

Were we wrong about Network Solutions? Certainly everything we published was correct and true. And until the company was able to demonstrate the vulnerability of the political system, it certainly looked like a $20 stock. All of the facts indicated to us that NSOL should *not* have been successful in retaining the interests that it did in the domain-name registry. The amount of money it was allowed to charge for its registry service is offensive. The terms were imposed on the market through the influence that Network Solutions has with the federal government. That's what makes this case completely different from any other company we've publicly shorted.

When you're dealing with the president of the United States and the secretary of commerce, you're beyond the law and beyond logic. These people create the rules. We bet not on ICANN but on free market forces. There was a lot of money involved here—and a lot of companies that could do the job. We believed that potential competitors in both the registry and registrar services were going to balance out Network Solutions' political power. But SAIC's influence in the federal government was greater than the force of the free enterprise system, stronger than those competitors that were willing and able to provide better services at far lower cost than Network Solutions. Who would have thought it? Not I—not at the time, anyway.

CHAPTER TEN

HOW TO SELL SHORT

Most people are tremendously confused by short selling. The process seems almost antithetical to the concept of a stock market, if not somehow unethical or illegal. We are accustomed to buying stocks. Even in gambling, we bet on teams or cards or numbers to win, not to lose.

So what is it, exactly, that I do?

When I sell short, it's exactly the opposite of my buying a stock. Basically, "long" investors buy a stock because they think the price of that stock is going to rise. I sell a stock short when I think the price of that stock is going to decline. And while long investors will profit from that stock's rise and lose when that stock falls, short sellers profit when the stock falls and lose when it rises.

Theoretically, longs never have to sell stock. They can hold it in their portfolio for decades and pass it down to their descendants. If the value of their holding increases, they can borrow against the growing value of the stock.

A short sale can become a long-term portfolio holding as well, and I have many of these. Certain stocks are so rank, so destined for extinction, that I believe I will never have to buy them back. I can hold them in my portfolio until they cease trading and then walk away with all the money I received when I sold them short to some unfortunate who didn't perform due diligence.

Upside, Downside

Longs theoretically can make an unlimited profit on a stock if they continue to move upward. A long's downside is the entire value of the original investment.

Short sellers can theoretically keep the entire amount for which they sold the stock—if and only if the price of the stock drops to zero. That's it. And if it goes to zero, short sellers have to find another short if they want to make more money. But if the stock price rises and continues to rise, short sellers' potential losses are unlimited.

Getting a Borrow (Wall Street's "Sacred Cash Cow")

When you sell a stock short, you are actually performing a two-step process. First, your broker is lending you those shares from stock held in other customers' margin accounts or from stock the broker borrowed from another broker. The reason brokers are able to lend these shares is that when customers sign a margin account agreement, they pledge (or hypothecate) the shares of stock in their account as collateral for the margin loan they are being provided by the broker. The broker is then free to lend these shares to another broker or to other customers.

These borrowed shares are then credited to the customers' own trading accounts. They are generally only available for the duration

The Math of Short Selling

Let's say Asensio & Company (ASMN) is trading at $10 per share, and you think it's overvalued. You sell short 1,000 shares. Your account is then credited $10,000, with corresponding liability to buy back those 1,000 shares at some point in the future at the prevailing market price.

If the stock declines to $9, you still have the $10,000, but your liability is now only $9,000, so you have made $1,000.

If, however, the stock rises to $11, your liability is now $11,000. You have lost $1,000.

If ASMN completely tanks, you end up with $10,000 and zero liability. If, however, ASMN ascends to the heavens, your losses are potentially catastrophic.

of the current trading day. If customers don't sell them, they have to give the shares back. If customers want to short that same stock the next day, they have to ask for a borrow all over again.

Sometimes a broker will say that the "borrow" isn't available, meaning that the broker either doesn't have the stock sitting in any margin accounts, or if he or she does, they've already been lent to another short seller. This often happens when stocks are tightly controlled by insiders or when a large number of shares have already been lent out to short sellers.

I believe the borrow requirement is an unacceptable constraint on the free market price-determining mechanism. If traders can prove they have sufficient funds to cover fully the risk of any upward price movement, why should it matter whether their particular broker or any broker happens to have shares of that stock available to borrow on a particular day? After all, the buyers of the stock don't care. Whether traders sell the buyers borrowed stock or not, if the stock goes up, the buyers make money and the traders lose money. But more on this later. For now, let's deal with the rules as they are, not as they should be.

You can increase your chance of getting a borrow by opening trading accounts at several different brokerages. There doesn't seem to be any rule of thumb as to which brokerages are more forthcoming with the borrow. Sometimes you will have more success finding a borrow with the fancy, full-service investment house, while other times you'll find the borrow with an $8-per-trade online broker.

You have to ask every day for a difficult borrow; it's best to try first thing in the morning. If a broker is consistently unable to provide the borrow, you have got to move your account to somebody who can provide it.

The Uptick Rule (Wall Street's Protect-the-Buyer Panacea)

Another way that short sellers are hamstrung is that a stock can't be sold short unless the price paid for the shares is above that of a previous sale or equal to the price of a previous "up" sale. This is called "selling on an uptick." Theoretically this is supposed to help prevent a 1929-style panic in which stocks plummet downward with no natural "brakes." But in reality, this rule once again artificially subverts the free market pricing mechanism. The preferential treatment of long sales vis-à-vis short sales reflects an obvious regulatory bias against short sellers.

Selling the Borrowed Shares

Once you have borrowed the shares, you have the same two options as a long seller, except you can't sell on a downtick.

How to Sell Short

1. You can sell them immediately at "market." This means you will accept whatever price is being offered for the quantity of shares you want to sell at the time the order hits the market. The sale will be executed unless you can't get an uptick on which to sell. A downside of a market order is that you cannot specify the price you will get for their shares.

2. You can sell them as a "limit offer." This means you are setting a minimum price that you are willing to accept for the shares. The danger is that the market might "get away" from you before you are able to execute the trade, and by the time you can find a buyer and an uptick, you might have to reset the limit offer price dramatically lower. Or perhaps the order won't execute at all, and you will be forced to return the shares at the end of the day and try to borrow them all over again the next day.

Margin Calls

A trading account will reflect a cash inflow from the money received when the shares were sold. However, you cannot withdraw or invest the proceeds from the short sale, nor can you apply them toward meeting margin requirements. Furthermore, you don't even get to keep the interest on these funds; the broker gets it.

The account will reflect a liability equal to the current value of the shares borrowed and sold. This liability will increase and decrease with the rise and fall of the stock. Most brokerages require traders to maintain an equity position in their account of at least 40 percent of this "market-adjusted" liability. For more volatile issues, some brokerages require 50 percent or more, sometimes even the total current value of the borrowed shares.

SOLD SHORT

If the stock price goes down, this equity requirement becomes smaller. All other things being equal, you will have no problem maintaining the margin requirement as long as the stock price declines. But if the stock price goes up, you are doubly cursed. Not only has your equity position shrunk, but the higher share price also means you're facing a higher margin requirement.

I strongly advise traders to maintain enough equity in their accounts to cover a substantial rise in the stocks they have shorted. This does not mean that I would ever encourage any investor to stay in a losing position longer than they should. Bull markets are full of high-minded martyrs nobly fighting losing battles. This does nothing for the efficiency of the markets or the net worth of the martyrs. However, there is nothing more frustrating than being forced to cover a stock that you know is a piece of garbage, just because it enjoyed an immaterial, temporary rise due to promotional activities.

Short Squeezes

I don't believe in "short squeezes." I've seen, and unfortunately experienced, market action that some investors and the financial press might describe as a short squeeze. But as a fundamentalist, I cannot believe that demand and supply of freely traded securities can be affected by the existence of a large short position in a rapidly and steeply rising market for an individual stock.

Sometimes a truly dreadful stock suddenly takes a sharp rise, and instead of the market "correcting" this anomaly, the stock will continue to rise. This rise, a situation often described as a short squeeze, might cause some tapped-out or psyched-out short sellers who have received margin calls to close all or part of their positions.

There is nothing pleasant about a short squeeze. But if you have done your research and are confident of the stock's downward destiny, you may be able to add to their position (at a higher price) and ride it back down. That said, it's never, ever, a good idea to suffer losses, no matter how small or how briefly. I don't believe in being right for right's sake. Short selling has one single purpose: to make money. That, not suffering losses, will add to the efficiency of the market.

In the end, all markets work to seek the correct price for every stock. No company can artificially pump up its stock with a short squeeze and expect to remain at that lofty price for long.

Covering

Not all shorts are terminal, or "zeroes." Just because a stock is over-valued, it doesn't necessarily mean it has *no* value. When a stock has declined to a point where I wouldn't necessarily want to short any additional shares, or when I feel there are better opportunities to deploy my funds elsewhere, I'll purchase the shares, an act called "covering" the short position. You don't have to cover your entire position. You can cover as many or as few shares of the short as you like. To cover, instead of placing a *buy* order with the broker, you place a *buy to cover* order.

Partially covering is a useful defensive strategy in a stock run-up. Doing so will both lower the margin requirement and allow you to resell the remaining shares at a later date.

Buy-ins

Unlike a stock purchase, which you can hold as long as you damn well please, a borrow for a short sale is subject to being called back by the broker at any time. This is a "buy-in" call, and there's not much even a seasoned institutional trader such as I can do about it. I might speak to my broker and try to find out how many shares are needed to meet the buy-in and how many shares are being held in total by his or her accounts. Then I'll try to make sure that the broker at least spreads out the buy-ins proportionately among all clients who are short the stock.

I'm hopeful that the looming specter of a buy-in will not haunt short sellers forever. The market would be well served if those who feel that a stock is overvalued could sell as much of that stock as they choose without being forced to buy it when they don't want to.

Puts and Calls

Sometimes it is simply impossible to find a borrow, but you just *know* that a stock is going down. Your alternative is to buy a *put* or sell a *call* option on the stock. Options aren't available for all stocks, particularly not smaller, lightly traded issues. But if options are traded on the stock you want to short, you have two choices:

1. Buy a put.
2. Sell a call.

A *put* is an option to sell a stock at a specified strike price at any time before the option's expiration date. If the stock price is below the strike price, the put is worth the difference between the strike price and the stock price. If the stock price is at or above the strike price of the put option on its expiration date, the put is worthless.

The advantage of buying a put is that potential losses are limited to the cost of the put. The disadvantage is that you have to pay a time-and-volatility premium for the put, often amounting to a few dollars a share.

The valuation theory of options is complex and, in a large, liquid market, highly efficient. In a thin market, you must be wary of market makers who offer options at allegedly fair prices. If you don't, you'll quickly learn the difference between a reasonable premium value and a roach motel. Like the roach motel, if you paid too much for an option, even if the stock moves your way, you may be able to check in but not check out.

A *call* is an option to buy a stock at a specified strike price at any time before the option's expiration date. If the stock price is above the strike price, the call is worth the difference between the stock price and the strike price. If the stock price is below the call's strike price on its expiration date, the call is worthless.

The advantage of selling a call is that in this case, you pocket the premium. The disadvantage of a call is that while potential gains are limited to the amount you received from the purchaser, your potential losses are unlimited. Selling calls is not a good substitute for shorting stock. Be careful. If you must, do it in small amounts as a potential addition to your account's income. Overall, selling calls is the fastest way I know to lose hard-earned money.

Most brokers will arrange for traders to buy puts if they fill out an option agreement, but special arrangements must be made to sell naked calls, that is, call options in which you do not own the underlying stock.

Boxing a Stock

Let's say I believe that a stock is heading down, though I'm not sure when. If I wait until I am sure, by then there may be lots of other guys also wanting to short the stock, and I might not be able to get the borrow. One way around that is to short the stock *now*, before the rush. However, a stock promotion often rises rapidly before its inevitable swoon. How do you establish a premature short position without exposing themselves to this risk?

The answer is to box the stock—simultaneously selling short and buying the stock. If you are boxed, then you neither gain nor lose no matter what happens to the stock price. Then, when you feel the time is right, you sell your long position and keep your short position.

If I think a stock is going to head up temporarily, right in the middle of a short-selling campaign, I might temporarily box it, either fully or partially. A borrow is a precious thing, and if I simply cover my short once the heat is on, I might not be able to get a borrow when I think the stock is heading back down again. Boxing the stock preserves a borrow and prevents losses during upsurges.

Boxing has its disadvantages, however. For one thing, it ties up capital while offering no possibility of any profit as long as you are boxed. For another, you never know when you are going to be bought in. If you are boxed and suddenly bought in, you'll wake up the next day with a long position in a stock you hate. Finally, you can completely mistime the box and find yourself short for the run-up and boxed for the decline—a sorry state of affairs indeed.

Short Interest/Days to Cover

Watch for the "short interest," updated and published for each stock after the fifteenth of every month. This tells how many shares of a particular stock have been shorted. It also reveals the "days to cover" index, which is simply the total short interest divided by the average daily volume.

Bulls tend to cite high days-to-cover ratios as indicative of good short-squeeze potential, since all those short sellers will be bidding up the few available shares. Believe it or not, in the raging bull market of the late 1990s, analysts at recognizable brokerages actually referred to high short interest as a reason for owning a stock. Now, I'm no babe in the woods. I know that there are plenty of wise-guy traders who talk about short squeezes and high-short-interest stocks. But what does the short interest have to do with how much money a company will earn next year? Isn't *that* what an analyst is supposed to investigate, evaluate, and discuss?

Bulls will tell you a high short interest is a good sign—that all those shares "need" to be bought back at some point, and the rush of buyers will buoy the stock. But the truth is, a high short interest represents negative investor sentiment—a lot of people think the stock is overvalued. And those short sellers are generally well-informed investors.

Strategy, Schmategy

In the end, the market sets the correct price of a stock. But sometimes, through misrepresentations of fact or withholding of material negative information, the market can be temporarily deceived, and a stock becomes grossly overvalued. These temporary disconnects, if thoroughly researched, are where short sellers make their money. And when my research tells me that a disclosure of material information that has been withheld or misrepresented might hasten the market's correction of an overvalued stock that I have shorted, I consider publishing this information. The rest is up to the market. May the best research win.

A Free Market Solution to Persistent Stock Fraud

It is unquestionable that there are public companies that trade at grossly overvalued prices. After researching and reporting on more than two dozen of these, and after watching the market's eventual correction, I believe more than ever that, in the end, the free market system is capable of weeding out misinformation by itself. Great forces are often massed in an effort to deceive the market, but these deceptions are only temporary. Short sellers can serve to hasten this inevitable clarity. As long as there is complete transparency of information and unfettered freedom for buyers to buy stock and sellers to sell, stock fraud is absolutely controllable.

This is not to say the system is perfect. Consider the following points.

- Speech is *not* free. Corporations with deep pockets stuffed with sometimes ill-gotten shareholder money can use those public funds to initiate Strategic Lawsuits Against Public Participation (SLAPP suits) in attempts to stifle public discussion of their businesses. Some states, notably California, have passed legislation barring these attempts to subvert the First Amendment, but I can tell you firsthand that this legislation has not helped. Even in California, SLAPP suits remain popular weapons in the arsenals of fraudulent corporations.

  Lawyers can turn simple defamation and libel claims into powerful vehicles to cause their opponents to spend millions of dollars defending themselves, even when there is no factual or legal basis for their allegations.

  No matter how frivolous a lawsuit or how abusive the litigator, the law does not allow a person who is wrongfully sued to prevent the lawsuit from proceeding or to recover damages afterward.

  Public companies should not be allowed to use their public shareholders' money to sue those who publish negative reports about their publicly traded stock. Period.

- Short sellers are *not* unfettered. Antiquated trading regulations force short sellers to go through the pointless ritual of "borrowing" stock to short. Traders of demonstrated means should have the ability to freely sell any stock short in any quantity they can afford. Likewise, the "uptick rule," which requires that short sales may occur only on an upward movement in a stock's price, places an artificial limitation on the free flow of stock trading. These regulations limit the power of the market to value stocks correctly by not allowing investors to freely utilize capital on the short side of the market.

These short-selling restrictions were first adopted in 1934, when the 1929 crash was still a vivid memory and the resulting Depression a current reality. They appeared in response to accusations that short sellers had caused the crash by manipulating the market. In reality, short sales were never proven to have caused or even exacerbated the crash. Regardless of what happened then, limiting short selling is not the answer because it harms the market's ability to price stocks fairly. Today's world is completely different from what existed in 1929, with far, far heavier trading volume, Internet trading, and instant access to company information and SEC filings. The market should be a democracy, not a manipulation-prone oligarchy like it was 70 years ago.

• Securities markets are governed by self-regulatory organizations. Any industry charged with regulating itself can at times fail to fulfill its regulatory obligations in a timely and effective manner. After all, the primary business of the NYSE and Nasdaq is to promote the business of its members—not to harass them.

The self-regulators resist the idea of punishing or expelling dues-paying constituents. This conflict of interest cannot be remedied until the listing side of the business, which earns income from trading, is separated from the regulatory side of the business, which should be its equally powerful adversary.

There are two things that every investor can do to foil stock fraud: Don't be cynical, be skeptical. And be informed. Due diligence does not mean perfunctory, one-source research. It does not mean taking as gospel the pronouncements of a broker or some financial pundit. And it most definitely does not mean taking the advice of some stranger phoning at dinnertime from a boiler room in New Jersey.

If you take nothing else from this book, I hope you have been inoculated with a healthy dose of realism. No matter how powerful the promoters, free market forces will cause stocks to trade at their fair value. I hope you now understand that major investment houses and their analysts may be downright excellent at their work, but there is no guarantee of complete integrity. Your brokers or financial advisers might very well be dispensing advice without any actual knowledge of the companies they are extolling. Or worse, they might have a hidden agenda—a personal financial stake, giving them an incentive contrary to yours.

You've now read this book. You have access to a wealth of company information. You can visit their websites, read their press materials, and examine their SEC filings. It's all out there, it's all free, and it's a great way for you to develop the skills to buy and sell with authority. If you're good at it, you'll become a vital cog in the great big beautiful machine known as the Efficient Market Theory. And you'll be well paid for your work. Every informed investor who participates in the market makes the whole system that much more effective.

EPILOGUE

GET READY
FOR A BIG ONE

On June 26, 2000, the *Wall Street Journal* ran a front-page story titled "A Short-Seller Trades Blows with a Target Who Just Won't Fold." The piece told of our struggle to expose a company called Hemispherx Biopharma (AMEX: HEB) and its CEO, Dr. William A. Carter.

Hemispherx, on which we first published in September 1998, has turned out to be by far the longest and most bitter battle in which we have ever engaged. Almost immediately on the heels of that first report, and ever since, Carter has dragged us through the courts in an attempt to silence us.

While we have continued to issue our ongoing opinions of Hemispherx and other questionable companies, the time taken by the litigation has meant that, in 1999 and 2000, we were able to publish far less often and on far fewer companies than previously. The idea that the truth can be suppressed by the misuse of shareholder funds and the justice system disgusts me to no end, but I still believe that the truth will ultimately emerge. And that's what we anticipate will happen with Hemispherx.

This story is still unfolding. Here are just some of the indisputable and damning facts:

- Hemispherx has been in business since 1996. During that time it has never brought a drug product to market. For at least 20 years, it has been testing a compound it calls Ampligen. Hemispherx has long promoted Ampligen as a potential cure for myriad diseases, including chronic fatigue syndrome (CFS), hepatitis, cancer, Gulf War syndrome, and HIV. Ampligen is over 25 years old and has never received FDA marketing approval for any use whatsoever. In fact, Hemispherx has never even filed a New Drug Application for Ampligen or any other drug.

- Carter was fired from the company in 1988 after selling $1 million of his own stock in the company, valued at $1.50 per share, for almost $40 per share to an AIDS patient who wanted to enter an Ampligen HIV trial. Dr. Carter deposited the $1 million into his personal trading account at Alex. Brown. The patient later sued Carter, but dropped his suit shortly after counterclaims were asserted against him. In sworn pleadings and other court documents, Hemispherx accused Carter of engaging in commercial bribery, fraud, and illegal and unethical conduct in conjunction with this incident, but Carter sued successfully to get his job back and later gained control of the company.

- DuPont invested $30 million in the development/testing of Ampligen with Hemispherx in 1987. The trials failed. Later, DuPont sued Hemispherx for material misrepresentations regarding the drug testing. Hemispherx countersued, using company resources, including residual funds from DuPont, claiming testing failures on DuPont's part.

- Hemispherx was brought public in 1995 by Stratton Oakmont, which was soon thereafter shut down by the SEC for violating securities laws. Its lead principals were convicted of stock fraud in 1999, including the fraudulent offerings of Hemispherx stock.

- A number of Hemispherx's board members, executive officers, and insider shareholders are career stock promoters, involved in many failed stock promotions in which insiders cashed in before the stocks became virtually worthless. The SEC has charged several with stock fraud, including the trading of HEB shares.
- Hemispherx has repeatedly received infraction notices from the FDA for illegally making claims of safety and efficacy for Ampligen. In addition to this illegal direct promotion of Ampligen, Hemispherx has also indirectly funded certain so-called patient advocacy groups that have promoted Ampligen.

I could run this list for dozens of pages and not be through. Suffice it to say that my research into Hemispherx indicates to me that this company's claims are seriously inaccurate.

The former chairman of the AMEX, a member of its Board of Governors, and one of its most prominent trading specialists have all held potentially compromising interests in insider shares of Hemispherx stock. The reporting of such conflicts in *Business Week* has helped prompt official scrutiny into this unacceptable situation.

But criticism of Hemispherx and those associated with it has had other consequences. Undoubtedly pressed by unfounded allegations by Carter and his colleagues, two years ago the National Association of Securities Dealers, which regulates member firms such as mine and owns the AMEX, commenced a wide-ranging investigation of our entire firm and all of its members. After inspecting virtually every trade we ever made for our clients and our own account, the NASD was unable to find that we ever improperly sold any stock short; nor could the NASD find that we or any of our clients failed to borrow any shares that had been sold short, nor that we executed any short sale on a downtick (see Chapter 10 for short selling rules).

Nor could the NASD find that any of our customers had ever filed a single complaint against me or my firm.

Yet, the years of extraordinarily intensive scrutiny did enable the NASD to assert a number of hyper-technical violations that were acknowledged and accepted without admitting or denying the alleged violations on October 20, 2000. Many of the violations involved failure to record affirmative determinations, which means recording in writing that the customer can borrow the security or will be able to provide it for delivery—not, mind you, that the actual security was not borrowed or delivered. Most violations the NASD alleged were of its advertising rules, where disclosure of risks or graphs used on our website were, according to the NASD, either not technically complete or not accurate in every respect. Our research itself was not challenged.

Though violations of this type are commonplace within the securities industry, I have accepted responsibility for our errors. Even the censure and fine imposed ($75,000) was not unusual for an active company. Full details of the NASD letter and sanctions may be viewed at www.nasdr.com. (Click on "Enforcement Actions" and then view under December 2000.) I leave it to the reader to decide how serious they are and to those knowledgeable in the industry to determine whether an inquiry of such intensity would have been instituted against a less outspoken firm.

Happily, Congressman John Dingell, ranking member of the House Committee on Commerce, has not been deterred by the Carter-inspired NASD inquiry. Congressman Dingell has encountered Carter once before: In 1989 he chaired a subcommittee investigating Carter for scientific fraud. The Congressman has now taken an interest in the listing policies and regulatory procedures of the AMEX and in Hemispherx in particular, and has contacted the SEC and Government Accounting Office (GAO) about these matters. The SEC is currently investigating Hemispherx and its officers in regard to possible securities fraud. The stronger the light cast on Hemispherx and the deeper an impartial third party digs, the sooner Hemispherx will be exposed as far from the value its promoters claim.

Notwithstanding Carter's objections, you can read our reports on Hemispherx (like all our other reports) at www.asensio.com. If all moves forward in a timely fashion, by the time this book in published you may have already heard a big noise regarding Hemispherx. If not, please check out our criticism and decide for yourself.

Index

INDEX

Index

INDEX

Index

INDEX

Index

INDEX

Index

INDEX